BEYOND IDOLS

BEYOND IDOLS

The Shape of a Secular Society

Richard K. Fenn

OXFORD
UNIVERSITY PRESS

2001

OXFORD
UNIVERSITY PRESS

Oxford   New York
Athens   Auckland   Bangkok   Bogotá   Buenos Aires   Cape Town
Chennai   Dar es Salaam   Delhi   Florence   Hong Kong   Istanbul   Karachi
Kolkata   Kuala Lumpur   Madrid   Melbourne   Mexico City   Mumbai   Nairobi
Paris   São Paulo   Shanghai   Singapore   Taipei   Tokyo   Toronto   Warsaw

and associated companies in
Berlin   Ibadan

Copyright © 2001 by Richard K. Fenn

Published by Oxford University Press, Inc.
198 Madison Avenue, New York, New York 10016

Oxford is a registered trademark of Oxford University Press.

Library of Congress Cataloging-in-Publication Data
Fenn, Richard K.
Beyond idols : the shape of a secular society / Richard K. Fenn.
    p.   cm.
Includes bibliographical references and index.
ISBN 0-19-514369-8
1. Secularism—United States.   2. Civil religion—United States.
3. Sociology, Christian—United States.   I. Title.
BL2747.8 .F463   2001
306.6—dc21   00-056684

9 8 7 6 5 4 3 2 1

Printed in the United States of America
on acid-free paper

For Bryan Wilson

ACKNOWLEDGMENTS

My primary debt here is to Bryan Wilson, to whom I have happily dedicated this volume. He has been a mentor and an intellectual father, from whom I have learned to follow a viewpoint that, although it is often uncomfortable, is filled with its own kind of secular hope. From Bryan Wilson I have received a lasting hospitality for which I am wholly grateful, and I have learned something of what it means to be steadfast.

Elsewhere I have stated what some of my debt is to David Martin, but more needs to be said. Paradoxical as it may seem in a book such as this that finds so little role for religion in a secular society, I have learned to trust what is beyond my own rather limited horizons. It is not simply David Martin's perennial kindness and intellectual vigor that inspires such a confidence; it is his attention to those who are otherwise of little account to academics like myself, but who embody, ahead of their time, the future. He sees what I and others overlook.

The editors at Oxford have been immensely supportive. Cynthia Read's interest has been essential, and Theo Calderara has supported the manuscript in many different capacities, each calling for imagination as well as attention to detail. Robin Miura has been excellent in preparing the manuscript for final publication. I am grateful to them all.

Robert MacLennan is a friend, scholar, and critic who has helped me to understand the secularity of the Jewish and Christian traditions and to be less afraid of the passage of time. Cally, my dear wife, and our children, Tom, Caroline, and Kim, have made the passage of time a joy. Thank you all.

CONTENTS

BEYOND IDOLS

INTRODUCTION

During the 1950s as Americans were being treated to an effort to purify
the nation of un-American tendencies, it became clear that the country was still hostage to the fortunes of fascism. That is, it was necessary for
Americans to find some way of personifying their own tendencies toward
violence and to punish their longings to break down the barriers that traditionally have separated people of various ethnicities and genders from one
another. In his recent study of relationships between Euro- and Afro-
Americans, for instance, Orlando Patterson makes it clear that the Euro-
American majority has long engaged in occasional ethnic cleansing. First
tending to lynch other Euro-Americans, the majority after the Civil War
found it both more convenient and more satisfying to lynch those whom
they blamed for their humiliation in the war itself and for their subsequent
degradation at the hands of the North. Negroes were thus lynched in increasing numbers, especially after the Jim Crow reaction in the 1870s, as
an outlet for class conflict, hatred, and humiliation, and as a focus for longings that were both sacred and erotic. Following the end of the Second
World War, Communists and McCarthyism filled what Patterson (1995,
255) calls "a Dionysian vacuum in American popular culture."

Later scholarship has reinforced our awareness that antidemocratic,
xenophobic, and authoritarian tendecies have long had deep roots in
American society. In the seventeenth and eighteenth centuries Americans
were living in communities that claimed to regulate the soul. As Barry Mc-
Shain has pointed out, the American colonies had more in common with
peasant societies of Europe than with the more enlightened tendencies of
England during the same period. While claiming for themselves freedom
from outside influences and federal intrusions, Americans were eager to
school the individual in the virtues held dear by the local community. De-
viants were then, just as some still are now, punished with various forms
of excommunication. Dragging an Afro-American behind a truck to his

death, or beating gays and leaving them to die strapped on a fence is merely the latest version.

In the post-war period there was also a renewed interest in the process of secularization. Some writers claimed that secularity was the mark of modern societies in general and of the United States in particular. The secular city was replacing communities based on more traditional forms of solidarity such as neighborhood and the family, ethnicity and race. New solidarity would emerge from the network of complex relationships that typify cities and bureaucracies, industry and the modern communications.

These same tendencies gave rise to speculation on the nature of a secular society. Religious intellectuals in particular were probing the notion that Christianity was not necessarily a religion after all. It could be a secular faith, and its early revelations could be translated into notions that would gain in clarity and relevance what they would lose in myth and mystery. To demystify Christianity one would simply have to place oneself in the existential shoes of the first-century Christians in order to strip their anxieties and hopes of their mythological disguises. Once demythologized, the faith could then be expressed in terms of a modern, Christian existentialism that called for less religion and more faith. Religious guarantees would be abandoned in favor of a faith that could embrace all the uncertainty and dynamism of life in a world without guarantees.

Not everyone liked the prospect of a world without the assurances of myth. Some subscribed to the notion that America was a new Israel and was enshrined in a sacred covenant. That this covenant was in some disarray was no secret, especially during the civil rights movement and the Vietnam War. But the notion of a covenanted nation could be used as a whip to arouse the consciences of a people that had grown lax with too much comfort and power for their own good.

The notion of a civil religion, variously defined and promoted by Robert Bellah and a number of influential colleagues, was merely one expression of a desire to return to the purities and rigor of an earlier faith. It is a desire that still has political consequences in American society, especially when it is shared by the Christian Right. Although Bellah would be embarrassed by a protofascist following of this sort, the desire for a society that transcends the passage of time and endows its people with peculiar rights and responsibilities often leads to attacks on those who have alternative tendencies.

The notion that the modern world was increasingly secular was therefore not only an expression of the intellectual preferences of a cultural elite. It was also a defensive reaction against the discovery that McCarthyite reactions were deeply entrenched in American society. The Robert Birch Society and white citizens' councils have now given way to a Christian Coalition that is more adept at speaking the language of civil politics, but the desire to purify the nation of unwanted influences and unworthy lifestyles runs very deep and strong. The occasional atrocity is merely an outward and visible sign of an inward and spiritual fear of outsiders that goes back not only to the immigrations of the nineteenth century but to the authoritarian and provincial communities of prerevolutionary America. For instance, in the 1950s Arthur Miller's play *The Crucible* made it very clear that these tendencies were as American as apple pie.

It is not surprising that some Christian intellectuals came to the conclusion that a Christianity steeped in myth no longer made sense in a secular and complex world. Such a faith also had a dangerous tendency to become fused with the nation and the state and to arouse aspirations for a messianic republic. Renewed announcements of the death of God were in part the expression of a devout desire to see Christianity freed from its political and cultural captivity. Religion had become too fused with the nation's central institutions to exercise its own freedom and to encourage dissent and rebellion.

I believe that it is no less imperative now than it was in the 1950s to articulate the nature of a secular society, to describe its benefits, and to suggest the conditions under which such a society could emerge. In doing so I will once again examine the notion of a civil religion, chart some of the debate about the possibility of such a religion in the American context, and explore its wider implications for other societies. The notion of a secular society, however, can hardly be developed only in reference to the American context. Other societies are far more secularized than the United States, and much can be learned from examining the relation of religion to their central political and cultural institutions. That is a very tall order for such a small book as this, and I hasten to disclaim at the outset any pretense of a broad historical or comparative study.

What can be done in this book is simply to suggest the way that secularization emerges in a variety of places, medieval as well as modern, European as well as American. To become secular is, I argue, to open oneself and one's society to a wide range of possibilities. Some of those possibilities are clearly interesting and even exciting, some are filled with the potential for liberation and the satisfaction of human desire and aspiration. Other possibilities are more burdensome or fill one with dread. They include a wide range of influences and dangers, threats and disasters, from infection and infestation to invasion and the loss of sovereignty over the self or over one's society. In their totality they constitute the Sacred, with a capital *S*. A truly secular society is therefore one that is wholly open to the Sacred.

To close these possibilities off, to contain them in a place that is accessible only to trained professionals, has been, of course, the strategy of societies that rely on religion and its institutions. Sanctuaries make the Sacred accessible in very small doses under the auspices of an elite that assumes privileges commensurate with the dangers to which it claims to be exposed by contact with the Sacred. Thus, I will be using the term *sacred*, with a lower-case *s*, to refer to the ways in which the Sacred is reduced to manageable proportions in most societies. In these reduced forms, uncertainty and mystery are made accessible and intelligible, if only to those who claim the vision and the training requisite to approaching the Sacred with impunity.

In secular societies one has a relatively equal opportunity to expose oneself to the possibilities that have been otherwise placed beyond the reach of mundane eyes and hands. These possibilities are no longer the property of a particular institution but are open to those who have eyes, so to speak, to see and ears to hear. Those eyes and ears may be trained on the Web, entertained by the media, stimulated by travel, or shocked by the arrival of outside ideas and people into formerly sheltered communities. The point is that when the sacred is diffused, the realm of mystery is dissolved, and what was once revealed only to the few is placed in the open, that is, demystified, demythologized, and thus profaned.

Difficult as it may be to describe, it is more difficult to define a secular society. At the very least, such a society is one in which *the temporal prevails over the lasting.* No obligations endure longer—or require more commitment and sacrifice—than is necessary. Where can we begin to look for examples of this shortening of temporal obligation? Certainly an obvious place is in the relation of the living to the dead and more generally in the veneration of heroes and celebrities. Thus, in the first two chapters I examine monks in the Middle Ages, individuals with multiple personalities in eighteenth-century France, and a wide range of others who have tried to break through the limits of experience and perception imposed on them by their communities and institutions.

In developing this picture, we will be trying to locate some of the orgins of secular societies. In the fourth chapter, therefore, I argue that the tendency for Christianity to secularize tradition, magic, and mystery is rooted in brotherhoods that are fundamentally antipatriarchal. Others have long pointed out that the secular city in the West could emerge only when the loyalties enshrined in brotherhoods were opened to the wider community, and the standards of the wider community were also applied to brotherhoods. As Benjamin Nelson brilliantly argued, the extension of credit on interest was a case in point. Strangers were deemed worthy of being trusted, and no one was given access to credit at no interest. The treasury of merit, so to speak, was widened to include others in the city beyond the pale of the sacred, and the sacred itself was opened to inspection by the sources of credit. Thus, brotherhoods are more or less secularizing forces—the more so when they are open to the political and cultural center but outside the chain of patriarchal command, authority, and inheritance.

Although I will not define a secular society, I will describe in some detail its shape and interpret what it takes to live in such an open and highly uncertain world. The stakes are always high: life and death, satisfaction and despair, relatedness to others and isolation, and the prospect of never knowing enough or being fully understood. The rules for engagement, so to speak, are very unclear. One never knows just what is required to open or close a conversation, to enter into a new relationship, to undertake a course of study, or to be taken seriously when one has something to say. The uncertainties are compounded by the change in one's environment; the rules, even if written down, will constantly be revised and updated, and much of what needs to be known about the rules, such as they are, can only be found by breaking them. One can lose one's religion in the course of acquiring faith. The costs of failure are high. One can become infected, acquire dangerous knowledge, become subversive, all in the process of encountering new fields, seeing new horizons, and acquiring a new sense of oneself and the universe. The more secular a society becomes, the more open to the Sacred it is, and the more risky, uncertain, and precarious life becomes.

Other societies have known times when its people face life-or-death decisions, when the rules for planting or going to war, for marrying or dying are at best vague and in dispute, when there are no guarantees for reward if one is successful, but when the penalties for failure are drastic and swift. At these moments societies have often called upon the dead for sustenance and support, reminded the populace of the example of heroes at decisive moments in the past, and called for varieties of human sacrifice in the present, all in the full knowledge that the future was about to begin. The Sacred can be overwhelming, and it is entirely understandable that societies have found it necessary to reduce it to forms that are human, accessible, and correspondingly more likely to evoke commitment and sacrifice from the people themselves.

However, for a society to exist more fully in time, to be more secular, it is necessary for the living to be free of appeals to sacred memory and eschatological hope. Rather than revere a continuing and fixed deposit of memory and tradition, a secular society turns its memories and traditions over to a continuing and democratic discourse about the past in relation to the present. Such a discourse is necessary if that society is to enjoy realistic degrees of freedom.

In this book I argue that there is nothing to fear—and everything to gain—from living in a society that is not bound together by sacred memories and beliefs, by sacred institutions and practices, or by a religious culture that seeks to collect the various manifestations of the sacred into a single, coherent order. A secular society is open to a wide range of cultural and social experimentation, to the suppressed anguish and grievances of those whose memories and injuries have not been honored, and to the full range of surprises, both positive and negative, that comprise the social and natural environment. In such a society, repression and calls to sacrifice would be at a minimum, but so also would be the former satisfaction of knowing that one's actions and values were enshrined in institutions and cultural memories. In a secular society one is continually exposed to the passage of time without the comforting illusions of transcendence. Thus to live in such a society would require a certain secularity of one's own.

In a secular society there may be much remembering of the past, but without the sort of nostalgia that makes people wish to make up for lost time or to settle old scores. There is, in a secular society, a great deal of interest in patterns of meaning, however obscure or fanciful, but there is little in the way of veneration or genuine wonder. Religion may afford glimpses of the firmament, but there is no guarantee of any meaning at all.

Some would say that such a society is a contradiction in terms: that social life is inherently serious if it endures for any length of time at all. Furthermore, social order requires a sense of its own worth as well as permanence. From this viewpoint the social world cannot be very secular. Even though the firmament may not be in the heavens any more, it still endures in the societies that human beings create in an effort to endow themselves with an illusion of transcendence. It is just such an illusion that I have in mind when I refer to a "civil religion," and I will discuss it at length later in this book. For some, as we shall see, a "civil religion" is real and a thing in itself regardless of its lack of devotees. For others, it is a survival of past attempts to enshrine the social order in a timeless universe: an ancient strategy for providing guarantees, setting rules, limiting knowledge, and legitimating sacrifice.

If all social life is inherently or inevitably religious in some way, how could a secular society be anything other than a contradiction in terms? In this book I will argue that a secular society is not a historical impossibility. However, to complete the process of secularization it will be necessary to remove any signs of the sacred that claim to be able to stand the test of time. Those signs, I argue, are the marks of idolatry. In sociological terms, a wholly secular society would be one in which the Sacred is largely demystified and is nowhere institutionalized. It has no place, so to speak, to lay its head. The Sacred would remain always as a set of historical possibilities, but they would largely be known, objects of choice, and neither mysterious or the object of veneration. There would be no need for the sacred, that is, for the institutionalized, reduced, and accessible forms of the Sacred. There would be no place for idols in a secular society and no need for unnecessary sacrifices of the heart and the mind, the soul and the body.

Societies that require these various forms of sacrifice create individuals with a faulty sense of their own being; indeed, some have a sense that they themselves are afflicted with a fundamental flaw. I argue in the first four chapters that societies provide an array of heroes, charismatic figures, and celebrities that model sacrifice and offer a substitute sense of solidity and worth to the self. These images are thus idols: an apparently solid and legitimate being in relation to whom individuals can acquire a sense of their own being. The hero embodies the wish to stand the test of time and to conquer death by having a being that can endure, like the bones of the ancestors, beyond the grave. Because the idols of heroism offer a cure while embodying the disease, however, they are classical symptoms in the psychoanalytic sense of the word.

In a secular society the experience of the Sacred would therefore always be possible but never necessary. Never imposed or obligatory, the Sacred in a secular society would remain ephemeral rather than institutionalized. This does not mean that a society, once secularized, would be immune to moments of awe or wonder and would be caught up solely in the endless and mundane events of everyday life. However, a secular society would describe and understand the momentous in terms that do not reify or sanctify the moment but allow it to remain caught up in the passage of time itself.

In a secular society idolatry might never be exorcised completely, but it would have a very short shelf-life indeed. Idols are, after all, a form of the sacred that has lost its potential for pointing beyond itself to what remains a mystery; instead, an idol forecloses further possibilities and inferences by pointing only to itself as sacred. The idol is no longer the beginning but has become the end of devotion. In speaking of the sacred, David Martin (1980, 125) puts it this way: "The images and pictures and icons which should mediate possibilities have become barriers, the narrow opening onto vision has become closure" Idols may seem to be the place where the Sacred is to be found, but instead they offer no absorbing or compelling vista of a distant horizon of human possibility. They act as limits. No doubt idols appear to gain strength on the way to a secular society, as a thick religious ethos gets reduced to the propositions debated by theologians or to the doctrines rehearsed in professions of faith. A truly secular society, however, allows images and icons to point beyond themselves to the Sacred; secularity opens the Sacred up to discourse rather than veneration.

Once mystery is reduced to information, there is still plenty to exercise the intellect and the imagination. The world becomes visible as a place of sufficient depth and complexity to warrant all the intellectual, moral, and emotional engagement of which humans are indeed capable. In this book, then, I am depriving the Sacred of any particular spatial or temporal reference; it is pure potential that lies for the time being beyond the ken and control of the individual or group, community or nation in question.

If Christianity is to fulfill its own inherent tendency toward secularity and remain a force for secularizing the larger society, however, it will be necessary to move toward what has been called "religionless Christianity," a phrase first used, I believe, by Dietrich Bonhoeffer. A Christianity-without-religion, I will argue, is capable of overcoming a society's idolatrous, reactionary, and authoritarian tendencies by opening a social system to the full range of its possibilities. I will also argue that a religionless Christianity can demystify social life at the local level and address the potential of the individual that lies beyond required or permissible social performances.

It will be obvious to the many readers who know Bonhoeffer's work how great a debt I owe him and his writings. His essays on the relation of the ultimate to the penultimate are the most thorough and systematic treatment of the problem with which I deal in this book: the task of re-maining open to the future, when the future itself promises not only to complete and correct what one has done or aspired to but will also judge and perhaps destroy it. It is the problem, in short, of living wholeheartedly in the present, knowing that the past and the future impinge on each mo-ment, and yet doing so with no lessening of commitment or concentration on the moment itself. It is the problem of entrusting oneself to the flow of time, without diminishing the moment, or sacrificing it to the future, although one knows that one is living in and for what is destined wholly to pass away.

For Bonhoeffer it is bad faith to confuse the present with the sum total of the possibilities that time alone can offer. That is the distortion provided by the idol. It is the idol who represents the vast array of possibilities, both positive and negative, and promises to reduce them to safe and manageable proportions. So for Bonhoeffer the penultimate that forgets that it is only the penultimate stands in the way of the ultimate rather than providing what is in fact always a necessary and never a sufficient preparation for the final things of life and of death. Conversely, any religion that proclaims it-self as the door to the ultimate in a way that denies time and nature, the things of this world and their proper importance, is guilty of turning itself into an idol: "The penultimate is swallowed up in the ultimate and yet it is still necessary and it retains its right so long as the earth continues" (Bonhoeffer 1995, 141).

There is an idolatry, then, in which religion presents itself as all that is necessary for wholeness or salvation and thus undermines the significance of time and of life itself, of the moment and of the partial and yet binding commitments of which an individual's life is made. There is also an idola-try of the secular, in which it presents itself as the sum total of all possibili-ties to which reason and imagination have access. It is in an attempt to find a third way through these two idolatries toward a radical openness to both the past and the future for the sake of an immersion in time itself that this book is written. I have no special pleadings to make for religion in general or Christianity in particular. That is, I would agree with Bonhoeffer (1995, 139) that "[t]he preparation of the way requires that the penultimate shall be respected and validated for the sake of the ultimate." By the ultimate, however, I do not mean to imply any revelation, any breaking-in of a di-vine word, and final historical judgment. It is enough that the ultimate is simply the sum total of all possibilities, conceivable and inconceivable, fate-ful and trivial, redemptive and damning, life-giving and life-destroying, that lie in front of all of us: the Sacred itself, prior to any of its reductions, however hallowed they may be by tradition or sacrifice, in the sacred.

However, the discussion of Christianity's relation to the secular remains a bit parochial unless we consider the possibility that other cultures, other religions, also have their own tendency to generate secular forms of self-hood and citizenship. It is therefore necessary to engage in a comparative, and occasionally historical, survey of the literature on civil religion. To what extent can it be said of other societies that they, too, have a dynamic that engages the secular with the Sacred and simultaneously blurs the boundaries between the two? Are other societies tending toward precisely that form of secularity in which it is difficult to distinguish the Sacred from the secular, but in which the two seem to be in a dynamic and open-ended relation with one another? I discuss the civil religion at length in chapters five and six.

Secular societies will grant only the most temporary victories over time. To freeze the memory of the people around certain times and events is to make them sacred; that is, it places them beyond the realm of historical inquiry. In a secular society the past is always being revisited and revised with the needs of the present and future generation in mind. It is therefore difficult to know which memories are sacred—that is, beyond adjustment and recall—and which are not sanctified and may therefore more readily be readjusted to the needs of the present. From celebration to discourse— that is the direction that the secularization of a culture will take. The end result is a society without idols.

The more secular a society becomes, the more it therefore permits the various peoples or communities within it to share memories in common without rank or privilege, category or invidious comparison. Thus, a secular society would have memories that recall the past, but without a tendency to find some parts of it sacred while the rest lies outside the temple of collective memory and is thus profaned. The sacrifices of previous generations of each minority would be remembered in a secular democratic pantheon of secular honor. It will be helpful, I argue, to imagine a spectrum along which societies may be ranged according to whether they have a well-institutionalized and traditional civil religion or a collective identity that is relatively fluid, pragmatic, humanistic, and lacking in any specific context. At one end of the spectrum lie societies with a clearly defined and well-institutionalized civil religion: a pantheon of heroes and sacred events, of texts and duties, of sacrifices and commitments, and of guarantees that the society will enshrine the individual's memory. At the other end of the spectrum lie societies where the Sacred is intermittent and problematical, and where individuals are largely left to their own devices to enter the future on the most ambiguous of terms and without guarantees that either they or their sacrifices will be remembered. In this latter group of societies it is difficult for an observer to distinguish the Sacred from the secular.

From this spectrum it will be possible to begin to develop a sense of the conditions under which modern societies may give wide scope to the fascist tendencies that are endemic in any social system that seeks to transcend the passage of time. Had there been no fascist movement in the United States during the fifties it would not be necessary now to reconsider the entire prospect of a secular society. Given the perennial attempt to erect enduring monuments to a society and its achievements, however, it remains a pressing task to try to imagine a social universe without a pantheon. What are the social conditions under which a civil religion can be expected to be absent from a social system? Under what conditions will societies be relatively free from myths of heroism, of sacrifice, and of symbolic victory over time? Will any of us yet be able to live in a society that does not institutionalize the sacred in its founding myths and documents, events and heroes, and does not call for the sacrifice of the self to the larger society? These are the questions that I take up and seek to answer not only in chapters five and six but in the seventh chapter, where I investigate the debates in the United States Senate over the impeachment of President Clinton.

It is precisely when a society's myths seem lacking, empty, or in need of articulation that the danger of an authoritarian regression becomes clear and present. Out of the memories of heroism and decisive events comes ample material out of which to weave a myth of origins. Out of times of crisis and near disaster there is usually enough song or speech to weave a myth of providential intervention. From the memory of past sacrifice comes the definition of the obligations that attend salvation. At least in the United States, the civil religion hypothesis has been a case in point: an attempt at cultural reconstruction and revitalization. This book is my own contribution to the debate over whether such a civil religion exists in the United States and what its consequences are for freedom and civility. I see in whatever vestiges of civil religion survive in the United States a threat to the possibility of a secular society in which individuals, groups, communities, and the nation itself live without illusions of their own uniqueness or superiority and in openness to the possibilities for a global human community. In the studies of civil religion in a variety of nations around the world, however, I find the empirical foundation for a conviction that a secular society is not merely possible; it is indeed the direction in which many, if not most, nations already are proceeding. It is a direction in which unnecessary mystery, sacrifice, and suffering are minimized. Although such a future is full of risk and uncertainty, it is full of hope. In the secular society of the future, I argue, there will be very little room for idols and ample encounters with the Sacred. It is a future in which a religionless Christianity begins to recover its original place as a solvent of communal hatred and as an opportunity for the discovery of new relationships and freedoms.

1

IDOLS, IDOLATRY, AND
UNNECESSARY SUFFERING

Among sociologists there are two basic assumptions about religion. Some assume that religion is primarily an elusive and ephemeral phenomenon. It is precisely in being fixed or identified that religion is transformed into something else. Sociologists of this persuasion prefer to use terms like the sacred, or charisma, or the numinous, to capture religion in their conceptual net. In their view religion is most truly itself when it is least understood and habitual. Once institutionalized, religion becomes something else, a shadow of its former self, or even a contradiction in terms. Charisma, as Weber argued, despises routine and the mundane, the world of work and of everyday responsibility. Once charisma or the sacred becomes entangled in the mundane, it becomes debased and degraded; some say the sacred is secularized in the process of becoming part of everyday life.

In this book I argue that the process of secularization indeed destroys the distinction between the sacred and the profane. The loss of the boundary between the two may not be due simply to the process of institutionalizing charisma, by which the sacred becomes a matter of routine and of everyday life. The boundary between the sacred and the profane may become obscure or problematic as social life itself becomes sufficiently fluid and complex to make any coherent or consistent pattern open to constant renegotiation and change. In any event, secularization increases as the boundary between the sacred and the profane becomes more permeable and less distinct.

For some sociologists the erosion of this boundary is a sign of decadence. Rituals become performances or games. Charisma becomes associated with celebrities rather than with those who bear awesome—indeed, supernatural—power and authority. If there is a bias in their view, it is in favor of those who regard this aspect of secularization as an appropriate outcome of the Christianization of Western societies. This is a point that has been forgotten or simply ignored by those who regard secularization as the enemy of Christian faith and life. Bonhoeffer (1995, 97) points out that "What has been utterly forgotten here is the original message of the Reformation that there is no holiness of man either in the sacred or the profane as such, but only that which comes through the merciful and sin-forgiving word of God." It is an old argument, but needs to be repeated here, that by envisaging a God whose ways are wholly other to the ways of humans, Christianity would have left the world without a reliable trace of the transcendent had it not been for the capacity of any social system to regenerate its own forms of the sacred and thus to manufacture idols.

Other sociologists assume that religion is the heart and soul of social life. Far from being antithetical to the world of the repetitive and apparently permanent, it is the vital and compelling expression of what transcends the passage of time. To find a social order that does transcend "the changes and chances of this mortal life" is to find the sacred itself. In religious beliefs and practices societies seek to harmonize sacred symbols. It is the task of a civil religion to bind together the fragments of the sacred that are found in smaller contexts, in the family, for instance, or in the community, in a region or ethnic group. Perhaps the sacred is found in certain places or at certain times, on days of sad or triumphant remembrance. Perhaps the sacred is found in people or in events that have become the object of popular veneration. The sacred may inhere in the recollection of the past and in affection or respect for ancestors. In any event, it is the task of religion to weave these fragments of the sacred into a coherent and authoritative fabric so that a group or community, an institution or a society may achieve a level of symbolic transcendence over the passage of time.

Sociologists of this persuasion may constantly contrast the sacred and the profane, society and the individual in order to demonstrate the difference between what is permanent and real from what is contingent and ephemeral. The process of secularization, in this view, undermines a society's attempt to transcend the passage of time.

Secularization is also therefore the enemy of religion. However, once again we have to recall the argument that immersion in the passage of time is precisely what Christianity has required, at least in its more Western variations. This is not the place to engage that argument in any detail. At the outset it is enough simply to refer once again to Bonhoeffer's (1995, 91) careful statement of the relation of the sacred to time under the auspices of Christian faith:

> The concept of historical inheritance, which is linked with the consciousness of temporality and opposed to all mythologization, is possible only where thought is consciously or unconsciously governed by the entry of God into history at a definite place and at a definite point of time, that is to say, by the incarnation of God in Jesus Christ. Here history becomes a serious matter without being canonized.

In this book I will examine the ways that societies continually throw up bulwarks or barriers against the passage of time. Heroes are included in sacred memory; critical events in the past are not only remembered but reenacted. The faith of the forefathers, so to speak, is revived in the present. Certain values are considered to be timeless. In all these ways, I suggest, the Sacred, that sum total of all possibilities both life-giving and threatening, is reduced to the sacred: to something that can be imagined, perhaps understood, and conceivably manipulated. In this way the Sacred is reduced, that is, to idolatry. The prerequisite of fascism is indeed to be able to evoke a realm of the sacred that embraces and transcends the entire nation and inducts every member of the society into the lists of those who may be called upon to sacrifice themselves for what is eternal. If we are to find a source of philosophical or theological resistance to this tendency, it is worth remembering Bonhoeffer's (1995, 91) additional reminder that:

> It is precisely in its temporality that it is history with God's consent. Consequently when we ask about the historical inheritance we are not asking the timeless question about those values of the past of which the validity is eternal. Man himself is set in history and it is for that reason that he now asks himself about the present and about the way in which the present is taken up by God in Christ.

On the subject of modernity there are also significant differences among sociologists who study religion. Some assume that modernity simply provides another stage on which religion can play out its life and perform at least some of its usual functions. Even though the appearance of religion may be drastically changed in the most modern societies, religion itself is still there. Religious commitment and even enthusiasm may come and go, showing up in critical episodes, but religion may also lie quietly in the realm of implicit understandings. In either event, commitment to common values or beliefs remains, in their view, critical for the support of the most basic exchanges in social life, and that commitment is nourished from roots that are inherently religious.

For others the persistence of religion is not due to an inheritance so much as to the alleged fact that people are fundamentally religious or that societies inevitably express themselves in symbols that command adherence and consent. In this view, the old religious symbols may have lost their appeal and power in modern societies, but new ones will have taken their place either because of popular religious tendencies or because of the inevitable attempt of any society to dignify itself in religious terms. Thus, we may have a religion that apparently functions without a god but nonetheless seeks to command universal consent and to endow some aspects of social life with the sacred. This sort of modernized religion may take the form, for instance, of a belief in—and concern for—humanity and thus would dignify the individual with the authority and power once reserved for the deity. Or religion may become a powerful ideology that provides meaning and coherence to a world that otherwise appears to be hopelessly chaotic or beyond the reach of human understanding and control.

Other sociologists are not so sanguine about the prospects of religion in modernity. Some appear to think that religion is an endangered species because it is poorly adapted to a social world that thrives on uncertainty and requires constant change and adaptation. It is of course not only sociologists who regard modern societies as jaundiced with change and uncertainty. Bonhoeffer (1995, 107) himself, although we have seen him exalt the plunge into time, finds a relentless present almost unendurable:

> With the loss of past and future, life fluctuates between the most bestial enjoyment of the moment and an adventurous game of chance. An abrupt end is put to any kind of inner self-development and to any gradual attainment of personal and vocational maturity. There is no personal destiny, and consequently there is no personal dignity. Serious tensions and inwardly necessary periods of waiting are not sustained. This is apparent in the field of labour and in the erotic field alike. Slow pain is more feared than death. There is no recognition, there is even contempt, for the value of suffering in giving form to life through the threat of death. The alternative now is health or death. Genuine tensions are not endured.

The plunge into time, then, must carry with it a sense of the past and the future as extensions of the present. The modern present, which has been reduced to a series of fleeting moments, lacks any sense of legacy or inheritance and bears no responsibility therefore either to the past or to the future.

In this book I argue that a secularized society leaves the individual free to become aware of the passage of time precisely because it does not freeze time into a series of sacred moments or events or sacralize certain personages or ways of life as exemplary for all times. To take time seriously, as Bonhoeffer put it, without canonizing it is to live within the dynamic of the passage of time.

Therefore, to live in the present as if it had no roots in the past would be tantamount to having had a psychological lobotomy; it would be a fundamental denial of the place of the individual in the passage of time and of his or her dependence on the past. Similarly, to live as if the future is not more or less than the next moment, to live without existential anxiety or the patience required for self-development and suffering, is to reduce oneself to the subhuman. In his letters from prison, for instance, it is clear that Bonhoeffer felt that the mark of spiritual maturity was to live wholly in the present and that the one who can do so gains a measure of spiritual authority in the eyes of peers and of younger men and women. However, it would be a tragic misunderstanding of Bonhoeffer at that point to assume that for him the present is a truncated experience of time devoid of the past and the future. On the contrary, his letters are full of hopes and reminiscences, and he lived within the tension between the seasons of the church year and the comings and goings of everyday life. For Bonhoeffer, time was indeed the medium in which the soul lives and breathes.

Perhaps an analogy would help to translate this understanding of life in a secularized society into other terms. In psychoanalysis the patient learns how to be patient in the sense described by Bonhoeffer. He or she is asked to enter into a direct experience both with the past and with the future. That is, the individual is required to experience the pain of old losses or the anguish of unfulfilled and hopeless desire as though it were present and yet with the full understanding that these emotions are "dated"; they belong to the past. In the same way the individual is required to understand that his or her grief, for instance, may be anticipatory. It may be the loss of someone who is deeply loved or the end of one's life that is bearing in upon the present and makes the patient anxious. Here again the psychoanalytic task is to enable the patient to enter the part of the psyche where time is put "on hold"; the libido, as Freud put it, is impervious to the passage of time, and it is the storehouse of unfulfilled and incomplete emotion.

Thus, to live in the present, with a full sense of the bearing of the past and the future on the moment, is to live with a sense of all the possibilities that inhere in the moment. The past impinges on the present without haunting it; the past is a source of possibility, like the present, but it does not weigh on the present as a source of heavy duty or of necessity. Similarly, the future also enters into the consciousness of time in the present, but the present need not be mortgaged to the future or seem to be merely foreordained by a future destiny. The present is only unbearable when it is empty of the past and the future, and thus lacks any other possibility than ways of passing or killing time.

There are theological reasons for believing in such a present, but one does not have to be a theologian to find one's way into a present that is filled with possibility and responsibility. It is of course from a theological point of view that Bonhoeffer (1995, 224–225) is writing when he says:

> To contrast a secular and a Christian principle as the ultimate reality is to fall back from Christian reality into the reality of antiquity, but it is equally wrong to regard the Christian and the secular as in principle forming a unity. It is now no longer established in advance what is "Christian" or what is "secular"; both of these are recognized, with their special qualities and with their unity, only in the concrete responsibility of action which springs from the reconciliation that has been effected in Jesus Christ.

To live in a secular society, then, is to live without the protections offered by religion against the experience of the passage of time. That is why some sociologists anticipate the eclipse of religion, if not its demise, simply because religion will be overshadowed by other institutions. No one will need the church or the clergy to establish the times and time constraints, the calendars of demand, sacrifice, and reward, by which a society learns to make promises, to work together, and to satisfy grievances. Secular institutions prove more than adequate in getting people to work together, in establishing basic trust, in making fair exchanges, and in controlling those who might disrupt the social order.

In this view the world has learned all it can from religion about the mechanisms of inspiration and authority, and societies can now do without the services of the sacred. One does not, however, have to adopt a theological viewpoint or to engage in religious apologetics for the relevance of Christianity to a secular society. That is, one does not have to begin from the premises of a Bonhoeffer. One can indeed opt for a larger view of the range of possibility in any society from an agnostic or atheistic perspective as well. As Herbert Marcuse (1960, 262) once put it,

> Philosophical structures had hitherto domiciled "the truth," setting it apart from the historical struggle of men, in the form of a complex of abstract, transcendental principles. Now, however, man's emancipation could become man's own work, the goal of his self-conscious practice. The true being, reason, and the free subject could now be transformed into historical realities.

This transformation of the true self and of reason into something real will require action to relieve suffering, and not merely the perfection of some kind of thought. That is because, at least for Feuerbach and the materialists following Hegel, Marcuse argues, the world was a fallen place, where humans could not freely and reasonably satisfy their needs. Until human suffering could be relieved and the conditions established for a genuinely free and satisfying existence, thought itself would be distorted and constrained. Outside the Garden of Eden, humans are strangers to their true selves, and religion itself reflects and reinforces their estrangement.

In this book I will follow the materialists in one respect; I believe that religion in general and the sacred in particular are socially produced. However, it is evident that the sacred seems to take on a life of its own. Although humans originally produced and continue to construct the sacred, the sacred then acquires its own authority, defines social life, and constrains the imagination and the heart.

For liberation, individuals will therefore have to look to a kind of thought that goes back to the beginning and seeks to understand how humans do become strangers to themselves and to real possibilities for satisfaction, freedom, and rationality. In that process, religion will be investigated along with politics and economics in order to find out how it started in the first place. How did religion flourish in the cracks and fissures of human existence, like the grass that grows in the crevices of the pave-

ment? How did the sacred emerge from social life? How does the sacred acquire an authority that appears to transcend its human origins?

Speaking of Feuerbach's attack on Hegel, Marcuse (1960, 268) points to
the sort of questioning that is part of any critical thinking that "would not
simply demonstrate and understand its object but would investigate its origin and thus question its right to exist." It would therefore seem reasonable
to hope that investigating religion critically would expose the origins of the
sacred. Seeing the sacred in this light should allow us to decide for ourselves whether or not to preserve beliefs and practices that for so long have
promised freedom and satisfaction but merely delivered further duty and
suffering.

A good example of this sort of critical investigation is Maurice Bloch's
(1989, 19–45) study of ritual. In ritual he finds an extreme form of traditional authority: a politics in which degrees of freedom both for the powerful and the subjected are reduced to an absolute minimum. In ritual the
participants sacrifice any freedom of will beyond the decision to participate. Their words and gestures are prescribed, and their assent is part of
the order of things. For those who speak with authority in such ritualized
occasions, however, there is also a loss of freedom. The priest becomes
depersonalized—a representative of an archaic priest or victim whose
words alone give life. The formalization of speech, the rigidity of prescribed
language, the inevitability by which the ritual proceeds from one stage
to the next, all these indicate that there is no way to interrupt, to stop, to
question, or to criticize this order of things. The seriousness of this speech
reaches a climax as the individual celebrant speaks the words of the
founder of the rite or gives voice to the ancestors' speech in tones that are
not his or her own but those indeed of the past speakers. Their words alone
have authority and spell the difference between life and death.

That is why in a ritual one has entered a zone that is virtually timeless,
in the sense that the clock of mundane calculation has come to an end.
One is also incarnating and reliving the past in such a way that the present
becomes a mere extension of the past. So also indeed, as Bloch points out,
does the future become a mere projection of the past. There is no other
way, no other possibility, no alternative response, no different viewpoint,
than the one being uttered in that particular context. Those words and gestures are timeless, then, in the sense of being out of time and for all time.

> The significance of this is that we should perhaps see the origin of re-
> ligion in this special strategy of leadership, the use of form for power,
> which we have found in a lesser form in our study of the communi-
> cation of traditional authority; we would then see the performance
> of religion as serving a special form of authority. (Bloch 1989, 45)

It would also seem reasonable to hope that once the sacred has been
subjected to this sort of critical investigation, it no longer will seem to be

part of another, transcendent world that is known only in its absence. The other world, whatever that is, becomes present, local, familiar, available, and open to investigation. No longer obligatory, the sacred should become clearly optional. Humans then can make choices about it, once they understand that the sacred is contingent, that it might never have existed, and that it depends for its survival on a set of conditions that humans have a right to change. In this book the name for this route is the process of secularization. Marcuse (1960, 268) puts it this way: "The prevailing state of man is the result of a long historical process in which all transcendental values have been "secularized" and made the aim of man's empirical life. The happiness he sought in heaven and in pure thought can now be satisfied on earth."

There is ample disagreement among sociologists as to how much progress has been made toward such a freedom or even whether that achievement should be called progress. Some would argue that religion never has been freely chosen but has always been accepted primarily by people who were never entirely familiar with themselves and who lived in circumstances that were sometimes oppressive and brutal. However, as some academic discussions of religion demonstrate rather clearly, some social scientists see the sacred as a "given"; it is therefore necessary and not merely a social product of a people's life together over a long period of time.

Even sociologists who agree on the relation of religion to modernity may disagree about whether they like what they see. Some may be quite delighted to see public religiosity persist in its new forms. Never mind that religion has lost some of the trappings and vestments and prerogatives of the institutional church, for instance; it survives in the pursuit of universal human rights that accord dignity to the individual and set limits on the authority of the social system. Those of this persuasion may be relatively pleased to find religion thriving outside of clerical control and welling up in the celebrations of a popular culture that is more electronic than sacramental. Religion may even take the form of aesthetics or science and achieve the sort of beauty reserved in the past for holiness itself.

Others, however, are worried by the transformations of religion and see in its revised forms either a secularized and decadent form of old religious beliefs or even the prospect of collective madness and new tyranny. For them there is little comfort in seeing masses of people swaying to the same tune or raising their hands as if with one accord in a new gesture of salute.

Theoretical and empirical studies of religion leave some social scientists convinced that there is something transcendent about certain beliefs and symbols, even when they can document the conditions under which the sacred was originally produced. Penetrating the veil of the temple and witnessing the manufacture of the sacred may not in fact lead to disbelief. We therefore will have to look further if we are to understand why idols do not always lose their luster when exposed to rational inquiry.

How far, then, can the process of secularization go? How far can societies go in allowing their members to think for themselves, to own and perhaps to control impulses and forces that in the past have seemed mysterious? How far can societies go in permitting freedom and in subjecting individuals only to those requirements and restrictions that are wholly necessary for the continuity of the society itself? Under what conditions would it be possible for a society to thrive and endure without the benefits and burdens of a religious culture that defines the nation and makes its people responsible for carrying out its purpose in history? More to the point of this work, what form will the sacred take in a society that fails to carry conviction about its own identity and continuity?

Answers to these questions will largely depend on whether the sociologist in question sees religion as something ephemeral and charismatic or as the very substance of social life. These answers will also depend on whether the sociologist sees religion in modern societies as transformed into something general and abstract that is still central to the larger society or as being relatively marginal and even moribund.

In this book I pursue these questions further by asking about the conditions under which public religiosity might be said to thrive or at least persist in certain societies. If we can discern those societies that are relatively free from public displays of religion, we can also speculate about the sort of conditions under which such commitments would be unnecessary. If we can find societies in which there is still public religiosity, but where the trappings of the sacred are relatively threadbare, we can speculate about the conditions that make such religiosity moribund. If we can find societies in which public religiosity persists but in which individuals see through the masks of the sacred, so to speak, to the interests and strategies that lie behind it, we can speculate about the conditions under which religion could survive without being convincing. It might persist and appear to be important even though its beliefs and ceremonies are beginning to command less conviction and assent. Finally, we may find societies in which public religiosity seems to be alive and well, of vital importance for the society as a whole and entirely credible and authoritative to its people.

Among sociologists there is an assumption that any form of social life rests on a certain amount of imagination. Since we cannot know all the members of a society, we have to imagine who they are and what they are like. Are they like us or are they fundamentally different? Do they care about the same things we do? Can we trust them with the education of our children? Will they value our sacrifices? Can we imagine ourselves as all sharing the same fate?

To make others seem real to us, let alone understandable or attractive, we need to adopt what sociologists have long called cultural fictions. Call them beliefs, because indeed they are: beliefs that allow a people to have confidence that, whatever their differences may be, they are part of a larger moral community that holds dear the same values and will make the same sacrifices. Those who have come only recently are likened to those who came and went before under the providence of God for a purpose that will long endure after their passing. The society will thus continue when we, like those who came before us, have raised our families, worked our fields, built our bridges and our institutions, and been laid to rest in the local cemetery. It is a cherished belief, and it dies hard.

Of course, not all those on the same shores do hold certain truths in common. Some may be serving an alien spiritual authority, a pope, a maharishi, a witch from Endor, or a gentile seer. At times, Americans have indeed feared that there was a fifth column among them, one that was sending information and secrets to a hostile foreign power. The Red scares of the 1950s were simply another sign that American cultural fictions were not as convincing as they had been in the war years. Now there are large numbers of Americans who fear that the cultural foundation of their country is being eroded by a more pernicious influence, secular humanists, who will teach the children foreign gods or, worse yet, no god at all. Cultural fictions are thus always susceptible to doubt and, sometimes, to panic. The more secular a society, the more vulnerable are its functions to doubt and disproof, and the more difficult it becomes to legitimate a call for sacrifice or resist the test of time.

A truly secular society is one in which these cultural fictions are understood to be just that: not merely illusions with the capacity to motivate or even captivate, but ideas and beliefs that are better understood than venerated. As topics of public conversation these fictions lose their power to enchant and become the narratives of particular groups as they commend their history, the sacrifices of previous generations, and the prospects of the living to the attention and honor of others who share the same territory and political system. The more secular a society, the more that society loses a sense of mystery about the life that cannot be seen or touched but that nonetheless dwells in its midst.

The Sacred is the world that lies alongside the one in which we ordinarily move, talk, imagine, and have what is left of our being. In the Sacred dwells all our knowledge of others who share our fate but who are not known to us directly and whose presence can only be signified. A symbolic world of signals and signs points to the Sacred; take, for example, the liturgy that points to an alternative society or kingdom alongside the one in which we live. In the words of the sacred we imagine and conjure up the presence of the departed and of generations to come and share with them a common fate. That common fate is articulated in our collects and other prayers, where we speak of the unspeakable to the One who can scarcely be mentioned let alone addressed with any ease or confidence.

When the signs and signals that point to the Sacred fail to give access but merely stand in the way; when the signs or signals turn into symbols that demand in their own right the sort of attention appropriately given only to the Sacred; when these symbols take up the space of the Sacred and bar the way to what is our common potential, our collective imagination, our hidden unity, they become idols. As David Martin (1980, 125) puts it,

> [T]he necessary instruments of openness can lead to closure. The partition which says there is more to come may cut off potentiality. The transfiguration may be used to diminish and not to alter, because the figures of grace have been translated into a completely foreign 'other' world expropriated and removed from their proper contact with human potentiality."

Martin has shown how the words and music of devotion address and suggest the Sacred world that is always just beyond the horizon of perception and direct experience. The other world is then brought into play in the present in a way that upsets the rhythms of everyday life, calls into question what otherwise passes for the inevitable, and supplies a rationality that tears apart what has been understood to be mere common sense. There is a new sense, held in common, of what life is about. Above all, Martin (1980, 116) makes it clear that theology and the liturgy, religion, in fact, are ways of speaking about the unspeakable. I would simply add that any religion seeks to tie together into a single system the sacred symbols and practices that point to, address, and embody the Sacred. Attempts to communicate that stand in the way of the ineffable, or seek to incorporate the transcendent with no remainder, inevitably distort the Sacred. They get in the way and act as barriers instead of offering the currency of communication with the beyond: I would call them the sacred, that is, idols:

> The world is deaf, dumb and dark: it does not comprehend the word, and does not receive the light. The message comes through the senses but it is in a new language for which we lack adequate translation. The language has an overtone which we recognize but cannot catch. We hear and touch, taste and see, but the word of grace remains elusive: "that seeing they may *not* see, and hearing they may *not* understand." (Martin 1980, 121)

That is why idols are typically regarded as "dumb." They cannot participate in communication about the ineffable. As Martin (1980, 122, 123) later puts it, "What transcends can only be partially understood. Therefore we cannot give a full account of the transcendent Word: we respond by analogy and paradox." As Martin points out, however, "the language of what they profess . . . becomes the lingo of their profession." Analogy and paradox become doctrine and received opinion.

That is what I mean by an idol: the turning of something that had suggested and pointed to the Sacred into something that stands in its stead and protects one from the full force of the unknown.

A secular society incorporates the Sacred into its public discourse by various techniques, including investigation, discourse, and entertainment, rather than reducing it to idols that represent the Sacred even while keeping humans at a safe remove from its power. Thus, a secular society is open to the Sacred in the form of a wide range of obscure meanings, of hidden intentions, of dimly disclosed motives, and of hitherto scarcely imaginable possibilities.

Take, for example, popular images of people who seem strange because they are often beside themselves and have sudden shifts of personality and character. Sometimes they develop serious afflictions: a paralyzed arm or leg, a habit of barking, or even bleeding from the hands and feet or the forehead. Ian Hacking (1995, 165–66) tells of a young woman, Louise Latour, who caught the French public imagination in 1875:

> She was called the stigmatic of Bois-d'Haine (a small Belgian village near the French border). She was famous all across Roman Catholic Europe for the miraculous stigmata that appeared on her side, hands, and feet every Friday. She was also famous for her devotional trance, and for the fact that she had eaten no food for years. Secular medicine tried to ignore her, but finally the Belgian medical academy established a commission to study her.

As someone whose stigmata could be marveled at or even venerated, the unfortunate Lateau could function as an idol. She could incorporate in herself the sacred, even at some cost to her physical integrity and comfort. However, she would also stand as a barrier between the public and the hidden forces that were producing in her these remarkable and unhappy effects. Because France was in the course of secularizing fairly rapidly, however, Latour became the object of concerted study into what later came to be known as multiple personalities. Understood at the time to be a case of double consciousness, Latour's bodily symptoms were thought to be hysterical manifestations of a psychological source; that interpretation made her a candidate for various treatments, notably hypnosis. It would not be unusual to find that such a diagnosis described her condition in a way that would also call for the services that the diagnostician in question was prepared to offer.

The more secular a society, then, the more the secrets of the heart and the soul are made available for public information, for scientific analysis, or for the imagination. One can venerate saints, but to learn from them about the potential of the ordinary individual is to turn veneration into something more analytical or discursive. There can be "no science of the soul," as Hacking (1995, 218–19) pointed out, but there can be "sciences of memory" that can provide the subject matter for public discussions of the human potential.

When the soul is discussed rather than approached with veneration, some of the possibilities that open up are touching and enlightening: a capacity for faithful love, enduring attachment, and a longing for restoration.

Other possibilities, however, are less savory: a capacity for cruelty that compares favorably with what sadists do to their victims or with soldiers on a rampage through conquered territory. Behind the veil of the Temple is the threat of death; that is why the priesthood has to be carefully selected and trained for the highest revelation. Behind the sanctuary railing an ancient murder is reenacted whenever the crucifixion is remembered; within the sacred precincts violence is enshrined, repressed, forgotten, and recovered, as though by holy magic. Without that magic, however, there is little mystery to be revealed: simply the raw features of abuse or the perennially murderous fantasies of the civilized psyche.

The Christian rites that venerate the memory of the crucifixion, as well as the ones that reenact the death of Christ as though it were a living human sacrifice, have therefore kept alive but also concealed the possibility of sadistic cruelty within the community itself. On the one hand, the liturgy reminds the Christian community that it is capable of that kind of violence: the rejection of someone who represents a range of possibility beyond what the community itself is willing to consider, understand, or tolerate. On the other hand, however, the reenactment in the liturgy shelters individuals from facing the extent of their own propensities, if only in fantasy, toward violence. Those propensities are hinted at but are then resolved within the format of the liturgy in a way that exempts or absolves the believer from a genuine acknowledgment of his or her own potential for inflicting or accepting such suffering. The ritual acts as a shadow play in which the negative potential of the community is summoned up and then exorcised.

This collusion between religious ritual, under the auspices of the church, and the violence of the community has seldom been better described than in *Rituals of Blood*, Orlando Patterson's recent study of the violence in American society inflicted on slaves and their descendants. Much of that violence, Patterson notes, was endemic to the southern community, in part a legacy from the Celtic traditions of Scottish and Irish folk, like the burning cross itself that became the idol of the Ku Klux Klan. The burning cross of the Klan was thus a vast reduction of the ambiguity and complexity of the cross to a signal defining the revenge of an ethnocentric, violent, and prostrate people. Prior to the Civil War lynching was directed by whites primarily against other whites, Patterson notes. It was in the aftermath of the defeat and humiliation of the Civil War that the Afro-American became the target for the violence endemic within the white community. The ex-slave became a scapegoat for defeat and a symbol of illegitimate aggression, frustrated and dangerous sexual impulses, and forces that were so dangerous as to be thought satanic.

It is important to realize not only that the Klan and racial violence were condoned and in some cases encouraged and even led by white clergy but that the rituals of the southern church became part of what Patterson aptly calls a southern civil religion. The issue he raises is a troubling one:

how could the cross of Christ could be associated with the lynching of the Negro?: "The cross—Christianity's central symbol of Christ's sacrificial death—became identified with the crucifixion of the Negro, the dominant symbol of the Southern Euro-American supremacist's civil religion (1998, 217).

To define the repertoire of social possibility is in itself a political act. Indeed, every society defines the limits of the possible in such a way as to limit public discussion of alternative ways of life and different distributions of power. To go beyond the limits of public discussion, however, is precisely what is needed if a society is to engage the full range of opportunities and threats, surprises, and repressed memories that constitute its environment. That is why, as Hacking (1995, 213) points out, so many movements base themselves on the recovery of past injustice and injury:

> Many wings of feminism, with their emphasis on survivors of incest and other forms of family violence, find in the recall of past evil a critical source of empowerment. Sects of Protestant fundamentalism impressed by tales of satanic ritual abuse, and of programming by diabolical cults, rely on the restoration of buried memory.

Where the devil is thought to be lurking, or for that matter where angels are assumed to be hovering, a wide range of possibilities for social transformation is on the verge of being admitted to legitimate public discourse. So long as they remain wholly Sacred, it would be a profanation for these unmentioned potentialities to be placed on the public agenda. To do so would be to risk the charge of blasphemy: a charge that was central to the indictment of Jesus. Thus, to entertain the possibility of a social order based on heavenly justice is just as subversive as it is to disclose the path of the devil through the streets of respectable neighborhoods. There are penalties for breaking the limits not only of what can be discussed but what can be thought to be a realistic possibility.

Societies set parameters on legitimate discourse, then, by setting up sacred markers that define the limits of what that society may aspire to or tolerate. These limits bear the marks of the sacred and define not only what the society will stand for in history and in the eyes of other societies but what it will not stand for.

Such an embodiment of the sacred at the level of the nation-state is sometimes called a civil religion: a well-defined, carefully articulated, and widely institutionalized set of symbols and practices that determine the range of legitimate possibility and aspiration.

When the sacred is more widely diffused, less institutionalized, more fluid and subject to the pressures of public interest or enthusiasms, it can take on a variety of forms. The presence of the devil or of angels thus can suggest a wide range of possibilities that are pressing on the public imagination and waiting to be articulated. So long as they remain off the limits of legitimate debate, however, they remain sacred. The process of turning them from objects of veneration or holy fear into the subject of public discussion is what I mean by the process of secularization.

It is not unusual, especially for sociologists, to take such an essentially positive view of the bizarre or the occult. Certainly, Hacking's discussion of the widespread French interest in double consciousness and multiple personality suggests that these personalities proliferated and became the object of scientific and public fascination in the aftermath of a devastating defeat in the Prussian War and after the communist revolt in Paris. By the same token, in the aftermath of the conflicts of the 1960s and the American defeat in Vietnam a wide range of religious movements attracted public attention, fear, and loathing in the United States. Devils and angels, occult religious groups, New Age religiosity—all these heralded the advent of new opportunities and threats, of new dangers but also of new possibilities for social transformation. Like the proliferation of multiple personalities in France in the 1870s and 1880s, however, these new demonstrations of eccentricity may be seen as the form that social experimentation takes when it is illegitimate or repressed.

However, it is quite possible to take a dim sociological view of these developments. The civil religion, as some argued, was declining, degenerate, or finished, and the sacred was taking on new forms that owed little if anything to official or conventional religiosity. The new religious movements would then seem to express a hunger for social discipline in the wake of the moral chaos of the 1960s. Fundamentalist Christianity could then be seen as an attempt to restore the virtues imagined to have dominated a simpler American society in the late nineteenth century, when men were men, immigrants were to be civilized, and those who served or even died for the nation-state were to be revered as well as honored.

So long as various forms of social protest lay claim to being sacred, they remain in a zone to be venerated or tolerated rather than examined and discussed. Only when they become thoroughly secularized do their impulses and aspirations, memories and longings provide the fuel and subject matter for public debate. Thus, it was a step in the secular direction for scientists to begin to discuss multiple selves rather than to venerate a stigmatized soul. However, science places its own limitations on the imaginable and hence on the possible. By "thoroughly secularized," therefore, I mean something more than subjecting the sacred to sociological or psychological inquiry. As Hacking (1995, 219–20) explains,

> Our present struggles about memory are formed within a space of possibilities established in the nineteenth century. If one metaphorically speaks of the structure of the possible knowledge that we can have, and which serve as the battlefield of our politics, they were put in place at that time. Today when we wish to have a moral dispute about spiritual matters, we democratically abjure subjective opinion. We move to objective facts, science.

More, however, is needed than scientific inquiry if a secular society is to be realized. In this book I argue a fairly simple thesis: that a society is only secularized when the religious self-understanding of that society has been tried and found notably wanting. What kinds of civil religion there may be, whether all societies have them, and what forms they take as a society becomes increasingly secular: all that will occupy us in later chapters. Here I am simply suggesting that societies have ways of imagining themselves that make them seem to have a historical identity and purpose. For some societies their place in history or the cosmos may seem to have been ordained by a deity, whereas for others it is an ideology, perhaps one as well developed as fascism or Marxism, that gives them a sense of transcending the passage of time. Without a religious self-understanding societies may seem fragile, precarious, and hardly worth the price of human sacrifice.

When a nation, such as France in the wake of defeat and rebellion, begins to disintegrate, individuals like Louise Latour become more commonplace; they, too, begin to disintegrate and develop a wide range of symptoms. It was no accident that first-century Palestine was also filled with individuals who were paralyzed or beside themselves, who could not talk or walk, and whose symptoms, being hysterical, were open to the sort of healing witnessed in the New Testament. The effects of powerful suggestion can not only paralyze someone but make them free once again to speak and to move about. That was precisely what the scientists found who were studying the celebrated cases of multiple personality in France after the defeat of the French in the Prussian War. The list of symptoms produced by one individual, Louis Vivet, reads like a list of the same demons who terrorized individuals in first-century Palestine: [e]very kind of pain, paralysis, anesthesia, contracture, muscular spasm, hyperesthesia, mutism, rash, bleeding, coughing, vomiting, convulsing; every kind of epileptic seizure, catatonia, St. Vitus' dance (chorea) . . . language impairment, animalization (the patient becomes a dog), delusions of persecution, kleptomania, loss of sight in this or that eye, restricted vision, taste, or smell" (Hacking 1995, 174) The list goes on. These are the stigmata of defeat, terror, hopelessness, loss, helplessness, and anguish.

Not only are these symptoms of what has been variously called battle fatigue or post-traumatic stress syndrome prevalent in traumatized populations, they come to preoccupy public attention much in same way that the victims of Agent Orange or the Gulf War Syndrome have focused public attention in the United States on the untold agony of recent wars. The stigmata of internal strife become the expressive symbols of what a nation has endured. Hacking reminds us that, at the time of these investigations of double consciousness and of hysterical symptoms, France was no longer confident of its historical destiny or even of its ability to survive. Suffering acutely from the experience of defeat, France faced the prospect of not being able to stand the test of time. It was becoming, in a word, secular. Speaking of the widespread interest in one case of double consciousness,

Hacking (1995, 165) places those participating in the debate over extraordinary mental states in the context of their time:

> They were part of a larger politics, a battle for the character of France itself, for a France that had just been disgraced in war, for a France that was obsessed by the problem of degeneration, for a France that saw its science in visible decline before the vigor of the German- and English-speaking worlds.

I would add that the boundary separating the sacred from the profane was itself under attack, and that no sanctuary would be immune to the forces of secularization.

A young woman with stigmata, who bleeds from the places where Christ was wounded, is a sentinel on the boundary between the known and the unknown. She is an idol, in the sense that she stands for the presence of powerful forces but also, by being venerated and set apart, keeps these forces at safe distance from the population. Once she is no longer venerated but turned into an object of study, however, such a person becomes a source of vital information about the range of possibility. In France, a massive report in 1874 detailed the cases of men and women who were traumatized during the war; some of them later suffered amnesia, and their cases became the basis for a new science of memory. According to Hacking (1995, 189), "Doctors of the day said that they were, to their own surprise, inaugurating a new field of study." In becoming objects of study, therefore, these individuals, with their extraordinary paralyses and hemorrhages, became secularized. As mysteries are revealed, so also is the human potential for self-destructive fantasy and for healing, for isolation and for profound connection with others, for helplessness and renewed vitality and movement.

It is not surprising, then, that the same individuals who become objects of study also may become the bearers of hope; some indeed become celebrities. The sacred, no longer contained in the few who are venerated for their suffering, becomes more widely dispersed. As the sacred is found to be more accessible and even commonplace, a population then finds within itself the capacities for spiritual heroism. Popular detective stories, novels, and plays take up the theme of amnesia, lost personal memory, and the rediscovery of the self.

If all of this sounds contemporary, it is perhaps because the topic of recovered memory is currently both popular and controversial. I do not intend to go into it here other than to point out that there is a connection between national disasters, traumatized populations, and new testimony by those whose agony has previously been unconscious and untold. Critics who deride public interest in these testimonies may miss their significance as emblems of a more widespread trauma. I am arguing, moreover, that the discovery of individuals who are able to recover themselves and acquire new aptitudes and associations is crucial for a society that hungers for a sense of possibility.

When the sacred becomes diffuse within a population, then, the capacity for amnesia and multiple selves, but also for self-discovery and spiritual transformation, becomes democratized, but when the sacred is institutionalized this capacity is largely placed off limits, as it were. Hacking reminds us that witch hunts in the West have often focused on individuals whose behavior resembles that of people with multiple selves: "sleepers," they were sometimes called, because of their resemblance to those who seemed to behave quite automatically when in a trance. This capacity suggests that individuals may have more than one identity within themselves. As Hacking (1995, 147) points out, therefore, "large parts of Western culture have been suppressed, even in the West."

As the stigmatized become accessible, the range of possibility opens up to include behavior that may be subversive, antisocial or criminal; one such character, identified by Hacking (1995, 154), merited the terms "impudent, mischievous, forward, passionate, and vindictive." However, these deviant types also may be more creative, playful, inventive, and resourceful in their altered states of consciousness, more vital and expert, than when they behave in a morally repressed fashion. The same character that was so vindictive was also at times "lively, vivacious, pert, gay, mirthful" (154). To suppress this sort of vitality is to lose the capacity not only for disruptive social behavior but also for creativity and renewal. One thinks of the popularity of Princess Diana, who was admittedly subversive of the royal family in England but whose capacity for play and for compassionate contact with the distressed made her seem to many not only glamorous but saintly. The diffusion of the sacred through such personages breaks the limits of human possibility precisely among those who otherwise lack hope.

When the sacred is well institutionalized, of course, these capacities are monopolized by the religious or other virtuosos whose aberrant behavior is protected or even revered. Fourteenth-century canon law protected a priest who murdered someone else in an altered state of consciousness; he was allowed to officiate at the Eucharist on the grounds that he had not been himself when acting in a spiritual trance and could not be held responsible for his actions. Thus, the sacred barred this state of mind from the sort of scrutiny that, five and a half centuries later in France after the Prussian War, opened the book on multiple personalities, suppressed memories, trance states, and hysterical symptoms and laid the basis for a century of psychoanalytic discovery about the range of human potential.

Thus, a secular society begins to emerge as the boundary between the sacred and the secular becomes irreversibly permeable on both sides. The sacred can permeate the secular just as readily as the secular can permeate the sacred. Indeed, under these conditions it would be exceedingly difficult to know where that boundary could be drawn. It may then be constantly defined and redefined, negotiated and renegotiated, to the point that no one can effectively say, "Lo here, lo there."

Of course, in every society there will be pressures to redefine boundaries that have eroded, and the boundary between the sacred and the secular is no exception. Just as the boundaries between genders become difficult to define, there will be movements to reinstate a traditional order in which the genders have different work to do and very different claims to dignity and deference.

However, in a secular society the sacred floats relatively freely. No longer monopolized by institutions and no longer confined between well-defended social boundaries, the sacred suggests possibilities that are always quite literally "beyond" those that are currently considered to be clear and present opportunities and dangers in a particular social order. Sometimes the Sacred is a negative possibility: the threat of disaster, a decline of the spirit, an Armageddon of sorts. Sometimes it is positive: the chance for renewal, an opening to new relationships, the discovery of new spiritual directions, a demand for justice, or merely the chance to leave the past behind. By floating freely, however, the Sacred enters public discourse where it becomes part of the world of the sacred; there it can be examined as a set of more or less realistic possibilities.

Some will mourn the passing of the Sacred because they long for an expanded principle of reality: "another reality principle" (Marcuse 1955, 146). Take, for example, Herbert Marcuse (1955, 147), who extols a reality principle that transcends even death and time and offers "the liberation from time which unites man with god, man with nature." In passages that are as lyrical as those of the poets, like Rilke, whom he quotes, Marcuse yearns for a reality principle that unites each person and thing with its own being and with the rest of the cosmos in an ecstatic vision that kills time.

For Marcuse (1955, 210) the source of a new reality principle, the basis of a new civilization, is in an imagination fed by the primary narcissism of the child seeking to reestablish the primitive unity between mother and infant. By imagination Marcuse does not mean merely the shrunken forms of fantasy life that are permitted in a rational social order; daydreaming and the like. He has in mind an imagination that recovers the primitive connection between the self and the world. He seeks to recover a memory of the self when its being, however infantile, was at one with the sources of life. In fact, he faults Freud for thinking that it is no longer possible to imagine these connections in which the individual is at one with all humans and with nature itself (1955, 133–34). Certainly, for Freudians it is only a regressive imagination that seeks to recover the lost harmonies of the womb and of a stage in human development that was prior to any social order. In Marcuse's view, however, this imagination retains the secret not only of the past but of the future; it is not only possible but necessary to remember the future if there is ever to be a civilization that lacks unnecessary suffering.

What is needed, I would argue, is not a new myth based on a more primitive imagination but a society that is able to learn from the unconscious. To recover the unconscious and to make use of it for fulfilling the potential of a society is indeed crucial, but there can be no return to a social order based on the primitive unities of the infantile matrix.

Instead, I would argue for demythologizing the unconscious as a preemptive strike against the idolatry that comes from mistaking delusion for reality. While it is possible to learn from dreams, one does not need to make them the basis of a new reality principle or social order. To learn from dreams is indeed to take the mystery out of them and to learn what it is they are telling us of truth and of falsehood alike. To free humans and societies from the burden of guilt for imaginary crimes will make it possible for entire societies to take responsibility for the crimes that have indeed been committed. To free a society from the burden of magical thinking will certainly lighten a society's burden of imaginary guilt. It may also make it less likely that such a society will pursue self-destruction under the guise of various idolatries: a visionary ideal, a special election, a manifest destiny, or simply the illusion that a favored society can beat the odds. To create a new future it will be necessary to know but then also to reject previously sacralized possibilities for distortion and cruelty.

For Marcuse, as I have noted, it is the attempt to recover the maternal world that is the source of a new reality principle, of an imagination that can provide the rational as well as the instinctual basis for a new social order. As he describes it, "Eros strives for eternalizing itself in a permanent order" (1955, 203). However, such a striving delivers only uncertainty about one's own being and stimulates a relentless demand for self-giving and sacrifice. The search for the sacred is the source of a fundamental doubt about one's own being.

Further, I am arguing that the search for an enduring basis for one's own being underlies idolatry. Therefore, it is necessary to demythologize the sacred in order to make it a source of information rather than of a binding imagination. It is the first step toward a society that no longer claims to offer existential guarantees or satisfactions and points to its own fragility, contingency, and impermanence.

In many Western societies, it is already difficult to discern precisely what is a source of fragility and impermanence. The pursuit of individual freedom and happiness turns out to be a persistent feature of these societies, even though communitarian critics see in this individualism the recipe for Western disaster. As Kenneth Minogue (1999, 3) so tellingly puts it, individualism and the nurturing of individuality were

how the modern Western world rejected castes, social hierarchies and even automatic respect for elders. It was a remarkable adventure, requiring a great deal of nerve, and conducted amid the wailing of those who believed that, unless we conformed to some ideal pattern of a good society, we should inevitably come to grief.

And yet it survived. Nervous passengers caught up in this adventure were forever holding their hands over their eyes as they discerned shipwreck ahead, but eventually the term "crisis" became a bit of a joke, because the ship sailed, not without turbulence but certainly without shipwreck, through so many crises. The difficult thing to explain is why these successes seemed merely to feed the appetite for building the perfect society, which, in being necessarily static, would equally necessarily amount to the suppression of the individual.

Minogue's point is extremely well taken. Certainly, the longing for a society that would conform to some ideal pattern is based on the yearning for a sacred social order: one that would visibly transcend the passage of time. The notion that certain models of a good society are not only perennial but transcendent goes back to Plato, of course, and the enthusiasm for making individuals conform to higher principles has fed a series of authoritarian solutions in Western societies. Not that Western societies have a monopoly on protofascist tendencies; they can be found as well in the hill tribes of Bolivia or New Guinea as in Western tracts calling for the discipline of the individual and the sacrifice of individual needs for the social good. (see Fenn 1997).

The key to a less repressive society is to take the mystery and myth out of the Sacred. The Sacred is the keeper of the dreamlike imagination and may also be, therefore, one source of unrealistic longings. These may include a desire for primordial attachment, for a release from pain, for an escape from panic, for the guarantee of rescue, for an unmediated meeting of minds, for the meeting of silent wishes, for the voicing of as yet untold agony, and for a sense of unity with all humankind and with nature itself.

In a society dominated by the sacred, attempts to symbolize the self in universal terms are in effect exclusive or demeaning. The sacred calls to a service that is perfect freedom but that in fact restricts the self within the fetters of unwanted custom and dead authority. A sacred society claims to be the source of all individuality but actually gives its priesthood priority in time and place over the laity. A truly secular society, however, would symbolize selfhood in ways that could never become the property or product of an institution of social system. It would be, as I have suggested, a society without idols or idolatry.

The Sacred is also the repository and expression of the fundamental wish for a primitive, certain, unmediated, and unequivocal sense of one's own being. Without this sense of solidity at the core of one's own being, one is vulnerable to sudden panic, to a need for rescue, and to the urgent hunger for direct access to another whose being can guarantee one's own. Unless the sacred is demythologized and made accessible, however, it will continue to offer spurious relief from unconscious fears and wishes. Where the sacred becomes the inaccessible and compelling source of obligation, these primitive wishes can be channeled into fascist movements; on the other hand, where the Sacred is opened to public discourse, it can feed the collective imagination of a social order that is more accessible and responsible. Channeled into public discourse, enacted in the theater or the mass media, examined in discussions of how to raise and educate children and care for the aging, these same wishes can foster the development of a society that might be humane. The Sacred is to the social order what the unconscious is to the psyche: a repository of crucial information about possible directions, continuing trauma, vitality suppressed, and longings demanding to be fulfilled.

Take a hypothetical society in which the vast majority of individuals want to live up to the standards set for them in school and at the workplace, at home or in the mass media. In this imaginary social order, everyone wants to be a licensed professional, or certified as having passed a series of tests that over a lifetime identify the individual as being conscientious and competent. Each person wants only those entertainments that are widely available, whether in the form of trips to theme parks or Caribbean cruises, blockbuster movies or innovative theater. To fulfill one's potential, whether for achievement or for satisfying experience, one has only to be an adequate worker and consumer. The society has more than enough opportunities and rewards to satisfy even the individuals who pride themselves on having unusual capacities and tastes.

In this society, of course, there are critics, but their energies are consumed by thinking negatively about subjects that are on the public agenda. Some focus on the latest obscenity in the entertainment industry. Others find more than enough to occupy them, whether in the activities of lobbyists and politicians who pollute public discourse or among industrialists and developers who pollute the environment. At one extreme are those who decry the intrusion of foreign people, food, microbes, money, and ideas. At the other extreme are those who decry public indifference to suffering in various parts of the globe, especially when it is caused by their society's own indifference or activity. At neither extreme does one find anyone imagining a world fundamentally different from the one in which they are living: improved, perhaps, revitalized or even revolutionized, but not fundamentally different.

In such a society there are possibilities for disaster, self-destruction, and decay that are not imagined in public discourse. Conversely, there is no widespread public awareness of the possibility of creating societies based on the universal satisfaction of basic needs, on the autonomy of the individual, and on the global expression of compassion. Such discussion as there may be is dismissed as at worst seditious or at best dreamy or utopian.

In this imaginary society, there is a false or incomplete form of secularity. Nothing is supposed to be sacred. That is, nothing is thought to be outside the range of what might be known or discussed; nothing, then, is considered inherently unknowable or ineffable. Books come out claiming to raise "taboo" subjects like sex and death, even though these subjects are under constant discussion in the public as well as private spheres. Politicians may challenge their followers to think the unthinkable, but what they have in mind fits entirely within the range of public options that might finally be regarded as "constitutional." The range of what is considered "constitutional," of course, expands or contracts along with the range of trust that the public puts in its major institutions and leaders. No one, however, considers the possibility of a society that is neither industrial nor industrious, or in which individuals should be entirely free to live or to die at their own discretion. Few consider the possibility that the truth may neither be already known through revelation nor a social product in the course of being invented.

Such a society might seem secular, open, and pragmatic, regardless of how many people engage in religious observances on a given Sunday or demand that the law reinforce their religious scruples. Indeed, religion might thrive on the rhetoric of protest against an allegedly secular society in which nothing appears to be sacred. "Appears" is the key word in the last sentence, of course. In this hypothetically secular society emphasis is placed on keeping open the gates of public opinion in the faith that reason, or the democratic marketplace, will produce a consensus that in the end reinforces the system's basic premises. Even religion, therefore, is reduced to a set of ideologies or interests that speak for a particular constituency rather than of a tribune before which the entire society might be arraigned for a final judgment. The society is, as sociologists might say, self-referential, and there is no place outside the system, no point of leverage, on which to base an attempt to change the society as a whole.

In such an "open" society there is presumably nothing that is unthinkable or unspeakable: nothing beyond the knowledge of the cognoscenti or the imagination of the aesthetes. There is nothing beyond the range of threats and opportunities known to be facing that society; nothing beyond the knowledge that local communities have of themselves and their own violence, nothing beyond the range of the human potential as it is defined by ethicists, genetic scientists, "secular humanists," or religionists. The entertainment industry absorbs the rest of public imagination in images of human beings that are partially alien or part animal. In a word, there is nothing supposed to be sacred: no mystery, no authority, no potential for transformation, surprise, or destruction that has escaped pubic attention. As Herbert Marcuse (1964, 8) put it, there is a "flattening out of the contrast (or conflict) between the given and the possible, between the satisfied and the unsatisfied needs."

With so many possibilities for selfhood, for the development of personal identity, and for a useful social character available in such a society, it would be difficult to explain why anyone should experience him- or herself as oppressed or repressed. The invitation to self-development comes from a variety of quarters and can be accepted under many auspices, from the military to the university. Scientific studies reinforce the prevailing religious nostrums that positive attitudes lead to better health or higher rates of achievement. The injunction to "Get a life" intimidates the negative and the gainsayers. Negativity seems to be trumped even when disaster occurs because the system, once adjusted, can be said to have worked once again. Here is Marcuse (1964, 9) once more:

> We are again confronted with one of the most vexing aspects of advanced industrial civilization: the rational character of its irrationality. Its productivity and efficiency, its capacity to increase and spread comforts . . . the extent to which this civilization transforms the object world into an extension of man's mind and body makes the very notion of alienation questionable. The people recognize themselves in their commodities; they find their soul in their automobile, hi-fi set, split-level home, kitchen equipment. The very mechanism which ties the individual to his society has changed, and social control is anchored in new needs which it has produced.

In this pseudosecular society even religious traditions once promised the individual immediate and direct access to a source of authority outside all those offered within the system lose their authenticity. Transcendence becomes mediated by church bureaucracies, and authoritarian ones at that, even within traditions that like the Baptists that once left the individual standing alone in unmediated relationship to the deity itself. The notion of transcendence is used to refer to a set of symbols that in fact refer to a society's ideals and imagined place in history. That it is a source of national self-criticism is considered to be transcendence enough, as if the beyond were not known solely by the signs of its absence in a world that still must exist only under its auspices.

In such a pseudosecular society, even the existential facts of birth and death do not propel the individual into a consciousness that asks for, imagines, even demands reinstatement into a universe that no longer exists except in haunted reminiscence. Those who go into terminal illnesses raging against the dying of the light seem oddly irrational when there is so much available in the way of support groups. Those who do not avail themselves of certain social supports, say for cancer sufferers or for the terminally ill, are found to die sooner than those who do and may be stigmatized as negative. The most popular book on how to die extols acceptance as the final stage of dying, which thus becomes the goal to be reached.

Such a society, even though it relegates religion to the status of a special interest, has taken over the functions of religion and administers them under what appear to be secular auspices. I am thinking particularly of the function of keeping hope alive for a different world while compelling assent to this one. Ritual accomplished this task by giving people roles to play that impose the attitudes that they presume; pseudosecular societies manage the development and expression of the attitudes and emotions that are prerequisite of the performance of particular roles in politics or on the job, in the family or in education. Religious rites performed the function of giving people apparent freedom to speak for themselves while prescribing the topic, the language, the right to speak, and the appropriate postures; pseudosecular societies define what it means to have a voice in public affairs and who is to have it on certain topics. Thus, the management of diversity includes ethnic and local communities in a symbolic universe that renders them increasingly marginal. These are the functions of religion that have been assigned to political, social, and economic institutions, in whose service modern citizens are supposed to find their freedom. As Marcuse (1964, 9) points out, [I]n the contemporary period, the technological controls appear to be the very embodiment of Reason for the benefit of all social groups and interests—to such an extent that all contradiction seems irrational and all counteraction impossible."

There is a way out, as Marcuse (1964, 5) also noted; it is to "recognize the disease of the whole and grasp the chances of curing the disease." One form of this "disease of the whole," I will argue, is what is now widely known as "civil religion." Different from one society to another, it nonetheless expresses the capacity of a society to identify the needs of the individual with the services and programs, the goals and requirements of the larger society. The civil religion reduces the ineffable and unimaginable to what can be remembered, known, understood, and emulated. It is thus a form of idolatry, and it offers a vast reduction of the imponderable and uncertain to what can be revered.

Only when individuals can see beyond these reductionist idols, this foreshortening of their perspective and horizons, can they become free from the weight of their culture. Only when they have become thus freed can they also become aware of their true rather than false needs, imagine a social life that embodies their true rather than false selves, and undertake projects that under present conditions might seem utopian but under the conditions of freedom would be entirely rational. What Marcuse (1964, 10) said of the economy of industrial societies and its apparent rationality applies to the civil religion: "The manifold processes of introjection seem to be ossified in almost mechanical reactions. The result is, not adjustment but *mimesis*: an immediate identification of the individual with his *society and, through it, with the society as a whole*."

What is a mechanical reaction, however, is only in part the need of the individual to "prove himself on the market, as a free economic subject" (Marcuse 1964, 2). In this book I focus on the need of individuals to prove themselves as citizens, as people who count for something, who can make a contribution to society, and who can, if called upon, surrender not only their judgment and autonomy but their lives to the larger society in times of national need or crisis. Thus, what Marcuse saw, following Marx, as an irrational diffusion of the demands of a capitalist society to destroy and produce, consume and distribute is only in part an economic problem.

To some it may seem strange to single out the sacred as the institution that must be uprooted if a truly secular society is to emerge without idols and without the mystifications of religion. Many would agree with Marcuse (1960, 283) that the final barrier can be found not in the sacred but in quite another institution, that of private property:

> The true history of mankind will be, in the strict sense, the history of free individuals, so that the interest of the whole will be woven into the individual existence of each. In all prior forms of society, the interest of the whole lay in separate social and political institutions, which represented the right of society as against the right of the individual. The abolition of private property will do away with all this once and for all, for it will mark "man's return from family, religion, state, etc. to his *human*, that is *social* existence."

Antique though this reference to private property may seem, there is a point to his vision of a society that is not fragmented by its own institutions. In a genuinely secular society, no institution outlasts its usefulness simply because it has acquired a purchase on legitimacy and can continue to exact tribute or loyalty from clients and the public, whose true interests may indeed lie elsewhere. Of all such institutions, the sacred is the one that is especially dependent on devotion, that freezes a sense of what is possible, and that stifles human potential under the weight of obligation.

I am suggesting that Marcuse's complaints against private property are better directed against the sacred itself. Private property, he argues, stands in the way of humans working together to make the best personal and collective use of nature. Patents placed on parts of the human genome might be one obvious contemporary example, but the point applies to the whole range of technology and natural resources as well as to the symbols and ideas that are produced socially, in laboratories and universities, studios and sanctuaries. In the following passage, Marcuse (1960, 282) is speaking of social institutions per se, private property being only one: "Every fact is more than a mere fact; it is a negation and restriction of real possibilities."

For instance, in services of Holy Communion, individuals offer themselves in prayer and song, and through gifts of money and of bread and wine. The minister then takes the bread and wine and, after corporate prayer and the pronunciation of certain sentences, lifts them up as consecrated. They have been rendered sacred. In this form the bread and wine stand for the love of God given to the world in Jesus Christ. They also stand for possibilities that come from beyond the capacities of human beings.

The possibility of creating a human community that is based on compassion and that fulfills the demands of justice is in this liturgy portrayed as coming from a source that is superior and external to this world. Those who have engaged together in the social production of the sacred now have to receive it from an authority and from a source that are beyond themselves. What had been human in origin is now presented as divine in provenance. That is how the sacred, like other social facts, not only limits the range of possibility but deprives communities of the authority to produce themselves on their own terms.

That is also how idols are produced. They reduce the social life of the community to a consecrated thing that stands for the possibilities of the human community once they are dignified by the presence of God. As such, the idol exercises a controlling presence that deprives the local community from producing itself on its own terms. Take, for example, the request of peasants in a Central American base community to have a Mass celebrating their own people. The priests told them that they could not do so; they could have an ethnic celebration, but the Mass was reserved for the community that could come together only under the auspices of the priests and be defined by the church itself.

In this way the sacred controls the way a community works to reproduce itself. Certain possibilities are enhanced; they are typically those that reinforce the existing boundaries between clergy and laity, the sacred and the profane, the public and the private, the inside and the outside. Whether the community produces a flag or a constitution, these symbols are regarded as sacralized. Even though the flag is as subject to as wide a range of interpretation as the constitution, and even though the constitution can be amended, the range of interpretation is limited, just as are the rules for amending the constitution. Social relations are turned into things like a text or a flag; in turn these things become the basis for the social order. That is why Marx, and following him, Marcuse, speak of them as "fetishes" (see Marcuse 1960, 280).

What, then, are the "real possibilities" that are denied by the institution of the sacred? The first and most obvious is that people may be able to come together to celebrate their unity without the permission or control of a clerical elite. The second is that, in celebrating their unity, people can do so without creating boundaries that relegate some to a world that is passing away and others to the sphere of the untamed or demonic. Some of those boundaries typically separate the gathered from those who are neither invited nor entitled to have access to these sacred precincts. To secularize sacred institutions is thus to call into question every boundary: between those who produce and consume the sacred; between what is social and what is natural; between what is human and what is animal; between the mental and the physical; between the public and the private.

By far the most invidious of distinctions are the ones that separate the human from the animal and the bodily from the mental. These demarcations allow the keepers of the sacred to consign those regarded as profane to a world that is subhuman and material; the profane become prey, or a resource for consumption and use. Along those imaginary boundaries a wide range of possibilities has been long denied admission to the human community. A whole repertoire of human feeling has been stigmatized as bestial, and whole areas of the body have been denied access to the mind. Under these repressive conditions the body experiences grief and anguish without the comforts of speech and symbol. No wonder that humans experience unnamed and untold agony. Similarly, various forms of human vitality have been stigmatized as mere "animal spirits" or as the bestial because they are outside the boundaries of the sacred.

Every society has the right to define what Freud called the "reality principle." The question is whether that definition will prematurely foreclose certain possibilities and thus impose unnecessary suffering on the individual. Some of these boundaries are internal and separate the more spiritual or purified members of the society from those who are held in lower regard. The former are thus entitled to tell the latter when to come and when to go; thus, the keepers of the sacred typically have power over time and timing. In removing the boundaries between the sacred and the profane, a community, even a whole society, expands the range of what previously had been considered possible and takes a step toward the fulfillment of its own potential.

The question I am asking is whether it is possible not only to imagine but to create a society that would be open to the full range of human potential, just as it is open to the entire range of threats and possibilities in the environment. There is, as Marcuse (1960, 2) pointed out, an as "yet uncharted realm of freedom beyond necessity." That is the realm of what I call in this book the truly Sacred, as opposed to the institutionalization of the sacred in particular forms, in certain practices and ways of life, in distributions of status and power, and in symbols or beliefs that are claimed to transcend the passage of time and to thus represent the society as a whole.

So long as the Sacred remains "uncharted" it also remains mysterious and can be alluring but also threatening, full of possibility but also of danger. It is that realm that the idol reduces to what is accessible and familiar, but in this reduction lies a fundamental loss of human freedom and autonomy. That idol, perhaps in the form of the civil religion, may speak of vast realms as yet to be conquered, but these territories are likely to be those not yet annexed by the state. Under the auspices of reality principle sacralized as a civil religion, the future remains a set of circumscribed possibilities. The imagination is allowed to soar only within the prescribed limits. Reform is thus imagined as an extension of laws already on the books or as a mandate to achieve freedoms that have already been prescribed. Change becomes reduced to the acquisition of new resources for production and consumption, or the mobilization of loyalties and energies that have hitherto remained in the private sphere. The unknown, the truly Sacred, remains beyond the realm of legitimate imagination; it is off the books of the civil religion and national ideology.

A truly secular society would therefore have open access to what at any given moment had previously been considered sacred. It would be a secular society, moreover, without idols that embody and mask the sacred. Without idolatry a society lacks the capacity to reduce the realm of mystery, freedom and uncertainty to known demands and opportunities. In such a society there would be no idolatry, no civil religion. Any attempt to create one would be seen for what it is: a politicization of religion, a sanctification of politics, a principle of cohesion that is also a principle for exclusion, an artificial means of mobilizing consent, and a license to practice on other nations. Like all idols, moreover, the civil religion offers individuals who lack certainty about their own being a surrogate form of selfhood, an ersatz substantiality that appears to be able to withstand the passage of time.

The chances of curing this disease, therefore, depend on a variety of factors: the capacity to unmask cultural idols as substitute forms of selfhood and therefore also the capacity to point to what is beyond, that is, to what is as yet unknown and mysterious. The beyond consists of hitherto unimagined forms of human potential, as well as of hitherto undiscovered threats and opportunities. In either case the loss of idols and the redefinition of what constitutes reality is a necessary, if not sufficient condition, if individuals are to be freed from servitude to the past. To move toward authentic secularity, then, requires the capacity to transform what is celebrated and venerated within a culture into what can be discussed, understood, and turned into politics. With further secularization will come the ability to demonstrate the tendency of all national symbols to marginalize and exclude. More difficult, perhaps, is the demystification of community life that reveals the silent and pervasive violence in a community, especially when that violence is masked by the sacred, and the ability to give individuals autonomy over critical decisions over life and death.

In a secular society, if there is to be salvation, it has to occur in the here and now. One cannot wait, whether for the judge in Kafka's trial to tell us our fate or for the priesthood to give us communion. Neither can we wait to receive whatever benefits the state will hand out or wait to acquire a place in society once we have passed the relevant qualifying tests. Sacred structures and a pseudosecular society are oppressive no matter whether the clerical order is ordained or has been certified by trained professionals. In a secular society even eternity just becomes a matter of time, and the world of the everyday and the mundane becomes the site of our salvation.

Under these conditions it becomes very difficult to know just what to take seriously and what to regard as relatively indifferent to our ultimate interests. The world becomes a place of infinite possibility and surprise; it also becomes a place of unnamed and potentially unlimited distractions and threats. Secularization domesticates the apocalypse and makes each day the scene of final struggle, torment, and liberation. Life itself becomes ultimately not only very interesting but fateful.

Genuine secularization thus requires the attempt to free individuals from a pseudosecular social order that has learned its lessons from religion on how to limit freedom, channel aspirations, and keep individuals within bounds so that thought and imagination will not lead to revolutionary questions or ideas. Opening the realm of what is possible and conceivable, however, and of what is considered desirable and worthy, places the individual in a condition of radical uncertainty as to what ultimately matters.

Secularization thus launches the individual into a world where the stakes are very high, indeed ultimate. However, it is a world in which there are no clear guidelines as to what one is to desire and loathe, pursue and avoid. Despite the lack of guidelines, however, individuals are to make an ultimate commitment to penultimate aims in the knowledge that they are risking the core of their being in a choice that may yet turn out to have been mistaken or false.

In the throes of secularization, one entertains the serious possibility that any moment and any person may be revelatory, but one also knows that each such occasion may leave one holding merely an idol in one's hands. The task is to distinguish the idol from the icon. Both are human products; both are cultural fictions. The icon, however, leads to the heart of as yet unnamed possibility, while the idol misleads and distorts the self by attaching it to an image that promises liberation but delivers, in the end, only confinement. The individual must become a spiritual adept at the practice of "testing the spirits."

For a definition of idolatry it would be hard to improve on Marcuse's (1955, 109) formulation of what is wrong with Western civilization: "the transformation of facts into essences, of historical into metaphysical conditions." Although Marcuse has in mind Nietzsche's contribution to this discovery, the point stands on its own. One of those facts, of course, is time, and with time the whole range of human failures, frustration, and mortality. To secularize the world is indeed to consign all human aspiration and endeavor to eventual decay and destruction; only the sacred is exempt.

Wherever the sacred is diffuse within the larger society, however, religious behavior may also conceal secular protest. For instance, as Martin has argued, when individuals join Pentecostal churches they are breaking with old forms of patronage-client relationships, adopting secular forms of training and self-discipline, and creating social networks that embody a wide range of possibilities for betterment to which they had not previously been entitled.

To demythologize the sacred, then, it is necessary to discover what forms of submission and sacrifice are being expressed in apparently secular forms. One may indeed discover idols under the guise of rational political behavior. However, one may also discover iconoclasm under the guise of new forms of devotion. The last place to look for the seeds of a secular society, then, may be in anticlerical or materialist political parties. Conversely, the place to look for the possibilities of a secular society may be among the enthusiasts of the spirit.

To engage in idolatry is thus to refuse to suffer the weight of longing for that which this world cannot yet give. "Yet" is the key word in the last sentence; it is there to ensure that "this world" remains a description of current possibilities and not a metaphysical principle. To imagine a world more responsive to human longings is immediately to be seen as unrealistic, and yet it is the only way to avoid the idolatry of the contemporary reality principle in any given society.

To be fully human is to suffer the presence of possibilities that the social order is designed to suspend, ignore, discredit, or destroy. To be fully human is to be an iconoclast, in the sense of destroying the facts that have been enshrined as metaphysical principles. In terms of Christian theology, then, the Incarnation of true humanity always ends up on the cross of some social system's set of imposed limits and cultural fictions.

What lies just beyond the veil drawn over the psyche or over suppressed aspects of social life depends, of course, on circumstances and point of view. In some societies the contents of the psyche are relatively inaccessible. One's inner life remains a mystery to oneself as well as to others. It is the place where unseen powers war for control of the self: demons and satanic figures, but also angels and the spirits sent by the deity for guidance and inspiration. In other societies, however, considerable effort is made to explore the unconscious mind. Dreams are told in the meeting room at the start of the day. In the local bookstore revelations are made by amateur and professional guides to the inner life. To say "I have a dream" is potent political speech.

Wherever the line is drawn, however, the sacred emerges as the name for the mysterious. The terra incognita may indeed be given a space: the bush outside the village where spirits roam and sorcerers do their work; the place inside the village where the spirits of the ancestors are allowed to return on yearly visitations; the inward and spiritual grace that lies hidden under the form of the sacraments; the sanctuary where only licensed religious professionals are allowed to probe the mysteries. However, the line demarcating the sacred from the profane or secular may set apart not places or levels but certain people: for example, those blessed with what now might be called a disability but was once considered a gift or visitation from unseen forces; or those who are slated for sacrifice in order that peace may be restored to the community; or persons invested with high office, on whom the future of the society depends; or even the guardians of texts whose meaning holds the secret of the society's origin and destiny.

To separate the sacred from the profane is thus a political act; power is being exercised and is at stake whenever some are consigned to the world outside the sacred. Much, therefore, depends on how that power is being exercised and on whose behalf. Where power is concentrated, access to people and places, to texts and secrets is relatively restricted. Only the brahmins or those allowed to practice before the Supreme Court may dare to interrogate and interpret the foundational texts of the society. When a group decides to distinguish itself from the larger society or even to secede, its own ceremonies, officiants, texts and language become equally sacred; they are to remain a mystery to those from the outside whose interest may be in controlling the subversive.

Where power is relatively decentralized, however, and information more widely disseminated, the boundary between the sacred and the profane is likely to be diffuse and variable. Shifting from time to time and place to place, the sacred may be more elusive, democratic, and unpredictable: a matter of evanescent spirit rather than fixed authority. What a society may need to know may therefore be broadly disseminated but still inaccessible, like the texts of the Ayatollah Khomeini's talks that were being played throughout Iran before the Islamic revolution that felled the shah.

The sacred may also remain widespread but inaccessible in various aspects of the psyche for which the society in question has little curiosity or taste. Thus, when a society lacks a public language for the psyche, personal resentments, longings, and despair may remain a potent but ineffable force that keeps people away from the polls, erupts in random violence, or occasionally mobilizes in fascist movements like the one that brought Hitler to power in 1933.

The sacred therefore may be centralized or dispersed. If it is centralized, it is a locus of devotion and a source of authority, if only for a few. If it is dispersed, the sacred may take on a wide range of forms: sects, celebrities, social movements, and multiple prophecies or revelations. Similarly, the sacred may be relatively concentrated or diffuse. In its more concentrated forms the sacred is identifiable at least in its surface appearances, but if it is diffuse, of course, it remains a more pervasive force that can put in appearances wherever the spirit, so to speak, wills.

In some societies the sacred may be centralized as well as diffused. Social life itself then seems mysterious, even threatening. Take, for example, a society in which the work of repression is covert. People disappear. Lives are blighted. Careers are thwarted and characters defamed without any visible agency. "Principalities and powers," as they used to be called, keep people divided and hostile, fearful and helpless. In a Kafka-esque world of bureaucratized cruelty, or in a police state, or even in a community ruled by gossip or a population prone to hysterical illness, the sacred is both central and diffuse.

2

STARTING ON THE
PATH TO SECURARITY

The Agony of the Possible

Many books justify themselves by claiming that there is a taboo on the subject that they are about to discuss. Perhaps it is death, and the author promises the reader a brave, unflinching look at a subject that has been protected by sacred taboos. Perhaps it is sex, and the author promises a version of the truth that is as revealing as it is unauthorized. Whether it is money, religion and politics, death, or taxes, the testimony of the author promises to take the reader further into unexplored territories on a vital subject. It is a promise to profane what has hitherto been regarded as sacred, by someone who is in a position to attack a profession's or an institution's monopoly on a given subject.

The Sacred, as I argued in chapter 1, is whatever lies behind the idols that societies set up to prevent too close an acquaintance with the unknown. In this book it is not the secrets of the Oval Office or the bedroom, of subatomic particles or the clergy, that I discuss. It is the Sacred itself: that indeterminate area in any society that lies beyond the horizon of public knowledge and discourse. It may consist of many things: state secrets; confidences given to a lawyer, doctor, or minister; knowledge of the inner workings of a bureaucracy; memories of old betrayals; longings for a love that is lost or merely illicit; an unsatisfied desire for revenge, seditious plots, and a potential for achievement or destruction that remains unknown and unutilized.

Because the Sacred lies beyond the veil of ordinary language and understanding, institutions like the church have long argued that special training is required if it is to be approached and mentioned by name. As the Sacred loses its mystery, however, one discovers that there is nothing there beyond the ken of ordinary mortals and that one does not therefore have to have special training or ordination to approach it. Anyone can preach or administer the Sacrament or interpret the Bible or speak of a revelation from God or discern what life is all about or what is worth dying

45

for. The process of secularization has to do precisely with this progressive loss of mystery that once enshrined the Sacred.

With this increased access to the Sacred and the ability to turn it from mystery into discourse goes the converse process: the discovery of the sacred in the precincts of everyday life or in the unconscious: in places, that is, where one previously would not have expected it. In his recent book *The Secular Mind*, (1999) Robert Coles discusses Thomas Hardy's novel *Jude the Obscure*, the story of the pilgrimage of a young man from the English countryside to Oxford, where he is denied admission to that sacred institution despite his very evident talents and accomplishment. It is clear to Jude, however, that he is a modern Job, being punished for what is not his fault and being tormented by a mystery that really is not beyond his understanding. The sacred halls of Oxford contain nothing that is in principle beyond his grasp.

Conversely, the town of Oxford itself is filled with enough mystery to baffle any Oxford don and the brightest students, who pass through the town wholly unaware of its complexity and depths. To be sure, the novel is a protest against the inequities of the English class system. It is also a herald of a generation that knew that the bounds of the sacred were not drawn in the traditional places and that they were standing on the holy ground of everyday life. That recognition opened to what had hitherto been the profane gaze of ordinary people the depths of psychological and social life as well as of nature itself.

Take the argument now one step further. To undergo the process of secularization is to experience what might be called the agony of the possible. Jude knows that he in fact could do the work of an Oxford scholar, as well as that the gates of the university are closed to him. He is in that sense haunted by possibility. In the same way, Adam and Eve came to realize, through the suggestion of the serpent, that the tree of the knowledge of good and evil bore fruit that would not be fatal; to eat of it would simply arouse the jealousy of God. The serpent is generally not on the side of the custodians of the sacred. At the same time, however, the myth of Eden concludes with Adam and Eve, like Jude, being placed on the wrong side of the gates to sacred knowledge. They, like Jude, know full well that they have been deprived of knowledge that is fully within the scope of their potential understanding.

Interestingly enough, Coles goes on to quote a poem by Hardy in which the poet criticizes the "Reverend Doctors" who scoff at the myth of the Garden of Eden and doubt that Adam and Eve ever existed. Although Coles does not pursue the reference to Eden, it is clear that Hardy understands the myth better than the divines who pronounce upon it. He understands, like Jude, the agony of being excluded from the realm of the possible.

If this were a book on biblical theology, I would review the successive revelations of both Testaments under this rubric: the haunting of the people of Israel by a sense of possibility. Some of those possibilities require understanding of the universe and its foundations; other possibilities require an understanding of the ways of God. Both seem hauntingly present and yet elusive. The stories of Cain and Abel, of the Tower of Babel, and of the sacrifice of Isaac look in another direction: to the depths of fratricidal, patricidal, and filicidal hatred and to the dangers of coming too close to realizing those possibilities. Israel is haunted not only by what it does not know about God and the universe but by what it does know, if only implicitly, about itself.

It is in the face of death that the door of possibility seems, like the gates of the Garden of Eden, to close with no hope of their reopening. It is particularly revealing, then, that the New Testament is full of stories of apparition and return after death. Indeed, Jesus is mistaken for a resurrected John the Baptist, and Jesus's own appearances strengthened the sense that the world was still haunted by possibility. It has been the function of the church to control that range of possibility and to limit the reappearances of Jesus to certain times and occasions under the control of the clergy. It has been the function of radical Christian movements, many of them populist, to insist that the times and places of Jesus's possible reappearance are known to the faithful and the poor rather than to the scholarly and the ordained.

The interest of the priestly editors in the myth of the Garden of Eden suggests that there is always a danger in unauthorized accounts of the possible. Take, for example, the transactions between the living and the dead: the whole arena of ghostly apparition, agonized grief, and close encounters with the souls of the departed. In his excellent study, aptly entitled *Ghosts in the Middle Ages,* (1998), Jean-Claude Schmitt describes the efforts of monastic orders to get a monopoly on this form of the sacred. To do so, monastic orders had to compete with the laity, who had their own experiences of the departed to tell about, as well as with the clergy whose services for pacifying the dead were often well remunerated. Indeed, for some orders, managing the relationship between the living and the dead through prayers and donations became the primary source of income, and any contrary accounts or practices could undermine the monastic economy. The point, to which I will return, is not simply that professional classes have long made a living off the dead. It is that the sacred is difficult to monopolize and repeatedly appears on its own terms without institutional permission or control.

Take, for example, the use of ritual to control the appearances made by the departed. As Bloch (1989, 22–23) points out, the function of ritual in many societies has been to speak the words of the ancestors:

> By this is meant that the elders are speaking not on their own behalf but on behalf of the ancestors and elders of the whole descent group whether living or dead. They are repeating the general truth which they have had passed on to them by previous genera-

tions. They are speaking in the style and often indeed with the very words which they believe were used by the dead ancestors at similar councils or at similar religious rituals in the past.[And, in trance-states . . .]Instead of the ancestors speaking *indirectly* through the *memory* of the living elders they speak *directly* through the *person.*

Now, if the speakers are to claim such authority, they will have to speak in a certain way. Indeed, as Bloch goes on to argue, their own options for speaking are very limited indeed. In the form of the ritual they are constrained to use certain words, to adopt certain tones of voice, to follow a certain order and sequence in what they say, and they are prevented from inserting their own ideas and strategies into the communication. The possibilities for interaction are very limited, both for the speakers and those, of course, who merely listen and respond in the stipulated fashion. The latter are particularly constrained, as anyone knows whose liturgical responses have been limited to saying prescribed words and, sometimes, simply "Amen."

Thus, to establish the sacred is drastically to limit the range of possibilities that are open to any community. In particular, the more the sacred is instituted in certain words and gestures, the less freedom is available to those who seek access to the sacred or certain benefits from participating in sacred acts and events. To contain the sacred, in other words, is to limit the degrees of freedom. In everyday life, by way of contrast, in the profane and the mundane events that lie outside the sacred, the range of possibilities is greatly enhanced.

Institutions, rites, ceremonies, and other practices that seek to control access to the sacred are therefore quintessential idols. It is the function of an idol to represent the sacred, to be sure. However, idols become the primary recipients of devotion and gifts precisely because they keep the Sacred at a safe distance and limit the possibilities, posed by the Sacred, for tragic or rebellious, creative or destructive intrusion into the scenes of everyday life. Thus, the Sacred is awesome and even haunting because it is the repository of possibilities that are still desired and can be understood to fall within the range of human capacity. That is the meaning, after all, of the Incarnation: the divine became human. It would be hard to find a more explicit doctrine to the effect that the possibilities foreclosed in the Garden of Eden were now reopened.

If the biblical witness is resolutely against idolatry, it is because of a cultural understanding that the realm of the sacred has been prematurely barred. The closing of the gates of Eden was not only an event in the mythic past; it was a fact of social life in a society where the range of possibility had been artificially limited by priesthood and patriarchy in the interests not only of their own strata and prerogatives but of a more pervasive social control. Thus, the idol becomes a place where the range of social and psychological possibilities has been limited to a known set of risks and responsibilities.

The appearances of the dead among the living can therefore serve the purposes not only of the rebellious and disenfranchised but of those who define the limits of the possible. As Schmitt (1998, 75) points out, in the case of ghosts whose appearances served the purpose of social reformers at the turn of the millenium:

> By telling all the reasons they were tormented in the hereafter, they tended to strengthen the social order as the abbot of Cluny dreamed of it: without murder or theft and with knights who respected clerics, who did not violate the consecrated walls of the cemeteries, who protected the poor, and who righted the wrongs they had done the weak.

The truly Sacred, however, is not so easily controlled. It is, in the jargon of the social sciences, an environment of the social system. By environment I mean the sum total of what must be taken into account: opportunities and threats lying in the future; the past; the deep terrain of the individual psyche; unsatisfied grievances and hitherto undeveloped or wasted human potential. These are far beyond what one normally thinks of as the geopolitical and natural environments. The Sacred may therefore present a mixture of the untold agony of a community or society and of its hidden potentials. Typically it is the bush, the environment outside of the village, that is haunted by possibilities that lie beyond the scope of the permissible and the ordinary.

Thus, idols tend to be counterproductive; they offer the illusion of access to and control over the Sacred, whereas in fact they are more like a Maginot Line defended primarily by those whose positions depend on the maintenance of such unreliable fortifications. To be sure, the Sacred is filled with possible threats, and it therefore is wise for any society to have some who are trained to decipher the code by which these threats are hidden and revealed. The difficulty with this arrangement, however, is that those who are entrusted with interpreting the secrets of the Sacred may rather prefer to perpetuate their own exclusive access to these mysteries and thereby keep the rest of the social system unnecessarily deprived of what could be saving knowledge and potentiality.

What is at stake is simply the entire range of social and psychological possibility that is repressed or neglected in any social system. As I argued in the first chapter, every system limits the range of possibility, and most systems do so in a way that preserves a particular distribution of power and authority. That is simply because knowledge of the full range of possibility might be the source of subversive satisfactions or of demands that would undermine the existing distribution of authoritative expertise. The Sacred thus includes not only threats and surprises but sources of impulse and energy, of creativity and other human capacities that remain unutilized because they conflict with the local monopoly of those who are required to guard the Sacred from the profane gaze of those who cannot be trusted.

The more there is a monopoly on access to the Sacred, the more will the Sacred be known by its absence. To be sure, there are signs set up to point toward it: indications of where the Sacred may be found. In his description of the appearances of the dead to the living, Schmitt tells us that the laity often received such visitations toward the end of the first millenium, but their accounts had to be assimilated to known—and approved—versions of the supernatural. Otherwise, their experience would not be conducive to preserving the official boundaries separating the sacred from the profane. Monks and clerics did indeed seek to ferret out accounts of ghostly appearances, but their purpose was often to strengthen the monopoly of the monastic orders on the messages conveyed by the dead to the living. Their "narrative schema was a horizon of belief that enabled the gathering and shaping of all tales that conformed to the desired end: the promotion of the Cluniac liturgy of the dead" (Schmitt 1998, 77).

There are institutions that specialize in approaching sacred mysteries and translating them for those who have ears to hear. The privilege of gaining access to the sacred is thus assumed by clergy or other specialists who justify their privileges by warning others of the dangers attending close acquaintance with the Sacred itself. The impure may die, as do all those who look directly on the face of God. These specialists therefore develop markers of the Sacred and engage in practices that allow access to the prohibited zones of knowledge and experience. These markers constitute the Sacred: a system of idols, where rationale is simple idolatry.

Idols point to the unspoken and unrealized aspects of any social system while preventing a more egalitarian, open, unregulated, and more intimate acquaintance with the Sacred. They consist, more often than not, of official accounts, holy texts, prescribed gestures and procedures, authoritative positions and places, all of which must be approached with care and, in the end, only by those who have been licensed to have a close acquaintance with the sacred. Here is Bloch (1989, 29) again:

> It is because the formalization of language is a way whereby one speaker can coerce the response of another that it can be seen as a form of social control. It is really a type of communication where rebellion is impossible and only revolution could be feasible. It is a situation where power is all or nothing and of course in society total refusal is normally out of the question.

As I have suggested, those are the trappings of the sacred, and at best they are only pointers to what is beyond. At worst, they become idols that bar access to the Sacred while requiring submission and sacrifice.

Thus, secularization begins with the weakening of the any institution's monopoly on what had passed for the Sacred but was, in fact, just a misappropriation and reduction of the Sacred to institutional proportions. Secularization continues with the discovery of the Sacred that lies beyond the current gaps in human knowledge and the limits of social control. What was once mysterious becomes progressively more fascinating and interesting, more intelligible and even useful, but that progress toward secularity does come at the expense of the Sacred. Take, for example, Schmitt's (1998, 78–80) description of the marvels that accompanied the eventual weakening of the church's monopoly on the sacred and particularly on exchanges with the dead:

> [T]he marvelous aroused the *curiositas* of the human mind, the search for hidden natural causes, ones that would someday be unveiled and understood. The development of the latter attitude [as contrasted with submission to the miraculous—rkf] at the turn of the twelfth century must be seen as an early form of the scientific spirit that valued inquiry (*inquisitio*), true accounts of facts, and even experimentation (*experimentum*). This approach was applied in a very broad field, to stones and to plants, to history and to geography, as well as to manifestations of spirits, fairies, and the dead.

It is thus because the realm of the Sacred increased beyond the idolatrous limitations set upon it by interested institutions that its mysteries could be imagined.

The church was not the only institution interested in construing all supernatural events to its own advantage; rulers also put their ear to the ground to hear what folklore and personal accounts had to say of the unknown and the mysterious. As early as the thirteenth century, Schmitt (1998, 87, 90) notes, the royal courts took official interest in apparitions and encounters of the living with the dead and engaged in what would now be called the gathering of intelligence. There were also official uses for occult revelations that might have a direct bearing on the safety and survival of the ruler:

> Thus the folkloric marvelous could be changed into a political marvelous and the tale joined with another tradition, that of revelations intended for the rulers of this world—kings, emperors, the pope. Visions of the hereafter, prophecies, and apparitions of Christ or of angels played essential roles in this realm. At the end of the Middle Ages, ghosts too were listened to more attentively. (Schmitt 1998, 92)

The tabloid function of the modern press thus has ancient roots in the desire of princes and prelates to know what is going on, what people are thinking, and what might be in store for them in the future. Those in authority do not like surprises, especially nasty ones, and it is entirely reasonable that they should take a keen personal and official interest in the Sacred. It is where secrets are buried, longings are stirring, and people are beginning to trust in their own perceptions, experience, and judgment.

To put it another way, the vast increase in what can be imagined as socially possible has been achieved only because the range of the marvelous has expanded to include what was hitherto beyond the horizons set by official inquiry. As the marvelous yields to inquiry, it does become a matter of fact; it loses its mystery and becomes ordinary, just as the unconscious ceases to be a diabolic realm of hideous impulses and becomes a playground or theater for what is left of one's earlier, infantile self. However, the horizon of the marvelous continues to recede as inquiry moves toward it, so long as the inquirer does not confuse the conventional or official representations of the sacred with the real thing.

There are simple ideological measures by which societies can define the difference between authorized—and hence idolatrous—representations of the possible and the full range of psychological and social possibility for which I wish to reserve the term "the Sacred." Consider the stock ideological distinction between appearance and reality or the similarly ideological dichotomy between this-worldly and other-worldly. These distinctions point to the separation of the sacred from what is before the Temple, the profane: the latter being the range of possibility open to the people and the former being that more esoteric and dangerous set of possibilities accessible only to the priesthood. Taken together these distinctions and dichotomies constitute the reigning reality-principle. As an ideology, the reality-principle places an illusory barrier between what can only be imagined and what can be known; between what may be full of fatal surprises or life-giving knowledge and what constitutes the mundane; between the potential of communities and peoples for harmony, solidarity, and universality and the particularities, invidious comparisons, and conflicts in which they live; between the individual as one senses what one might yet become and the person one knows oneself to be.

It takes time for the marvelous to become ordinary and for the horizon of the Sacred to recede beyond its more familiar distances. Take, for example, the long, slow progress of the West toward allowing individuals to explore and discuss their own psyches, including their unconscious, on their own terms. Certainly, the psyche of the individual has been one area where the Sacred has dwelled: hidden from profane view, but known by its occasional emanations as a source of great human potential but also of deadly surprise. The unconscious is full of longings for the renewal of old loves, the restoration of broken relationships, the satisfaction of old emotional scores. Often it is with the dead that individuals have the most unfinished business, and it is the dead whose reappearance in dreams or apparitions has stimulated longings for another way of life, a renewed social order, or for a revolution from above. As a source for the Sacred, the psyche confronts a society with a wide range of possibilities and problems, threats and opportunities.

It is not only the seditious or even revolutionary aspect of the dream world that accounts for the church's hostility to the unconscious throughout most of the first millennium of its existence. It is the possibility that individuals, in becoming more closely acquainted with their own unconscious, unspoken, and therefore unacknowledged and unrecognized selves, will gain the authority that has hitherto been reserved for the church alone as an interrogator of the mysteries. As Schmitt (1998, 42) so tellingly puts it, "What was under fire with regard to dreams was the recognition of the subject, of his or her autonomy, of the unconscious that was liberated during sleep, of the admission of the inadmissible impulses and desires of the sleeping body."

If a society is to capture the imagination and loyalty of its members, it must, above all, gain a monopoly on the legitimate interpretation of personal experience. The question has to do with authority. Whose account of psychic experience is to be believed? If someone returns from the dead, so to speak, who will believe him or her? It is an old question, as the New Testament reference suggests. It is a perennial question, since societies generally seek to authorize accounts of personal inspiration and imagination, whether through the clergy or through psychiatric professionals. By the end of the first millennium of its life, the church had largely succeeded in controlling authorized versions of psychic experiences in general and particularly of dreams.

For a long time the cleric or the literate monk had confidence more readily in a written or even an oral tradition, in authorities (those of the Bible or the church fathers), in narrative models that established a requisite chain of "trustworthy" witnesses. The same held true for tales of ghosts: rather than noting one's own dreams, one would reproduce in writing the tales passed on by an *auctoritas*—an "authorized" text or person—whose necessary mediation intervened between the individual and the mysteries of the hereafter." (Schmitt 1998, 42)

Individuals, left to their own devices, do have visions and dreams. In their sleep they encounter the dead and converse with the departed in ways that often fail to pass institutional or communal muster. The dream in particular has been a contested ground between individuals and societies: societies claiming the right to control the telling and interpretation of dreams; individuals, more often than not, succumbing to these pressures, even when they reserved the last word for their own secret—or silent—interpretations.

To turn these imaginings to good social use is the task of any social order that aspires to elicit devotion and even sacrifice from its members. Any society that is unable or unwilling to do so must repress them. Moreover, the more open to the Sacred—in this case, to the psyche and particularly to the unconscious—a society may be, the less vulnerable it will be to unpleasant surprise.

Not only the avoidance of surprise is at stake, of course, but the ability of a society to imagine itself over time. The creative use of the past in defining the present and shaping the future depends on the constructive use of the sources of social imagination. The dead tend to return to their former societies in times of crisis or—more annually—when life has to be renewed.

For centuries, we find from Schmitt's account, the Church succeeded in suppressing all but the authorized accounts of dreams and of imaginary encounters with the dead. At least "during the early Middle Ages both dreams and their subject were objects of oppression. One of the reasons was that the dream gave direct access to the revelation of hidden truths about the hereafter, without the mediation or the control of any ecclesiastical authority." (Schmitt, 42–43).

The church, I am arguing, functioned as an idol to the extent that it claimed to embody the sacred and barred access to the unmediated experience of the individual with his or her own unconscious. To bar the way to direct access to personal encounters with the dead in dreams and to limit such accounts to those that pass institutional muster is an understandable effort to maintain social control over the individual. It is also costly, however, in terms of information and opportunities that are lost to the social imagination and to public discourse. Finally, it places the church in the precarious position of attacking idols while functioning as an idol in its own institutional policies of repression, censorship, and control over the interpretation of personal experience.

What is often called "civil religion" emerges from the attempt of the larger society and its dominant institutions to maintain such a monopoly over the ways that individuals imagine themselves to be related to the living and the dead. The greedier the larger society, the more it will consider to be threatening all those personal affections and animosities that endure beyond the grave, and the more it will seek to make use of these passions to inspire commitment and sacrifice to the social order. Thus, the early Middle Ages found the church, along with other institutions, attempting to suppress the independent sources of visionary experience and to restrict public accounts of dreams to authorized versions.

These institutions also were able to channel the experience of the supernatural or the sublime into the existing orders of affiliation and service. Few, if any, of the spirits advised the living to go easy on their filial, feudal, or religious obligations or to avoid opportunities for heroism and self-sacrifice. Thus, relatives and superiors would profit from the messages of returning spirits. Schmitt recounts various dream narratives that, in their telling, had the function of reinforcing high standards for administration, for truth telling and satisfying one's debts, for the giving of alms and gifts to the church. These dream accounts also reinforced ties not only between spiritual kin but also between natural kin, vassals and lords, parents and children, godparents and godchildren, the living and the dead (Schmitt 1998, 46–47, 190ff.).

In all its attempts to get the spirits of the dead to return only at the proper time and place, the church was never more than partially success-ful. I have already mentioned Schmitt's (1998, 173ff.) discussions of the church's preference for certain times at which to celebrate the dead, but it would appear from that same account that the dead were often not so easily channeled. Either the time at which the person died or "more an-cient calendrical rhythms" and the historic preference of the dead for the dark season took precedence over the church's official calendar.

It was not only difficult to control the times at which the dead appeared; restricting them to the proper space was also more difficult than it might seem, given that the departed apparently sought more control over their own affairs. Some escaped from purgatory to ask the living for relief; oth-ers, perhaps only a few, from hell itself (Schmitt 1998 179–80). What is en-tirely clear from Schmitt's account is that individuals were developing their own accounts of purgatory and the stages of the soul's progress from life into death and back, finally, into life eternal. As the dead increasingly ap-peared on their own account, individuals developed their own accounts of the progress of the soul.

Conversely, as individuals came to explore new possibilities for them-selves outside the range of what had been prescribed for them by birth or various institutions, so did ghosts come to be more inventive about their own prospects. If individuals could stray from the narrow paths offered them by the larger society, so could ghosts begin to wander. Thus, ghosts would show up in the domestic bedroom or the monastic dormitory, places where affections for the dead naturally outlived them. These troublesome passions, however, could disturb the peace of the home or monastery, and the dead were therefore supposed to stay, if not in purgatory or hell, at least in the local cemetery, where occasionally they could be found dancing. Not only the dead, however, could dance in cemeteries; so could young people, in dances that the church often found wholly repugnant and pernicious. The rebellion of one generation was thus not only symbolized in dancing but established through a dance in which the young attempted to make their own connections with the dead quite independently of the media-tions of the church itself.

It was not always easy, therefore, to confine passions for the dead to the proper channels, where old affections could be used to reinforce loyalty to ecclesiastical or feudal superiors or affection between the generations. Out-side these channels, passions for the dead might be even more disruptive. Schmitt (1998, 181–82) speaks of "the furious troop of the dead" that could sometimes be observed in the streets. Thus, it is in these unregulated channels that the dead also were to be found without the permission or control of the church. Sometimes in roadways, especially at crossroads, or in riverbeds and ravines, and certainly in wild places, the living and the dead found their own ways of recognizing one another in affectionate or antagonistic encounters. In modern societies, of course, the young still dance in rebellious fashion, identify with the "grateful dead," and establish their own identity and authority through channels, through media, that they can in fact own and control.

Again, none of this need seem particularly foreign to Christian tradition. The first followers of Christ found themselves meeting on the margins of institutions and particularly in the streets, where they demonstrated their independence of the grace mediated by the Temple. While they might meet on the grounds of the Temple, it would normally be in the porticoes along the edge, and in the roadways of Jerusalem and Galilee. There the spirits, so to speak, ran more freely; the living and the dead could recognize one another, and individuals could discover themselves outside of prescribed channels for the formation of personal identity. The seeds of secularization, then, were sown in the experiences recorded in the synoptic Gospels, long before the church sought to become the new custodian of—and a barrier to—the Sacred.

Of course, we need to be more alert to the differences between complex, contemporary societies and the earlier Middle Ages, especially with regard to the diffusion of these spiritual encounters outside the channels that bind inferiors to superiors, children to parents, godchildren to godparents, the laity to the clergy, and the living to the dead. At the one end of an imaginary spectrum, then, let us place early medieval society and its more or less successful attempt to channel the presence of ghosts into useful social purposes and to control the public account of contacts between the living and the dead. At the other end of the same spectrum let us place a society in which the media that link the living to the dead are multiple, open, and difficult to monitor or regulate. The dead may appear in dreams or on celluloid, and the public may establish its own ways of recognizing the dead that have little to do with official holidays or religious observances. Indeed, at that end of the spectrum secularization has vastly expanded the range of what can be publicly discussed, if not wholly understood.

In the United States, as in other societies of comparable complexity, there are multiple channels open between the living and the dead. The relatives of soldiers who have died in various wars may indeed visit the official monuments, but they may also return to the old battlefields, commemorate their losses, and document their grief in ways that invite publicity. Whether in talk shows, where individuals confess their grief, or in movies that dramatize the return of a dead friend or lover; whether in novels or memoirs, in retrospective exhibits or television documentaries; whether in public fascination with archaeological exploration or in continued digging into the circumstances of the death of public leaders, the dead are no longer restricted to certain times and places or relegated to riverbeds and crossroads. The channels for memory and affection have become multiple and open, and the sacred has become more diffuse and dispersed.

It is all the more striking, then, that in the twelfth century the Sacred—in particular the life of the psyche and the experience of encounters with the dead in dreams—became open to a wider discussion. Individuals relied less on authorized accounts and felt far more able to tell their own stories as part of a confession of their experience and their faith. Granted that even these new accounts, often written by lay persons rather than by monks or clergy, were unauthorized; many of them still expressed in Christian symbols their devotion to the dead, their guilt for not having loved them enough while there still was time, their own suffering at the departure of someone dear to them, and their desire for reunion with the dead. In the laity's accounts of their dreams, traditional Christian symbols of fidelity and infidelity, love and loss, were mingled with images of familiar persons made strange by separation and death. Despite the uses of tradition in these unauthorized accounts, however, dreamers could engage in the "precise analysis" of their own dreams and come to their own terms with longing and grief (Schmitt 1998, 57–80).

It is clear from Schmitt's account that from the thirteenth century onward the Church was losing its monopoly on the description and interpretation of the psyche. In memoirs and autobiographies, individuals could come to their own understanding of their continued relation to the dead. Thus, the range of social and emotional possibility was beginning to expand. The less the larger society could define and shape the relation of the living to their own conscious and unconscious experience, the less it could also control the relation of the living to the dead. Even the Church's insistence on penitence and introspection served, in the long run, to increase the degrees of spiritual freedom (Schmitt 1998, 51).

In this book, then, I am expanding the notion of the Sacred to include all the information that has been repressed in the interest of maintaining the fictions of solidarity and the illusion of a society grounded in what is uncontrovertibly real. Secularization is far more than the collapse of the cultural fiction that there is a symbolic whole that unites and is greater than the sum of the parts that make up a particular society. To understand secularity it is necessary therefore to grasp more than the obvious fact that a particular society has become a set of special interests, divergent ways of life, and competing notions of the sacred. In the process of secularization, to be sure, the public sphere may have co-opted the historical experience and imagination of a wide range of groups who have been marginalized precisely because they deviate from or conflict with the majoritarian institutions of the sacred. That co-optation, however, is only one aspect of the process by which secularizing societies have gained access to the implicit, hidden, or suppressed aspects of their social and psychological environments.

Secularization also includes the process by which the public sphere gains knowledge of unresolved longings and unsatisfied grievances that call for recognition lest they become a source of inertia, cynicism, occasional explosions, and other unpleasant surprises, or even of volatile movements for revolutionary social change. In the epidemiology of public injury

and complaint, I am arguing, it is necessary to understand that secularization makes room for inquiry into the violence and hurt that have not been
made public but that may account for widespread chronic fatigue, depression, cynicism, alienation, suspicion, and withdrawal from public life.

In a secular society, moreover, there may be a wide range of impulses
seeking satisfaction that are relatively neutral or benign but appear to
serve no redeeming social purpose. To allow these full play is not merely
to sanction deviant sexuality, bizarre art forms, diverse spiritual practices,
alternative medicines, experimental utopian communities, a world full of
games played on the internet, romance in cybernetic chat rooms, and fantasies of extraterrestrial life. It is not only to lift the burden of positive or
negative sanction from a wide range of activity and thought. It is not only
to suspend judgment but to *dispense* with judgment altogether.

This is not to say that a secular society lives in a world of fantasy; it is to
suspend the reality principle long enough to allow imagination and experimental practice full play in public life. Nothing, in that sense, would be
Sacred, that is, beyond the access of thought, imagination, and speech.

Of course, the more secular a society becomes, the more it is possible for
individuals and groups, corporations and institutions to make inflated
claims of their own role in relation to the possible. The notion, popularized
in some commercials, that in America anything that can be imagined can
also be done is a case in point. That corporations routinely portray themselves in advertisements as the carriers of the hitherto unimaginable
future is also a case in point. Individuals also are likely to have their own
sense of reality confused by an unrealistic sense of unending possibility: a
chronic sort of adolescence incompatible with the hard facts of mortality.
Popular entertainment that features time warps caters to the public
fantasy that time can be reversed or transcended. Indeed the cinema, like
late medieval accounts of ghosts, popularizes personal experiences of a
continuing conversation of living with the dead.

To open the gates of public information and sociality, therefore, is to risk
that interest, affection, and compassion will flow in unusual channels. A
sense of anguished affinity for human suffering may require public engagement in global ills for which the nation itself is ill prepared. Conversely,
the increased range of public discourse will require a willingness on the
part of the nation to entertain the possibility of danger from a wide range
of sources, from the microbial to the psychological. Tendencies toward national self-destruction will be as much a part of public discussion as studies
of individual depression. The dangers of terrorism are already mooted in
various talk shows. However, it will require the full attention of the government in public sessions to give the people a political education in precisely
what they may be facing in the way of biochemical disasters or nuclear explosions even in remote parts of the country. There will be no sanctuaries
in the future from hatred and revenge on a global scale.

The sacred has always been a fragile defense against violence. Even those who have sought sanctuary at its altars have found that they have come to a place where sacrifice is made, and on occasion the sacrifices have been human. The sacred does provide a veil, however, over the awareness of human anguish and of the violence that often permeates both the local community and the nation. It is this most carefully guarded veil, I am arguing, that must be lifted if a society is fully to become secular. Only then will the secrets of the Sacred, the community's untold agony, be open to public inspection and discourse. That is a long way from the sort of veneration that sacred violence has inspired in the past.

The sacred, once it is institutionalized, offers up only a dim and distorted image of the human being. Social life under the auspices of the sacred is therefore a bit perverse. Individuals working together consecrate bread and wine, but they receive it as though from another, transcendent source. It is their own sociability that they find reflected in the communion of believers, but it comes to them as though from beyond, a gift from God, rather than clearly being what it is: the fruit of their own labor together to build a common life. What might otherwise be recognizable as a profoundly human emotion is regarded as bestial. Individuals find in animals the feelings of desire and grief that they can no longer recognize in themselves because their own "animal spirits," so to speak, have been sacrificed and suppressed in the name of a higher spirituality. On the walls of churches are pictures, perhaps, of an idealized or crucified humanity, but it is the individual's social condition that has been distorted beyond recognition.

That is why there is something dreamlike about social life. In dreams, after all, the self is disguised in a number of ways. Other persons appear in our dreams who embody one or another aspects of ourselves. It is not only persons but things that represent us in our dreams. Planes and locomotives, hammers and knives, vessels and houses, all speak to us in code about aspects of ourselves that we have learned to ignore or despise. Dreams, like social life in Marcuse's description, tell us a lie about ourselves by turning us into things or by making what is really our own nature seem foreign to us and beyond our knowledge or control. That is why dreams seem a bit uncanny. They show us that which seems somehow to be really familiar, because it is simply ourselves, but which, under the impact of repression and a distorted social life, also seems to be strange.

Freud and Marx agreed that social life holds up distorted images of the human community but differed on "their origins, their mechanisms of perpetuation." Marx was perhaps more optimistic than Freud about "the possibility of their transformation," but even Freud believed in the long, slow process of self-analysis as a way of removing Sacred mysteries from the psyche and, in the end, from social life. What Marcuse (1960, 280) said of the production of commodities thus applies to the social construction of the sacred as well: "It sets forth the actual social relations of men as a totality of objective relations, thereby concealing their origin, their mechanisms of perpetuation, and the possibility of their transformation. Above all, it conceals their human core and content."

Studies of fascism and a variety of other mass movements have argued the case that individuals acquire an ersatz selfhood through these abstract social identities in order to make up for the lack of a self that is truly related to the universal human community. Each of these movements promises a "new social order," but each is merely "a new form for subjugating individuals to a hypostatized universality" (Marcuse 1960, 283). Marcuse is thinking about changing the way a society organizes production, but I am applying his point to any aspect of the social order that claims to be external, superior, and constraining to the individual, that is, the sacred.

Wherever the sacred is well institutionalized, however, boundaries separate the public from the private, the sacred from the secular, the believers from the unbelievers, the human from the animal, the social from the natural, and so on. The institutionalized sacred thus offers an image of humanity that claims to be authentic and universal, but is in fact the expression of a very particular community and of the interests of those who control it. Every crucifix or cross hanging on the wall of a hospital room not only links the patient with the human community of all who suffer but separates that patient from non-Christians and legitimates the authority of the religious professionals who run the hospital and tend to the sick and dying.

To take the mystery from the community and thus to disclose the more universal aspects of its humanity it is necessary to begin with the symbols of violence that adorn its shrines. Let us return to the crucifix, for example. Usually it is taken to be a sign of the violence that made possible the creation of a community freed from suffering and torment. In the context of ritual, furthermore, it stands for the possibility of restoring the purity of the society's origins at a moment of perfect, supreme self-sacrifice:

> A successful ritual stops time at the perfect creation moment. It repeats and freezes the retrospectively golden moment when the group was created out of sacrifice. In this moment the debt to the blood-thirsty god was paid. The group was pristine. This was the moment when sacrifice was truly enough, when we were delivered from time and death (Marvin and Ingle 1997, 777).

As the authors point out, however, the same hostilities will increase once again, and the nation will need another purge in order to achieve a respite from internal tension. With each new performance of this ritual, once again "the slate of internal hostilities is wiped clean. The group begins again. The external threat is met. Our bad feelings toward one another are purged. Time begins anew, space is re-consecrated" (Marvin and Ingle 1997, 775). There have been two such major purges, in the opinion of these two authors: the Civil War and the Second World War. Certainly the Vietnam War had the opposite effect. Instead of lessening internal tensions it increased them.

The need for these periodic purifications, I would argue, is quite simply in the violence that remains relatively unspoken within the society. Even within the local community, there is violence done to the dignity of the individual: not only by the more obvious forms of abuse but by more subtle forms of indifference and humiliation that create a desire for retribution, if not chronic despair. Knowledge of these forms of degradation is often widespread in a community or institution, but because it remains unspoken, individuals remain haunted by a sense that there are unseen forces, often hostile, within the society itself (see Bollas 1992). I will return in the next chapter to the relation of violence to the Sacred.

Thus, the notion of the Sacred as the site of hidden and dangerous forces acquires new currency in every generation. The path toward secularization is thus constantly barred by the fresh experience in each generation of the violence done to the individual by institutions that seek to curb individual autonomy and to discredit the authority of personal experience.

3

HEROES, CHARISMATIC FIGURES, AND CELEBRITIES AS CULTURAL IDOLS

A t best, the relationship between a society and its heroes is going to be ambivalent. No one makes this more indelibly clear than the Afro-American cultural hero, as Orlando Patterson (1998, 235ff.) has most recently argued. Clearly the object of pervasive, systemic rejection over two centuries, nonetheless the Afro-American has at times been accorded the status of cultural hero. That may be because Americans wish to deny the cruelty that they have inflicted on Afro-Americans, but it also is because the Afro-American is the object of more erotic and positive feelings as well. Thus, eliminated from the body politic, the aggressive Afro-American figure is idolized on the playing field. A safe target for class or ethnic hostility and a screen on which Euro-Americans can project their own animosities, the Afro-American is also the embodiment of the longings for a more playful and accessible selfhood or for freedom from the repressive forms of social identity based on one's social class or gender. As Jews have long known, it is the function of a marginal and oppressed people to be whomever the dominant majority wants them to be.

Heroes, then, are the embodiment of a society's sense of possibility. Of course, some of those possibilities may be widely regarded as illegitimate or illicit. The hero is thus one who ventures where angels fear to tread. Such a hero may do the dirty work of a society, like Dirty Harry, unfettered by the codes of a bureaucratized law enforcement agency but emboldened by a community's innate sense of justice and its loathing for certain outsiders. Such heroes are often countercultural. Not only do they cross certain boundaries, as Patterson points out. Like Dennis Rodman or Michael Jackson, they may act as if those boundaries no longer exist. These are the Dionysian heroes that Patterson finds in American culture, particularly among the Afro-American community.

Such heroic status is an honor that comes with certain risks attached. In the past it has been extraordinarily dangerous for Afro-Americans to disregard boundaries. Indeed, the use of profiles by state police to target minorities in general and Afro-Americans in particular on the roadways is particularly symbolic of the dangers that Afro-Americans still encounter when they enter areas where the boundaries are not clear—roadways, like other passageways, being particularly open and therefore dangerous. As we have seen, they are the places in which ghosts are often seen: those beings that seem to be part of neither the living nor the dead but who travel freely between them. Note that "spook" is an old-fashioned racial epithet in American society as well.

It is not surprising, then, that heroes so often turn into idols with clay feet. Indeed, it is the function of the idol to convey the full range of possibility in any society, the negative pole of that range being only hinted at in the form of symbolic transgression. Thus, Jesus is the hero whose ways are uniformly good, and yet it is he who disregarded the Sabbath and mocked the honorific status and titles of those who, like the Pharisees, wore long robes and hogged the places of public honor.

In American society, Patterson notes, the status of Afro-Americans as cultural heroes fully embodies this ambivalence that can turn into rejection and violence. The source of mother's milk, the Afro-American nanny, is transfigured into a male whose fluids are both desirable and loathed: hence the disfigurement and castration of Afro-Americans lynched well into the twentieth century. The mocking engagement of Afro-Americans in minstrel shows was the flip side of the coin of racial hatred that produced lynchings where the body of the slain Afro-American was regarded with the mute horror accorded to a sacred victim. From imitation, incorporation, and mock affection the society raises up the opposite idol who must undergo disfiguring rather than imitation, rejection rather than incorporation, and unaffected derision. The hero embodies the sum total of these possibilities, although seldom at one and the same time and place or in a single incarnation. There usually has to be a second coming; the god slain must be born again.

When a society has a monopoly on the sacred, it can fairly well define what the individual is supposed to be and what is worth not only living but also dying for. When a society loses its monopoly on the sacred, however, and the sacred becomes more like a genie or a free spirit, the sacred may be found anywhere at any time. The wells of personal inspiration will overflow, while the reservoirs of societal authority begin to run dry. Drawing from an underground stream that surfaces in a variety of places, personal inspiration produces an extraordinary, if sporadic and uneven flood, of virtuosity. These virtuosos may be living or dead, friendly or malicious, but they always live in the realm just outside ordinary possibility. In their presence and in their shadow, individuals will develop their own notions about their identity, about what is worth living or dying for, and about their ultimate destiny.

Let us start with the dead. So long as a society can monopolize the careers of the dead, there will be relatively few surprises, and the dead will only confirm the arrangements made by the living to control individual virtuosity, antisocial impulses, and longings for various kinds of satisfaction. The dead, if they reappear at all, will arrive on schedule and stay only so long as their presence is wanted. A number of societies have shown considerable skill in managing these reappearances, so that the dead have largely been useful in settling quarrels or fertilizing fields for another year's crop. As I noted in Chapter Two, the medieval church, for instance, mounted a concerted effort to coordinate the arrival and departure of the dead with major feast days and observances. As Jean-Claude Schmitt (1998, 173) has put it, the times of ghostly apparitions "intersected with the collective time of living, that of the calendar and feast days, the days of the week, and the division between daytime and nighttime activities." Even the church, however, did not succeed entirely in orchestrating the appearances of the dead, who seemed to have a preference for the Christmas season and, "more widely, winter, the dark part of the year" (Schmitt 1998, 174). Whereas under Roman auspices the dead may have acquired the habit of appearing during winter, the church, on the other hand, was interested in turning old Roman festivals of that cold season, like the *parentalia*, into celebrations focused on the church itself and particularly on the bishop of Rome. As a compromise with folk traditions, then, the church moved days of commemoration of the dead to the fall, where they could be honored on the day after All Saints without competing with the church for attention. Schmitt (1998, 174) notes:

> Interestingly, it does not seem to me that these commemorative days served as privileged anchoring points for apparitions of the dead. Regarding November 2 [the day after All Saints—rkf], apparitions were even less forced to bend to the constraints of the calendar, since that date was relatively recent. . . . In sum, the time of apparitions depended principally on individual logic . . . or on more ancient calendrical rhythms, which the liturgy of the church only partially resumed.

Why this focus on the dead? The dead, after all, represent the Sacred, the world of unfulfilled human potential. They are part of the environment of every social system and can be the source of unpleasant surprises or of untiring motivation. As the object of affections that will not die, the dead themselves hold the key to wellsprings of motivation that can mobilize a society for long, hard work or for the disciplines of war. The dead remain familiar but strange, unwanted and yet invited to return. The living have unfinished emotional business with the dead that can be used to arouse a sense of duty or to encourage a people to undertake new risks. To ignore the dead is therefore fatal for a society; it is tantamount to being blind to a major source of opportunity, threat, and surprise in the social environment.

One would think that reverence for the heroic dead would be superfluous in a complex social system like modern Europe. However, although the European monetary and economic system is rapidly developing, old forms of solidarity are becoming more rather than less important. Although cultural boundaries are changing, old ones are being reasserted. To counteract what the Indian press used to enjoy calling "fissiparous tendencies," it is necessary even for the European community to claim for itself some traditional form of solidarity. Thus, there has been some attempt to resuscitate a Celtic cultural heritage as a foundation for the modern European system.

The Celtic revival is odd, if only because large parts of the new Europe are not now and never have been Celtic. Celtic heroes also might seem an odd choice of cultural chic because the Celts have been notoriously resistant to encroachments from larger societies. Brittany and the Basque country are obvious examples. In the nineteenth century those who extolled the virtues of the countryside over the metropolis, of the people against the state, fashioned a Celtic heritage of opposition (Dietler 1994).

As French language, bureaucracy, and education began to erode Brittany and Breton identity, the old assumption—that Bretons and Gauls were tied by kinship—was changed in favor of a model that argued that modern Brittany was populated by immigrant Celts from Wales, Cornwall, and so on. As Michael Dietler (1994, 594) explains, "Militants consider Brittany not as a province of France but as an independent Celtic nation allied by ethnic kinship to other 'oppressed' insular Celtic nations."

Not to be outdone by resistance on the periphery, French romantic nationalism resuscitated "our ancestors the Gauls" and "focused on the character of Vercingetorix" (Dietler 1994, 588). Vercingetorix became "a national martyr and symbol of revenge," while the Celtic motif enabled cultural mobilization of French, Belgians, and Netherlanders against Germany (Dietler 1994, 591). Today, especially in southern France among the followers of Le Pen, Vercingetorix stands as a symbol of resistance against the Germans. Some there still remember the Second World War and live in fear that the Germans will come back. Vercingetorix is understandably the hero in that part of the country where the crossroads still are marked by crosses commemorating those who died in the Resistance.

Typically the center seeks to co-opt and then subordinate the cultural heroes of the periphery. Certainly the Gallic center sought to co-opt Celtic identity for its own purposes. Earlier, perhaps because Napoleon had modeled himself after Roman heroes, Napoleon III heightened "the dynamic tension between Celtic and Roman identities." While he compared himself favorably to Caesar, he also sponsored the study of Vercingetorix and the Iron Age settlements of the Celts. Napoleon III even sponsored a statue of Vercingetorix by Millet "with the face modeled after his own." In the end, then, the center seeks to prevail over the periphery by stealing its heroes. We need not be surprised to find that Napoleon III subordinated Celtic to

Roman identity in the interest of French colonial policy; indeed, he argued that it was a good thing for the Celts to be subsumed by the Romans (Dietler 1994, 588–90).

The changing face of Vercingetorix, from hardy Celt to the more adaptable Napoleon III, was a fitting prelude to the fate of this hero during the time of Vichy. Petain, who had initially celebrated Celticism, finally had several statues of Vercingetorix demolished. Vercingetorix lives, however, in the comic book *Asterix the Gaul*. No wonder, then, that European cultural exhibits, promoting the Union, claim that the Celts were the proto-Europeans, despite the ambiguous and problematic nature of the evidence (Dietler 1994, 594–95).

It is not entirely odd that the statue of Vercingetorix should have had its ups and downs in France. If it has been legitimate to speak of a cult of the dead in any European country, it has been of France. Auguste Comte not only sought to establish a secular religion of humanity but believed in a continuing spiritual conversation between the living and the dead; so, indeed, did many socialists who were otherwise thoroughly at home with the notions of positivism and materialism (Kselman 1993, 137ff.). Shrines may thus spring up on what would appear to be very infertile soil indeed. How can we move beyond a continuing veneration for the dead and a sense of obligation to the past? How can we create a secular society that remembers the past without reverence or remorse, without celebration or repentance: a society without heroes?

If the dead represent a wide range of social possibility, so do others, however, whose energies and loyalty remain important to a society but whose commitment may be unreliable and problematical. In a patriarchal society, of course, it is women who are both insiders and outsiders; they are essential to the continuity and survival of the community but are also the carriers of passions and loyalties that always remain somewhat suspect. Women are for this reason often the ones to be cast in the roles most closely associated with the dead. They dress the corpse, tend the grave, perform the services of memory and devotion, and bear the burden of social ostracism associated with death. It is their association with the dead that links women and others to the ambiguous realm of social possibility that I am calling the Sacred.

In rounding up the usual suspects in order to outline the parameters of social possibility, we must not of course forget the poor. Not only women but the poor have represented an aspect not only of the social system but also of the environment. Indeed, with the poor it is difficult to know whether one is inside the system or outside. As a source of dangerous surprises but also of resources that have yet to be put to use, the poor represent an area of social possibility that is full of both threat and opportunity. Being representatives of the Sacred, the poor also represent the burdens of unfulfilled human potential.

It is therefore not surprising to find that the medieval church linked the poor with the dead themselves. Schmitt (1998, 176) notes that more than one abbey invited the poor to receive food and drink on days of devotion for the dead: "[T]he poor were considered to be substitutes for the dead, and the material food they were given symbolized spiritual 'food,' that is, the suffrages that shortened the trials of the dead."

In the commemoration of the dead through attention to the poor, however, the monks were also making a perhaps larger point that emanates from the New Testament itself; Jesus, after all, had identified himself with the least of the brethren and with the poor themselves. In other words, the New Testament provides an impetus for any institution or society to expand and explore the range of social possibility by incorporating into its own immediate consciousness the needs and aspirations of the poor. Societies that ignore the potentials of the poor, both for commitment and disruption, for useful work or subversive activity, place themselves at unnecessary risk.

There is a continuum of increasing marginality from patriarchs to women, children, the poor, and the dead. Ghosts, after all, are people who are asleep; they are virtually dead, but not quite. They can still come among the living and cause consternation, create surprise, and demonstrate extraordinary vitality. Their potential is fulfilled only to the extent that they are allowed to walk, although asleep, among those with whom they once had lived their lives. So long as they feel the need to fulfill this unmet potential, their torment will continue. Who or what, then, in modern societies could represent this incarnation of antisocial possibility?

Like dissatisfied ghosts, the proliferation of multiple selves, and widespread public interest in these aberrations characterized France during the years immediately after its defeat in the Prussian War and the Paris commune (Hacking 1995). The point of the stories was that, when the nation-state loses its monopoly on the sacred, what was once venerated but left unexplored can then be examined and analyzed. The more the Sacred is secularized, the more it becomes part of public discussion. There it can feed the imagination not only of individuals who can see alternative lives for themselves as feasible, but it can filter into the discussion of what sort of society the nation might yet become.

In this process even the unconscious becomes open to inspection, and individuals tread on psychological territory previously reserved for angels. For instance, One French writer and painter, Henri Michaux, seeking "to conquer the obscure and shifting territories below the surface of rational consciousness, wrote of explorations into territories and worlds that were largely imaginary if not actually hallucinogenic (Cardinal 1999, 18). Like some of the multiple personalities discussed in the previous chapter, he, too, seems to have come of age during wartime; like some of them, too, he took trips to faraway places like the Amazon Basin or China and India. Unlike them, however, he had a language for his own multiple selfhood. Not only did he doubt the reality of a single or unitary self; he thought it preferable not only to have more than one role in life but more than one self: "Albeit subscribing to a model of the creative rebel dating back at least to Rimbaud, Michaux defines his vocation in terms of a refusal of antecedents, and a hunger for situations of estrangement and discontinuity" (Cardinal 1999, 18). Now, we know from Hacking's (1995, 251) discussion that public interest in multiple personalities entered the mainstream of French thought through the doors of science; Bergson himself was influenced by this research, and so, perhaps, may have been Proust. The possibility of becoming more than one self had entered the realm of human possibility. No longer being accused of entering a sacred realm reserved for religious virtuosi, the individual could now intend to be more than one self without even necessarily being considered a victim of involuntary distraction or aberration. One no longer had to be a patient in order to expand the horizons of the self.

When the sacred becomes diffuse and secularized, not only does the stigma of sainthood become open to clinical description and public inspection; individuals can imagine for themselves and intend a wider range of possibilities for selfhood. Sanctity becomes celebrity, and what is celebrated no longer requires the presence of clergy in order to be valid or efficacious. One can do it for oneself, all the while following what has become, as Cardinal put it, a "model" for creative rebellion. The path to idiosyncracy and eccentricity has been paved with what can finally be called good intentions.

It is always dangerous, however, when individuals begin to create for themselves the roles that break up old constraints and open up new realms of possibility. In this regard we have so far examined several categories of those who seem to ignore the barriers between night and day, between the invisible and the visible, and between this world and the next: the ghost, the sleepwalker or those with double consciousness, saints, patients, and the geniuses of self-development. These are virtuosos at expanding the range of social possibility, and institutions like the church with a vested interest in the prevailing distribution of rights and responsibilities have sought, more or less unsuccessfully, to keep them under control. We have also given honorable mention to two other categories of socially problematical types who seem to exist in two worlds, the one conventional and the other outside the bounds of ordinary conversation and control: the poor and women. There are other virtuosos, however, that have represented the constructive and destructive potential of the Sacred.

These are the heroes: a category of virtuosi that stands right on the border between the possible and the impossible. Heroic feats typically are those in which an individual takes on risks, encounters threats and surprises, and realizes a human potential, all of which are far beyond the ordinary limits of knowledge and prowess. In doing so these individuals may in fact avert a terrible danger from a society or people and change the course not only of battle but of history. Consider, for example, Moses at the Red Sea, David and Goliath, and less single-handedly but no less spectacularly, the soldiers of the Second World War who redeemed Europe from fascism. On the other hand, these virtuosi may expand the range of social possibility in another, more subversive direction, by revealing the known world to be composed far more of illusion than reality. Still other heroes show the way to a social order that is based on no ordinary ties of affection and affinity and that acknowledges no visible authority. Both the subversive hero and the one who has saved the nation is an emblem and vehicle of the sacred, but the sacred is a sword, as I have argued, that can cut two ways.

If it seems strange to link heroes with ghosts and sleepwalkers or individuals with double consciousness, consider this passage from Schmitt's (1998, 176) treatment of ghosts in the Middle Ages:

> For the military aristocracy, whose place we have seen in the Cluniac tales of apparitions, Pentecost was the great holiday of knighthood, that of the collective dubbing of young warriors. The ritual of entering into knighthood was a rite of passage, thus a sort of symbolic death through which the young man "died" in his first "state" to be "reborn" into the order of knighthood under the direction of his elders and the invocation of the lineal ancestors. On this occasion the new knights indulged in war games, notably in the tournament, but the clerics avidly denounced the violence of these rituals, and many ghost tales in fact feature knights who met a violent and untimely death in a tournament."

Thus ghosts and heroes are tied together in liturgy and in moments when the times are out of joint. Their liturgical connection in Pentecost dated from the time before the church sought to move all celebrations of the dead to the fall season, and there had been a long association of Pentecost with the celebration of Christian martyrs (Schmitt 1998, 175). It would have been understandable if the church, attempting to transform renegade warrior youth into chivalrous knights or even crusaders, should have attempted to model their coming of age on patterns of Christian sacrifice and heroism.

To channel the risky behavior of violent youth into roles that serve to defend or expand the security of a community or nation is a way of taming—institutionalizing—the sacred. Thus, to turn their behavior into a defensive operation is one way of defending the boundary between a society and an environment full not only of extraordinary human potential but of nasty surprises. The sacred—as embodied in knighthood—becomes an idol: a vast reduction of the range of possibility in the service of the existing social order.

There is nothing particularly antique about these reflections, despite our focus on the Middle Ages. Heroes in modern societies also are likely to be turned into idols that defend a society from the subversive and illegitimate exploration of the possible. Take, for example, the moral career of Augustus Pinochet, the sometime Chilean dictator. There was a time when he was a national hero, of sorts, enshrined in a national pantheon of his own creation.

According to Marcela Christi and Lorne Dawson (1996, 324), the Pinochet regime created a "Chilean civil religion [which] was an episodic politico-religious discourse fashioned by one 'civic group' over and against another." Supported by the Catholic Church, it succeeded in casting Pinochet in a priestly role. Although it was reflective only of the values and interests of one conservative faction, it nonetheless drew on widely available religious symbols (Christi and Dawson 1996, 324).

Crucial to the success of this new "civil religion" was the ideologues' attempt to initiate an entirely "new social, political, economic and even moral order" with Pinochet as the new Moses. Children were required to participate in rituals in the schools and to sing anthems "'thanking the valiant soldier' for the liberation of the nation." Not only was Chile a chosen nation, but Pinochet was a priest, a wise leader and representative of Providence: leader of the movement to extirpate Marxism from the country and the globe. Although the authors conclude that the movement failed to create a moral community, it did dramatize the capacity of a civil religion to institute authoritarian rather than democratic values (Christi and Dawson 1996, 325–28).

I bring up the Pinochet regime here to dramatize what is at stake in movements to enshrine political and military figures as national heroes. The stakes are indeed high: the freedom, even the life of the citizenry. Although we can imagine that the machinery of ritual clanked audibly, still we must also be able to hear the voices of young children chanting their praises to Pinochet-Moses and to the soldiers for freeing them from the curse of international communism. To create national confidence it is necessary to inspire faith in national heroes, and to ensure a steady supply of civilians willing to sacrifice themselves to the regime it is necessary to start children singing heroic praises before they have a chance to think about the words as well as the music.

In the current enthusiasm for bringing heads of state like Pinochet to trial for their crimes against humanity, it may therefore be difficult to remember that he himself was the object of highly contrived and well-orchestrated national devotions during his regime in Chile. It has only recently become true that

> The new international law has arrived, with the rights of individuals at last taking their proper place among the other rules that regulate international relations. Those who resist these changes—or choose not to take a position—will find themselves left behind by a process that has become inevitable. (Byers 1999, 27)

These words were written while England was waiting for a ruling from the House of Lords that would indicate whether—and to what degree—

Pinochet could be tried for the torture and murder of citizens not only of Chile but of other countries during his ruthless tenure as head of state. The author cited a number of developments, not all of them as yet having the force of English law behind them, that would make it possible for individuals to prosecute heads of state who had violated their fundamental human rights.

Is the process "inevitable," as Byers suggests, in which not even heads of state can hide behind sacred mystery and authority? It is well to remember that the regime of Pinochet was as effective and enduring as it was in part because the state organized and carried out not only a program of severe repression but also one of endowing Pinochet and his military regime with the trappings of the sacred.

If the process by which human rights become enforcible in international courts is "inevitable," as Byers suggests, it does not follow that the process of secularization is irreversible. Mystery may continue to join hands with authority to require human sacrifices. The sight of young people dancing in the streets of Belgrade wearing targets on their bodies to suggest their willingness to be bombed rather than renounce national claims to Kosovo suggests that there is nothing irreversible about secularization. Indeed, it is that sight that makes it necessary to understand the mechanics of heroism. As Christi and Dawson (1996, 328) put it regarding Chile under Pinochet,

> [T]he general tendency to characterize civil religion as a national, non-sectarian faith loses validity in the face of dictatorial regimes, as does the portrayal of civil religion as a canopy of common values fostering social integration. In line with Weber, we must remember the dual functions of legitimating ideologies and theodicies. They serve to reconcile subservient groups to their fate. But they also serve to assure ruling groups of the righteousness of their rule and privileges. The latter was probably the primary function of a civil religious discourse in the case of the supporters of Pinochet.

The strength of Pinochet's fascist civil religion was also its weakness. Closely tied to the interests and values of his military regime, it was insufficiently differentiated from the church and existing institutions to develop a life of its own. It failed to develop its own symbols and rituals, and was more like Franco's than Hitler's version. It focused on the virtues of the regime (military discipline, anti Marxism) and failed to invoke the core values of a broad spectrum of the people. As Christi and Dawson (1996, 329) put it, "In line with the Durkheimian approach to civil religion, then, we suggest that the inability to create a sense of moral community was instrumental to the demise of Chilean civil religion." It was too Rousseauian.

In this view, national fascism has a better chance to be established in the United States, where the civil religion may reflect a broader, more deeply held set of values. That is another way of saying that a secular society may be a crucial defense against fascist tendencies in a country that has already flirted with the likes of Senator McCarthy. In any society, however, there is a latent demand for individuals who appear to have taken on a certain life after death by entering a society's pantheon of heroism. In relation to them, by emulating them or submitting to demands made in the name of these heroes, individuals can acquire a surrogate identity and a sense of their own being as solid and perhaps enduring. In return a society gains access to a vast reservoir of longing that can be turned into loyalty. By tapping the individual's desire to stand the test of time, a society can acquire the vast resources of potential sacrifice. The more the sacred is diffused, however, and dispersed throughout a society, the more widespread will be the distinctive grace—the charisma—of heroism. If a regime wishes to monopolize the potential for loyalty and sacrifice within the population, it must therefore centralize and concentrate the symbolic manufacture of heroism.

Indeed, the idol is the prototype of the individual to whom special consideration must be made: an individual who has been shorn of any particular characteristics and stands as an emblem of the social order. By paying tribute to the idols the individual regains access to a form of selfhood more stable and enduring because it is anchored in the larger society's pantheon, but nonetheless it is a surrogate selfhood acquired by sacrificing the individual's own particular psyche. By joining the ranks of devotees, the individual acquires a social status endowed with the sign of good faith, but this bona fides is purchased at the price of original selfhood.

It is no accident, therefore, that a society should enshrine the individual as the source of all political legitimacy in a social system that reduces the individual's voice to a polling statistic and the individual's vote to a mechanized symbolic operation. It is also no accident that the individual's ideas and creativity should be extolled in a system that requires individuals to be certified for participation in the labor market. Similarly, it should not seem strange that "individualism" is considered the besetting sin of a society in which individuals are increasingly subject to pressures for conformity, to competitive evaluations, to corporate downsizing, to bureaucratized education and medicine, to mass political appeals, to the manipulation of politics through the media, and to litigation or imprisonment.

The individual becomes an idol to the extent that the person is stripped of particularity and dignity. Crowds idolized Princess Diana for her unique selfhood, for her own peculiar blend of royalty and folk appeal, of public duty and publicized pleasure, but in turning Diana into a folk princess they also displayed the signs of their own marginality and subordination. Indeed, it was Diana's ability to place herself in the midst of those who lack public dignity that heralded her own extraordinary worth. The dynamics of idolatry were played out on a stage that dramatized the individual's lack of singularity while magnifying the special graces of Diana herself.

The point of these comments, however, is simply that the idolatry of the individual is a substitute form of dignifying the person. It appears that the individual per se is being given dignity, even while the persons in attendance are as visibly abject as those visited by Diana in her lifetime or, after her death, displaying their grief outside of Kensington Palace.

To put it another way: There may indeed be, as some have suggested, a civil religiosity that enshrines the individual in the rules of etiquette and thus accords to the individual the sort of consideration that is due to someone who bears the sacred mark of humanity itself. This is a view that has been attributed particularly to Erving Goffman, who gave his own form of exquisite consideration to the rules of interpersonal etiquette in bars and mental hospitals, island villages and public streets: "An idol is to a person as a rite is to etiquette" (qtd. in Chriss 1993, 261).

However, as Goffman went on to demonstrate in painful detail, each social order has a way of demeaning the individual that it enshrines. Mental hospitals deprive individual patients of the signs of personal worth and dignity that normal persons take for granted; patients are kept waiting and are deprived of autonomy and privacy. Their movements are monitored, and the satisfaction of their needs is calibrated to the convenience of the staff. Similarly, those who have been stigmatized but are not in institutions have developed ways of maintaining their dignity, even though they, too, have to suffer the indignities that accompany the special status of those who are seen or suspected to have some physical or moral defect. Idols, especially those whose clay feet are visible, are prone to humiliation.

To sum it up, we might put this argument in the form of two simple propositions: (1) To the extent that a society needs individuals to sacrifice themselves for the nation or the state, they will create a pantheon of heroes. (2) To the extent that the society recognizes particular individuals as heroes, persons are to that extent in danger of losing their personal dignity.

The ideological expression of these propositions can be found in Durkheim's discussion of the religion of humanity, within which the individual is seen as the embodiment of all that is sacred. Durkheim attacked a utilitarian or anarchist individualism while supporting the individualism that sees in the individual the embodiment or carrier of humanity. His notion of the individual is Kantian: the individual being an example of the human condition, of the universal in the particular, and of the abstract in the concrete. The individual is sacred because he is that embodiment or incarnation of humanity itself (Prades 1993, 421).

Durkheim's idea of the religion of humanity is essentially an Incarnational sociology. Because the individual incarnates humanity, which is sacred, the individual is approached as if he or she were sacred, set apart, to be respected. Note, however, that the individual could only be thus enshrined as an idol of humanity if the individual is subjected to the collective will by a pedagogy that inculcated respect for moral authority, for law, and for legitimate authority, and that makes the child grasp the joy of collective action (Prades 1993, 420). In other words, the idolatry of the individual gives what the larger society has already taken away in self-respect and self-determination.

What form does the idolatry of the individual take, however, when the state lacks a clearly defined pantheon of heroism and a strict discipline for allowing individuals access to the sacred? When the sacred is embodied in less traditional forms; when the sacred lacks an elite that is trained to gain access to it and to provide revelations; when the sacred is not institutionalized, therefore, but is widely diffused in the population; when the sacred thus takes on forms that are mundane, popular, and temporary: what form does the idolatry of the individual take under these conditions? These are the conditions under which some observers view the civil religion as corrupt and others question whether in fact one can speak of a civil religion at all (Prades 1993, 423; see also Wilson 1986).

Under these conditions, for instance, one would find a civil religion being discussed in terms that hardly distinguish it from the more idolatrous forms of popular culture. Take, for example, Flere's (1994) observations about civil religion in Yugoslavia between the end of the Second World War and the country's disintegration in the 1990s. Except for a political ideology largely restricted to communist cadres, it was a populist civil religiosity focused on public celebrities (charismatic figures) in politics, sports, and music, with traditional religious elements, and was found primarily among the less educated members of the population. It was apparently a pantheon of heroes that was easily assimilated to nationalist aspirations, if later developments in Serbian politics can be taken as a guide to earlier forms of celebration.

Remember that the core of the civil religion is the victory over death: the veneration of individuals who took on important roles during events that were decisive for the creation and maintenance of the nation or the state. Derek Davis (1997) observes that even the more complex discussions of civil religion "usually drew upon civil events such as the Fourth of July, Memorial Day, and presidential inaugurations, documents such as the Declaration of Independence and the U.S. Constitution; personages such as Washington, Jefferson, Madison, and Lincoln; and common religious beliefs such as the belief in God and the chosen nation status of the United States.

This cult of the dead, so to speak, gives individuals the illusion of belonging to a society that will survive the ravages of time and thus furnishes them with a surrogate sort of existential satisfaction.

With this in mind, the discussion of differences in the idolatry of the individual from one society to the next will not seem too confusing. The question is simply "To what extent can a society succeed in mobilizing the loyalty of individuals, even to the point of self-sacrifice, by giving individuals symbolic victories over death?

It is considerably more difficult, I would argue, to attract allegiance to the major emblems and figures of the nation-state than it is to small collectivities—for example the church—or to the totem of a particular clan. We have discussed the role of images of the self, of control over devotions to the ancestors, and the use of heroes and other charismatic figures to galvanize collective devotion. In some states, however, the process must proceed in the full light of informed and public scrutiny where an indigenous opposition to collective piety has already formed.

Consider the manufacture of heroism in the United States during the 1960s, a period when the nation was also in need of a reservoir of loyalty and sacrifice if it were to mobilize its forces for the various "wars" not only in Vietnam or the Peace Corps but on domestic poverty and pervasive racial injustice. Kennedy had asked people to think not of what the country could do for them but of what they could do for the country, and Johnson had gone out of his way to pin medals on veterans in order to contrast them with those whose opposition to the war he deemed traitorous. It was the period in which Robert Bellah published his first article on American civil religion in an attempt to revitalize basic commitments to American traditions and ideals.

In this climate it is understandable that the nation would have used whatever resources it had to stimulate reverence for national heroes and to increase the reservoirs of sacrificial commitment. In the view of one observer, the national space program, and particularly the Apollo mission's success in walking on the moon, "broadened the civil religion, pointing to a potentially new form of the public faith, one appropriate to the realities of the late twentieth century" (Wilson 1984, 225–26). Indeed, C. R. Wilson (1984, 210–11) argued that "science and technology are not necessarily antithetical to, but indeed supporting forces for, the religious maintenance of American political culture, even in the global age."

The state was thus sorely in need of heroes and turned the astronauts into exemplars of the civil religion. President Kennedy spoke of the space program much as Winthrop had spoken of the early Pilgrims, as being the focus of the "eyes of the world"; for Johnson the astronauts were "those brave pioneers who . . . captured the imagination of the people around the world"; and for Nixon they had brought heaven into this world in the greatest week "since the Creation" (Wilson 1984, 214–15). Even the astronauts themselves acted as exponents of civil religion. Neil Armstrong saw in the program "a sort of enlightenment," and Glenn saw the program giving us a chance to become "the kind of people God intended us to be," and Borman on Apollo 8 read from the Creation verses in Genesis (Wilson 1984, 218). There were even echoes not only of national religiosity but of a more universal civil religion: the plaque left by Apollo 11 read "Here Men from the planet Earth first set foot on the Moon, July, 1969, A.D. We came in peace for all Mankind."

In the American case, however, these rhetorical gestures indicate that American civil religion was not a treasury with vast supplies of social merit. There was nothing in the United States at the time that could be compared with the resources of sacred heroism available, for instance, to Rama VI in Thailand during the First World War. Rama VI, otherwise known as Wachirawut, ruled from 1910–1925. During his reign, there seemed to be no escape from the First World War. Wachirawut needed to mobilize the population, overcome pacifist tendencies within the Buddhist tradition, legitimate the war, recruit a military force, and keep civilian discipline.

> In the case of the monarchy, Wachirawut [Rama VI] evidenced little direct concern with the cosmological conceptions that had been so crucial to the traditional charisma of kingship . . . but rather devoted his attention to recounting—primarily in dramatic, semi-historical form—the deeds of the great Thai royal heroes of the past, such as Phra Ruang (who defeated the Khmer and established the first great Thai kingdom, Sukothai) and Uthong, the founder of the kingdom of Ayutthaya. Again, as one might expect, given Wachi-rawut's immediate concerns, the military virtues of these royal he-roes and their followers were singled out for special attention and praise. (Reynolds 1977, 277)

We have here a case of the manufacture of heroism out of resources largely, and traditionally, controlled by the Thai monarchy for many generations. During the formation of the dynasty in the late eighteenth century, the sacred had been more heavily centralized in the kingship and the court, along with the brotherhoods of monks that were the custodians of sacred texts and ritual. Although there previously had been a tendency to concentrate the sacred in the person of the king, who alone had access to the claims of divinity, Rama I (1782–1809) had also insisted on the recovery and restoration of sacred texts, access to which would be made available only to monks who had passed increasingly higher standards of education and discipline. Only occasionally was the sacred also dispersed among monks with popular followings, and these seldom presented a threat to the monarchy even during the nineteenth century.

Whereas the Buddhist kingdom of Thailand had over two centuries of monastic traditions, the careful custodianship and interpretation of sacred texts, and sacred ritual that had already stood the test of time, the American case suggests a desire to make the most of whatever heroism could be celebrated. The war in Vietnam would not produce a pantheon of heroes, and the conspicuous democratic leadership of Martin Luther King, like that of the Kennedy brothers, could not transcend politics, the deconstruction of national celebrities, and finally the force of assassination itself. American political legitimacy seems to depend heavily on the presence of charismatic leaders that command, however briefly, national attention. Unlike the heroic pantheon of Rama VI's kingdom, however, these heroes are temporary and their memory is more likely to be evoked in crossword puzzles than on regular occasions of national celebration.

No doubt the pantheon of heroes in the United States is intended to serve the same functions as the more traditional set of heroes at the disposal of Rama VI: the attraction of public loyalty, stimulating the will to sacrifice, and the opportunity for individuals to identify with those whose being has been officially certified as transcending the passage of time. In the United States, however, the construction of the pantheon is more visibly contrived; the scaffolding of public relations is more apparent than the monuments themselves. Furthermore, the content of the public ground is contested. Like the right to be buried in Arlington Cemetery, there is a taint of suspicion that the dead to be honored have not all been interred under the right auspices. Some may be buried in this heroic soil on the basis of false credentials or in recognition of favors given the party in power.

It is the weakness of the religious foundations of the country that compels political leadership to cloak events in the occasional appearance of religious meaning: "Form and symbolic gestures frequently take on their greatest significance after their substance has been lost" (Fairbanks 1981, 219). However, since it is typical of American politicians to drape their own goals and policies in the vestments of national religiosity, they are frequently targets of those who wish to keep their religious traditions from being put to such explicitly political use (Fairbanks 220). I will return to this subject in the next chapter, where I discuss in more detail the divisive aspects of a national, civil religiosity.

The contrived and potentially divisive cultivation of a pantheon of heroes can be found in the American public schools. In observing a series of national holidays the schools seek to link the seasons of the child's life and of the year with a cycle of commemoration that honors those whose lives and deaths have been critical to the survival of the nation. However, the meaning of these events and their local significance is temporary, negotiable, and varies greatly from one context to the next.

One particularly keen observer, Adam Gamoran, (1990, 241) has described the calendar of national holidays that introduce elementary school students to the heroes of American history: "Each holiday served to mark a period of time, setting the tone for the days preceding the holiday with its unique symbols." Historical events are blended with the seasons of nature in a way that might seem to give them cosmic significance or metaphysical guarantees. Thanksgiving and Presidents' Day, like Memorial Day, are blended in with Christmas and Easter, with St. Patrick's and St. Valentine's Day, along with the increasingly important observance of Halloween.

The individual's experience of time is thus orchestrated in the course of the year with the country's sense of the periods of time, and both are set in the cement of religious holidays that evoke a world that is no longer subject to the passage of time. These sacred or quasi-sacred times elicit memories of critical events and recurrent seasons, and children are thus seemingly inducted into a community that is national and local, personal and institutional.

In textbooks children are also given a sense of the major founders of the country, the myths of origin in the life of Washington and of salvation or redemption in the life of Lincoln. Thus, children appear to be inducted into a national community "under God." Because the nation originated in acts of courage and sacrifice, it therefore should be the object of loyalty, and individuals are obligated to sacrifice themselves for—or at least to tolerate— other members of the national community (Gamoran 1990 245–47).

However, the temporal web binding the child to the community and the nation is neither as strong nor as seamless as it might appear to be from the routine orchestration of national holidays in the public schools. The plethora of symbols and holidays is abstract, empty of specific content, and its meaning is therefore flexible, variable from one context to another, and dependent both on circumstances and the subjective appropriation of them by the individual. Who is to say what precisely is the meaning of a "nation under God," of the flag, of specific holidays, of the pledge of allegiance, or the moment of silent meditation? Certainly their meanings are not the same for all, and civil religious observances may antagonize not only groups like the Seventh-Day Adventists but also Hispanic Americans, Native Americans, Unitarians, and Jews. Indeed, Gamoran (1990, 237) notes the civil religion is not always tolerant of some "societal subgroups." One is reminded of Robert Wuthnow's comment that civil religion is now "a confusion of tongues speaking from different traditions and offering different visions of what America can and should be" (quoted in Billings and Scott 1994, 178). It is particularly difficult for a state to make moral and emotional, let alone physical and spiritual, demands upon individuals when its storehouse of heroes is relatively empty.

In order to license, so to speak, the state's attempts to colonize the individual, the state produces an array of heroes and their national holidays. However, this attempt is not restricted to the political sphere. Note that under the aegis of Pope Paul VI the Roman Catholic Church has added a large number of saints to its own treasury of merit: a number disproportional to any other period of comparable length in the history of the church. Unfortunately, I must only remark on this in passing. It would be well beyond the scope of this discussion to try to analyze the institutional and demographic weaknesses of the Roman Church that have led to such an extraordinary flood of beatifications and canonizations in the last several years.

If it seems cynical or harsh to suggest that the state, like the Church, employs heroes in order to gain access to the deepest reaches of the psyche, consider the argument of Robert Bellah in advocating the renewal of American civil religion. Bellah (1995, 7–8) believes in "a conception of religious traditions that are deeply formative of individual and social identity and demand profound loyalty from their adherents." Hence, he does not like people attending church without a deep commitment, or shopping for more satisfactory congregations, or choosing for themselves what to read and believe, and so forth. True religion for Bellah is the immersion of the self in roles that in their turn are embedded in the community and the larger society; and this ligature is tightened and strengthened throughout the society by religion. Indeed, for Bellah (1995, 3) "religion cannot be a separate sphere of largely private experience."

Lest there be any doubt that Bellah-as-sociologist is speaking in a theological register, consider his final comment, delivered in an afterword to volume 4 of the *Theological Institute Annual Series* (1995, 163): "What is needed makes more demands on us human beings than in any previous period of history. It is perhaps not too much to say that we stand under the millenial pressure of the approaching year 2000, and that judgment of God is indeed near." I mention this here simply to underscore the desperation that attends some discussions of the problem of recruiting the psyche in modern societies.

What, then, are the conditions under which we might find a society that does not require the unnecessary sacrifice of an individual's self? A truly secular society does not prematurely foreclose the possibilities for human aspiration and development; neither does it provide an unnecessarily limited array of options for selfhood. The more secular a society, the less does it pretend to have reduced the uncertainties and threats, the possibilities and opportunities of life to a known and highly-to-be-desired pantheon of cultural heroism. In the case of Australia, for instance, it appears that ideological discussions are relatively exhausted; even if ideology has not ended, it is very tired indeed, and the state is sufficiently secularized that it is simply excluded from discussions of the relation of the individual to eternity Crouter 1990, 162). If there is to be a society that allows the Sacred to be demystified rather than turned into idols, it will be one that keeps open the question of what it means to be a mature and highly valued person.

It is no accident that even modern societies cultivate a social character that will fill its roles more or less smoothly. If those roles call for unquestioning obedience, the larger society may dignify those individuals who come when they are called. A doctrine of vocation, which awards each person the charismatic dignity of one who has a calling, will be turned into a script for vocational training. Thus, the grace of being elected to a divine commission can be reduced into a prescription for unthinking compliance with a job description. The heroes of such a society will be the ones who keep on keeping on, who answer the call to defend the country, who endure stultifying labor or undertake the hopeless task of cultivating fields that yield only a poor or uncertain harvest, or who ask not what the country can do for them but what they can do for their country. Those who refuse meaningless work or decline to vote for candidates that offer only a prohibitively narrow range of ideas and policies: these will be notably absent from the pantheon of cultural heroes.

Of course, that is only half the story. Along with the larger society's interest in determining the will of the individual, we must assume that there is something about the human psyche that is not only willing but seeks to be determined. What Erich Fromm called the "escape from freedom" begins with the experience of birth and the perennial longing for a return to a condition in which one's existence was guaranteed with a minimum of tension. Beyond the longing for that original matrix is the need of the growing self to have stable, reliable, firm, but flexible others with whom to interact: for parents who can provide scope for—and limitations on—one's aggression or an ideal to be served in the interests of being loved. Later comes the need for the society to provide substitute satisfactions for the ones that are originally sought but prohibited: a place where the oedipal project of possessing the parental object of one's affections and displacing the parental rival can be played out on a social stage where ambition is rewarded and the more disastrous effects of competition are avoided. There the conflict between the generations can be worked out on the playing field or in the office, in the classroom or in the laboratory, wherever new insights, discoveries, and procedures supersede the old ones.

When the sacred is properly institutionalized rather than allowed to float free, individuals will be more willing to barter their imaginative and emotional freedom for a prescribed role. So long as the sacred is kept within safe bounds, the individual is far more apt to collude with the demands of the larger society. That leaves sorcerers and rebels to remain in each other's company; they persist in the bushes rather than enter the village, to erupt in moments of disappointment or crisis rather than be celebrated in the normal course of liturgical events. It is when the bush, so to speak, is found to be burning that the fundamental question of individual identity and destiny is finally asked. Only then do individuals have borne in on them the full range of hitherto excluded possibility.

The point is simply that there is a conspiracy, then, between the psyche and the social system to keep the individual from being wholly conscious of impulses and wishes, fantasies and notions that—were they to become conscious—could fuel demands for a fundamental change in the current distribution of authority and satisfaction. That is the reality principle, and it is always at war with the pleasure principle. Once the sacred is institutionalized, there is an apparent peace between the real and the possible, between desire and reality.

In a common effort to avoid painful disruptions either of social convention or mental equilibrium, the social order gives the psyche reason for postponing gratification, enshrines some aspirations in the sacred, and consigns others to a world that is marked as either secular or evil. The secular world is thought to be running out of time, and the world of evil will come to a terrible judgment at the end of time.

It is this collusion that constitutes the reality principle. Like any compromise, it remains a symptom and binds together what is not easily reconciled: the desires of the heart with an order that protects the prevailing distribution of status and power. The sacred, once it is concentrated and institutionalized, is also vulnerable. Its statues can be beheaded, its shrines violated, and its stained glass windows broken by those who have decided that they have waited long enough for a different social order.

When the sacred is not well institutionalized, however, it is easier to see that there is indeed conflict between the psyche and the social system. When what has passed for the Sacred is opened to question, the reality principle becomes unstable.

The sacred, even though it suppresses and distorts human longings, also serves as a reminder of what this world is not organized to give. Even if it enshrines the facts of this world in a metaphysical system, the metaphysics provides a continuing suggestion of another world, a different kingdom, of a day that will come and not pass away, and of a love that satisfies all thirsts and hungers. That can only be subversive, no matter how long it is contained in vessels and hidden behind sacred curtains and vestments.

It is therefore crucial to know whether certain longings cannot be satisfied because of what passes for reality in a particular social order or because of the inevitable decay of life and vitality. The two forms of reality are easily confused; indeed, Freud warned of a primary masochism in which the psyche longs for a return to the inanimate world and for the satisfaction of a tension-free nonbeing. It is all too easy to confuse that more primitive longing for one that remains unfulfilled because the social order, through the sacred, has locked in certain privileges and locked out others.

When the Sacred is not institutionalized, of course, individuals begin to have thoughts and aspirations that are not so easily channeled into social uses. They seek satisfactions that the world of work and politics is not likely to provide; they imagine themselves in roles that far exceed the ones they are likely to be offered. They dream of a social world in which their very being is recognized without having to be proven to the satisfaction of those who grant degrees and give licenses or award medals. They become romantics or even charismatics if they do not become certifiably insane.

Of course, some repression is always necessary simply for the sake of getting along or getting by. What Freud—and later Marcuse—wished to eliminate was the unnecessary suffering that Marcuse called surplus repression. Surplus repression is the amount of energy wasted in performing unnecessary tasks, in unnecessarily postponing satisfactions, in useless work or make-work, in privations that are unnecessary, given a society's ability to take advantage of nature and given its level of social organization. A society with a well-developed system for assuring order, with more than enough people, with the means to ensure its survival and growth, and with more than enough food and other supplies to go around can afford degrees of freedom for the individual and can provide levels of support unheard of in previous societies. For such a society, to insist on the privations and discipline associated with a struggling nineteenth-century economy and society is vastly to increase the amount of unnecessary, surplus repression.

Marcuse (1955, 80) puts it this way:

> Within the total structure of the repressed personality, surplus-repression is that portion which is the result of specific societal conditions sustained in the specific interest of domination. The extent of this surplus -repression provides the measurement: the smaller it is, the less repressive is the stage of civilization.

In a complex society it is hard to point the finger precisely at the source of unnecessary domination. The world is a complex place; there are many jobs to be filled, and each requires more or less specialized training. That is simply the way life is, and so parental authority becomes apparently less constraining and arbitrary. One is no longer being forced to work within the scope of the family enterprise or, otherwise, to seek adventure in the wider world. The job of the parents is to outfit the young for their adventure in a complex world of jobs and specialties that has a rationality and appeal of its own. As Marcuse (1955, 81) points out, "In the same process, repression too is depersonalized: constraint and regimentation of pleasure now become a function (and 'natural' result) of the social divison of labor."

The hero, then, embodies a combination of icons. One image is that of the self that seeks to live forever and is capable of confronting and overcoming death. The other image, however, is of the self that manages, through heroic confrontation with the enemy, to fulfill the desire for self-immolation and return to one's native state. On the one view, the hero is the one who has overcome the fear of running out of time. On the other view, this fear, like so many others, disguises a more elementary wish: the desire, in fact, to run out of time. The two views are compatible theoretically; in psychoanalytic terms, fears are often the flipside of wishes. If we are to understand the possibility of a secular society, of a society without sacred heroes, however, we will need to come to terms with both views of the self in search for a being that is solid: the one seeking the capacity of ancestors to endure over time, the other seeking a return to the solidary attachments of the original, maternal environment.

If the first view is correct, individuals will hurt themselves and inflict terrible damage on others in order to score a lasting victory over mortality. For a society to lose its grip on the sacred, then, would be to raise existential anxiety about time and death to a point that might be unbearable. So long as the sacred is well established, some will have to be consigned to a secular world that is passing away so that others may have their victories over death.

In a secular society, however, time is all there is. At the very least, the line cannot be clearly drawn between those who are slated for inevitable extinction and those who might be loved and honored, remembered and enshrined, at least for a while after their death. For Andy Warhol to allot everyone fifteen minutes of fame reduces the idea of secularity to a near-absurdity, but his point is clear. In a secular society time is all, and the only question is whether the social order distributes time equally and fairly.

On the second view, for a society to lose the sacred would be to open the way to self-destructive impulses. Remember not only Jonestown but also the widespread popular push for Christian martyrdom during the more re-pressive and hopeless periods of the Roman Empire. Deeply coded, behind the memories of Christians taking their violence on crusades, are other, even more sacred memories of wholesale self-mortification. The desire to end all tension and striving and to return the self to its atomic state has at times been allowed to become conscious and to flourish without disguise or displacement onto others. As Marcuse (1955, 69) put it,

> In the primal horde, the image of the desired woman, the mistress-wife of the father, was Eros and Thanatos in immediate, natural union. She was the aim of the sex instincts, and she was the mother in whom the son once had that integral peace which is the absence of all need and desire—the Nirvana before birth. Perhaps the taboo on incest was the first great protection against the death instinct: the taboo on Nirvana, on the regressive impulse for peace which stood in the way of progress, of Life itself."

Now, however, there are fewer protections against the death instinct. That is precisely what is bothering Marcuse. Rather than determine for themselves what activities would be satisfying and would give them a sense of achievement, individuals are well socialized into a complex division of labor that offers a series of well-administered choices. One can do this or that in a seemingly wide range of occupational futures, but all the choices remain remarkably the same, and none allows the self the right to choose his or her own way of life or sense of achievement. What counts for achievement, what counts for a reward, what passes for satisfaction, all these are well administered through the schools and guidance counselors, through social workers and one's "smiling colleagues," through adminis-trators and the advertising agencies, all of whom have roughly the same idea of what matters (Marcuse 1955, 69). What has happened to the spirit of revolt in societies that have so much security and material well-being as those of the modern West?

In such a well-administered society the self has nothing solid to push against and so becomes weakened. There is no strong father or chief to hate or love, so the self does not build up a strong ego or conscience, let alone a strong reservoir of unsatisfied love. The weakened self is therefore a prey to its own aggressions and cannot defend itself against guilt and hos-tility from within. In a world that seems rational and inviting, reasonably fair and productive, there is no place for the poet and rebel who can imagine an entirely different social order. Dreams and fantasies are reduced to personal and idiosyncratic variations on a common theme. As Marcuse (1955, 69) puts it,

> with his consciousness coordinated, his privacy abolished, his emotions integrated into conformity, the individual has no longer enough "mental space" for developing himself against his sense of guilt, for living with a conscience of his own . . . The individual pays by sacrificing his time, his consciousness, his dreams; the civilization pays by sacrificing its own promises of liberty, justice, and peace for all.

Marcuse is describing not a social hell but a well-administered purgatory filled with individuals who are only shadows of their former selves. They lack substance and have no weight. Their past weighs heavily on them with a sense of guilt for failing to have become the persons that they might once have been. Burdened by their past, they are prey to the old sadistic impulses of the human species, and these impulses can gain expression only by crushing what is left of the self. There are no real dreams of an alternative future; the hope of beatitude is itself too shadowy to have any substance or to galvanize any thought or energy. Everyone wants to show that they have pulled their weight, been productive, or satisfied their social obligations. None wants to seem truly rebellious or to have a mind other than the prescribed set of wishes and emotions. To blame the individual or individualism for the ills of Western societies would be to blame the victim. A world without heroes, then, frees individuals to find their paths toward selfhood, but it also may release a diffuse masochism that seeks to immerse the individual in the world of others and thus to obliterate the self.

In a secular society appeals to basic trust are minimal, although they are never totally eliminated. Because they are minimal, there is less danger of a society exploiting that trust in order to mobilize energy, to attract loyalty, or to call for sacrifice. Delusions of solidarity are replaced by a lively awareness of differences, by mutual respect for others, by a common memory that honors the sacrifices of past generations in other ethnic groups and communities, and by a continuing attempt to generate clarity, consent, and commitment toward common goals.

It is all the more disturbing, therefore, to find democratic leaders calling for a recovery in Western democracies of the kind of solidarity that is based on primordial attachments. There indeed may be a universal human longing for transcendence, a longing that embodies memories of prenatal experience. Societies do indeed provide individuals with a semblance of that early memory of the self as solid. Social movements, sacred institutions, the high symbols of church and state do promise that those who identify with them will recover an experience of the self as solid, so long as they remain in solidarity with the larger society. That is precisely the danger rather than the hope: that in search of guarantees for the self individuals will return to the primitive solidarities that underlie the most authoritarian, even fascist regimes. The seeds of idolatry are planted in the psyche when individuals not only seek but find in their societies an image and guarantee of their own innermost being.

Consider, for instance, the world of Moroccan authoritarianism, so well described by Abdellah Hammoudi in his recent work, *Master and Disciple: The Foundations of Moroccan Authoritarianism* (1997). It is a world in which sultans vie for authority with rival leaders: tribal chiefs among the Berbers, or heroes of the resistance against French colonialism, or leaders of reformist brotherhoods who demand representational government, or even radical brotherhoods for whom very little is sacred and who are more than willing to engage in conversation and exchange with foreigners.

In a society like this, Hammoudi argues, the authoritarian principle runs deep, even within movements for democratic reform. Underlying all these institutions, whether they are subversive brotherhoods or a centralized sultanate that seeks to monopolize power and authority, is the relationship of master to disciple. In that relationship the disciple virtually loses his identity and his manhood; he becomes a "woman" open to spiritual and often to physical penetration by the master himself. It is only when the disciple has matured enough to become a genuine threat to the master that he is allowed to create his own community of brotherhoods. Thus, the proliferation of rival brotherhoods is due to the inherent tensions between father and son, older and younger generation, master and disciple.

Thus, Moroccan authoritarianism sows the seeds, as it were, of its own destruction by forcing the younger generation first into abject submission and then into rival communities of brotherhood that are alternative centers of power, authority, and influence. These latter brotherhoods are the sources and carriers of alternative sources of charisma that undermine the idols of sacred authority in the political and cultural center.

The master, then, is the prototypical charismatic authority, the hero, the source of identity and power, against whom the younger generation of disciples must push hard in order to establish their own identity. In their struggle for the succession to the authority of the master, the younger generation virtually dies to its own selfhood and masculinity. The hostility of the son for the father, of the young disciple for the older master, is directed against the self. The young dies spiritually and psychologically in order to please the master, in a long masochistic process of self-abnegation in the hope for a final victory and right to succeed to the place of the master himself.

That is indeed a far cry from a more secularized society in which authority is diffuse and thus harder to resist directly: more pervasive and hence all the more subversive of the individual's own spiritual autonomy. Nonetheless, a modern society that partially blurs the distinction between sacred authority and profane resistance is not fully secularized. On the contrary, there is a strong popular demand to be placed on probation, to be given the credentials of those who have been tried and not found wanting. That is precisely what is bothering Marcuse: that modern, partially secularized societies seem more open and liberating than they are. What passes for freedom, a wide array of existential and occupation choices and the latitude to claim for oneself a more satisfying lifestyle, becomes an array of relatively restricted and meaningless distinctions within the range of what is socially useful for the larger society.

In such a society masochism and self-destructive tendencies become more diffuse and thus more difficult to identify. Nonetheless, they still represent Freud's notion of a primary masochism: the wish of the individual to return to an inanimate state and to mingle with other matter. In the world that Marcuse (1955, 93) is describing, individuals themselves are inanimate: "The human existence in this world is mere stuff, matter, material, which does not have the principle of its movement in itself."

By fitting into the world on the world's terms, moreover, individuals are also reduced to something less than what they could be. That is not only because specialization and routine have made so many social processes automatic. It is also because responsible social roles typically do suppress or bracket the personal, which becomes noise or static in the system. Relations are governed by the protocols of the workplace, and these make it inadvisable or even dangerous for personal affections and antipathies to be displayed in the normal course of human interaction. The purely personal goes underground, where it may be subversive, but where it also begins to disappear into a purgatory of its own, filled with regret for a life that could have been led but is literally no more.

The uniquely individual, then, is dying a slow death in the course of becoming irrelevant to the routines of a well-administered social order. It becomes graffiti or other highly stylized forms of protest. Men march on Washington in large masses less to protest the blight imposed on their lives by racism than to demonstrate that in the future they will keep their promises and be good husbands and fathers. Politicians organize to make it impossible for children who do not wish to pray in the public schools to be immune to administered forms of civic piety. Interest groups lobby to make it possible for the Constitution to be amended in a way that would allow Congress, by a simply majority vote, to overturn courts in which individuals had succeeded in getting at least one of their rights vindicated.

In the very bleakness of this picture, of course, we find Marcuse warning us about the boredom, despair, and death of the soul that ushers in fascism. Repressed psychic wishes return with a vengeance. Old chiefs long since consigned to history return with boots and flags to strut in postures of the defiant individual and to impose a terrible new form of repression. In their ceremonies, their music and anthems, marches, and banners, we find the trappings of the sacred amid the newly imposed and ratified uniformities of a totalitarian society.

However, it is also the very elusiveness of the Sacred that makes it impossible for such an order to acquire more than an artificial and temporary monopoly on charisma. As I write this, students in Iran have been demonstrating against the authority of their clerics and of the state itself and have been demanding democratic political and social reforms. The appearance of the sacred can be conjured up to support such a movement, but it is only an appearance: a halo effect, as Weber once called it. So long as the Sacred is not successfully contained, however, it remains as a potential reminder of another way to live, a different social order, and of a human potential that cannot be fulfilled no matter how many school prayers are said or uniforms worn or banners displayed in public places. Despite every effort to contain the sacred in the Temple in Jerusalem, it showed up in the streets and in the countryside, in the exchanges of everyday life and in unauthorized speeches by inspired prophets. Despite the attempt of the emperor to place his effigy and standards in the Temple, the sacred also showed up in the same places among those who possessed an alternative source of charisma. It is difficult for administered forms of the sacred to maintain their monopoly and to avoid being revealed as a public contrivance.

A secularized society need not entirely dispense with the Sacred. Indeed, if it does so, it loses a vast amount of information that may be crucial to its growth, protection, and survival. In every society the individual is a repository of ideas, imagination, impulses, insights, and skills that are indispensable for work and politics, social reproduction and military defense. The more specialized the roles of a social order become, however, the less relevant is the wide range of human capacity to its functioning. By losing access to or interest in the aspects of the individual that seem irrelevant to specific role performances, the society loses a reservoir of information that could help it to anticipate and respond to crises and opportunities. Equally important, by assuming an indifference to the inner self, the society loses access to the experiences and the language around which basic trust can be generated.

Trust can only be generated in part by the manufacture of heroes and heroism. Indeed, one of the standard laments on the media—at least in the United States—concerns the loss of heroes. At the death of Joe DiMaggio there were the usual invidious comparisons of the past with the present, the past being the scene of heroes who, like DiMaggio, exhibited a will of steel and whose love of the game took precedence over any personal consideration. Now sports figures are alleged to be motivated more by money than by love for the game.

Even Satan as an antihero has suffered the same fate. Traditionally, Satan was a figure whose self-interest and greed could divide communities and tear apart the soul with insatiable desires. Now the self-determining individual whose passions inspire a career of self-fulfillment and innovation is a necessity for a society based on personal choice, individual freedom, independence of thought, and the need for continuous change in technology, organization, and lifestyle (see Del Banco 1995).

It makes sense that heroes would disappear in a social system that requires not only continuous experimentation and adaptability but high levels of coordination and control. Neither the manager nor the entrepreneur, the bureaucrat nor the specialist is a heroic figure. To stand steadfast against all odds is to be neither experimental nor adaptable. Where boundaries are shifting, horizons expanding, requirements changing, systems becoming more complex, and management more risky and technical, there is little demand for the hero who sets out against overwhelming odds to save the bridge, stem the tide, and finally to turn back the enemy.

4

BROTHERHOODS, SISTERHOODS, AND SECULARIZATION

Creativity, Secularity, and the Creation of
Space for the Present Generation

The Sacred is always getting out of the sanctuary. Like the proverbial genie who, once released from the bottle, is capable of generating extraordinary effects and fulfilling wishes that have long been deprived of fulfillment, the Sacred promises to usher in a new day in which old rivalries and distinctions are finished, once and for all. Like the Christian belief in a sacrifice that ended the need for all sacrifice, performed by a high priest who was also the victim, the Sacred puts all local and institutional cults out of business. Once its day has arrived, there is no need for more anticipation or further delay. The time has come.

That is why the Sacred is the enemy of all idols and puts an end to all idolatry. The idols of the church or the state are shown up to be mere substitutes for the real thing: markers that remind the faithful of what once was worth living or dying for and what may yet come again. That is why David Martin (1980, 24) argues that "Christianity is a form of secularization." It always undermines the distinction between the sacred and the profane, the real and the possible, this world and the next.

In previous chapters we have been seeing how the range of social possibility becomes congealed whenever a society seeks to gain a monopoly on what is regarded as heroic or vital, legitimate or authoritative. Whether it is the dead or those who are virtuosos of multiple personality, these incarnations of a wider range of association and thought have threatened the institutionalized versions of the sacred. Texts and priesthoods have a tough time standing up against the fresh revelations of those who are from the beyond and who have new messages and visions to give to those who have ears to hear and eyes to see.

Acting as a counterpoint to this argument, however, is the insistence of Martin that even the more restrictive, authoritarian, and ossified forms of the sacred are inevitable and necessary. They are inevitable because the Sacred is fulfilled only when its potential is realized; faith requires occasional demonstrations, and the spirit is always on the way to becoming flesh. It is also necessary for the sacred to exist within certain containers and constraints for its own protection; the world is often inhospitable to dreams of equality and freedom, and that dream, if it is to be sustained, must at least be given the shelter of institutions in which it is cherished no matter how imperfectly it is realized.

In this chapter we will consider how secular and religious brotherhoods have both carried the hope for a new society and kept repeating the past. They have kept alive the hope for more freedom and yet preserved traditional forms of obedience. Not only have brotherhoods expanded into new forms of association, they also have created new boundaries between those who were included and those who were kept out. As Martin (1980, 24–25) put it, "Christianity relativizes and undermines the whole structure of holy laws, holy priesthoods, holy places and holy lands," and it has done so largely through the operation of "the radical brotherhood." Even these brotherhoods, however, submit to an order that is recognizably patriarchal in origin.

Christianity is not alone in having brotherhoods that obliterate idols, disturb the prevailing notions of the sacred, and open the society to outside influences that are inevitably secularizing in their impact. Wherever the central power in a society is considered sacred, those who oppose it are likely to be considered dangerously secular. By the same token, when a society considers its own authorities and institutions, its way of life and its traditions as sacred, it will be hostile to sources of internal division and to outside influences. On both counts, brotherhoods are good candidates for the label of secular and subversive. They are subversive because they are often open to outside influences and opposed to the central authority, especially when that authority is patriarchal. They are secular because they do not derive their own authority from the traditions that legitimate the powers of the center. Instead, they may draw the waters of their own inspiration and authority from wells that are to be found in the countryside rather than the city, in the periphery rather than the center. Their own notions of a sacred king have little to do with the ones who sit on the throne or claim a certain lineage. Instead, they remember ancient authorities and kings from a mythic time of national purity and heroism: an Arthur or an Alfred rather than a George or a Charles. They also look forward to the return of a divine king from a mythic future: one who will reveal the incumbent for the imposter or fraud that he is.

No doubt many of the secularizing tendencies in the Christian faith come from its origins in a seditious brotherhood on the Judean periphery. Jesus was often interpreted by some of his followers as a king from Davidic times rather than from the contaminated lineage of the more recent Hasmoneans and Herodians. His was an authority that far surpassed that of the scribes and local rabbis, because he derived his authority directly from the patriarchs and could supersede even Moses himself. Not only was his brotherhood subversive of central authority; it was also open to exchanges with gentiles and thus could be a dangerous conduit for outside influences.

Perhaps a more contemporary example will illustrate how serious are the stakes in the conflict between brotherhoods and patriarchies. In his acute observations on Moroccan society, Abdellah Hammoudi (1997, 15ff.) points out that the sultan's authority in Morocco during much of this century has been derived from a struggle not only against French colonial influence but against the internal divisions presented by Berbers as well as by various interest groups such as trade unions. The sultan also had to defend his authority against rival leaders, chieftains, who enjoyed extraordinary popular support because of their own leadership in the struggle against the French. Around Mohammed V, a resistance leader who returned from exile and was named king in 1927, grew a myth of a monarchy above sectional and partisan influence and wholly resistant to outside influence: a myth of national unity. The very existence of brotherhoods who did not revere the monarch as a sacred figure and who were open to exchanges with foreigners was thus both secularizing and subversive:

> In the early stages of the protectorate some religious leaders—particularly the heads of Sufi brotherhoods—stopped resisting and allied themselves with the colonial administration. The nationalist groups, in organized demonstrations during the 1930's, fought the Sufi brotherhoods in the name of religious reform (*salafiya*), accusing them of excessive ecstatism, anthropolatry, and collaboration with the occupying forces. (Hammoudi 1997, 17)

It is remarkable how similar were the charges brought against Jesus and his followers. They, too, were accused of ecstatic behavior, drunkenness, consorting with sinners, and so on. They, too, were accused of making humans the measure of the sacred: why not, in view of Jesus's admonition that the Sabbath was made for humans? They, too, were accused of consorting with foreigners, and their internal operatives, the tax collectors. If there were a first law of sociology, it would be that "Brotherhoods are trouble."

Even when some brotherhoods are not open to outside influence, they spell danger to patriarchal authority especially when—like the sultanate—it becomes concentrated, owns a powerful administrative apparatus, and develops its own sources of revenue and support. The Sufi brotherhoods in Morocco had a tradition of resistance to the sultan. Hammoudi (1997, 17) goes on to recall one Kettani, who led an Islamic reform movement based on "brotherhood Sufism" and offered the sultan an allegiance that depended on the sultan's willingness to accept their demands for a representative and constitutional government. It may seem strange to suggest that brotherhoods, especially monastic ones, were the cutting edge of secularization. Brotherhoods did, as I suggest, become the vehicles for deviant sources of inspiration that challenged the authority of tradition. On the other hand, however, brotherhoods are notoriously authoritarian in their own internal practices.

In his study of Moroccan brotherhoods, for example, Hammoudi points out that they are often fundamentally authoritarian for several reasons. For instance, in addition to conflict between the generations, there is conflict between men and women. Hammoudi thus argues that the authoritarian nature of Moroccan brotherhoods is due to the need of an entirely male society to reproduce itself without women. That means that younger members of the brotherhood need to take the place of women as bearers of the seed of the older generation of men. Understandably, it is the young initiates in the brotherhoods who become the bearers of the older generation's ideas and practices, disciplines and duties; they are feminized figuratively and in many cases quite literally as the bearers of the older generation's powers. Eventually, when they become sufficiently mature to start their own communities, they become as aggressive and "virile" as the older generation of men in the brotherhood.

This process is very much akin to the "rebounding violence" discovered by Maurice Bloch. The older generation requires the younger generation to die to its former existence: to give up the satisfactions of female company, lose its prior identity, and surrender all forms of autonomy and initiative. It is only when he has been inducted into the world of older men that the young male can be restored to a place of authority in the community and can regard the world as his to be consumed or destroyed, as the case may be. In some societies, Bloch notes, the second stage, in which violence "rebounds," does not take place, and the younger generation continues to be suppressed by the older one indefinitely. That is, a character is formed that is chronically submissive, throughout a lifetime, and asceticism becomes not a requirement of initiation alone but a way of life.

The question, then, is how brotherhood in some societies can become a force for social change rather than a largely authoritarian institution that replicates the more crushing aspects of a patriarchal society from one generation to the next. When does brotherhood become subordinated to the master-disciple relationship and when is it likely to become more creative or even perverse, playful, and inventive? Hammoudi (1997, 148) suggests that "the feminine presence as a divine principle of continuity in Indian religions and cosmologies" has made it possible for the notion of brotherhood to be less authoritarian. The contradiction inherent in a society of men seeking to reproduce itself without women may have been less apparent, and the need for authoritarian assertion of patriarchal privilege somewhat less intense, than in Moroccan society. It might be that the devotion of monastic brotherhoods to the Virgin Mother performed the same function of softening, if not neutralizing, the more aggressive assertions of patriarchal authority in the monastic community and allowed visions of equality and liberty to coexist with those of fraternity. This inherent conflict is not contained within brotherhoods; indeed, it is often acted out in Morccan society in fights of fathers with sons; the prize being access to younger women who have often been monopolized by the older generation of men.

The lack of this "feminine presence" as a basic aspect of religious brotherhood would suggest why it is that brotherhoods remain authoritarian, lose their openness to outside influences, and return to locating the sacred in traditional practices. Without the pervasive presence of the feminine, whether in the form of the Virgin Mother or a goddess, there is reason for a more radical conflict between older and younger generations of men for access to women. This conflict thus intensifies the inevitable rivalry between the generations over succession to positions of authority. To be sure, the older generation needs the younger in order to perpetuate its authority and control. However, if the brotherhood is to continue, the younger generation will eventually have to take the place of the older one. Thus, the young are by definition, therefore, rivals of the older generation.

Although Christianity is not alone in having radical brotherhoods, Martin is no doubt right in suggesting that there is something particularly secularizing and universal in the way that Christian brotherhoods have disturbed all existing markers of the sacred and pushed idols aside to make room for a society that is wide open to all who seek access through commitment to something worth living—and dying—for. Speaking of these Christian brotherhoods, Martin (1980, 25) sees them as having

> been called out of every tribe and every tongue to be a new and holy nation. This in itself creates a much tighter frontier between the church and world than the frontier between the Jewish nation and other peoples. A community of faith is not demarcated by natural ties or by a territory, but by the sharp edge of commitment.

Thus, with every attempt to establish a wider and more inclusive society comes the fresh assertion of a boundary, and those who have not shared the vision are relegated to the status of dim outsiders. For Martin there must always be a distinction between "the church" and "the world." Otherwise, "the power of grace will be assimilated to the realities of our social nature" (1980, 25).

A truly secular society, then, will emerge only through the continued tension between the Sacred, untrammeled and unfettered, and every attempt to turn the sacred into an idol. The Sacred is not to be located, and hence it is to have no boundary. One is never to say of the kingdom, "Lo here, lo there." If the Son of Man had no place to lay his head, who is the church to quibble? On the other hand, if there is no institution that preserves the memory of the Incarnation and seeks to demonstrate it, the Christian hope will float like a ghost: an occasional apparition whose presence and message will have at best an unsettling effect on the visited.

The Church, however, is only a vehicle for a truly secular society in which there will be no further need for the sort of contained and protected version of the sacred that the church usually offers. This means that the church is required to live in the present as though the future had already begun: to live as though its cherished boundaries were no longer necessary. To ask the Church to live this way would be like asking France to live without the Maginot Line prior to the First World War. I have no illusion that the church is about to take seriously the Gospel as the charter of it own demise. Nonetheless, there have been groupings in Christian history that have lain alongside the church and have competed with it for the honor of being out of touch with the times. These are the brotherhoods that Martin has mentioned: the radical ones, which have lived in the present as though the future had indeed begun.

Spiritual fraternities indeed exist in a time zone of their own. The past and the future are part of an extended and dynamic present that frees the brotherhood from the ordinary passage of time. From the past they draw a permanent store of accessible blessing and authority: not a long line of succession from father to son but an immediate and accessible reservoir of spiritual merit. The dead indeed are part of the same time frame as the living; they are coeval with one another.

The future, like the past, does not depend on an extended succession from one patriarchal authority to another over the generations; the hereafter constantly informs the present, just as surely as the ghosts of dead monks come back to comfort and cajole the living members of their fraternity. As Schmitt (1998, 70) puts it;

> The lesson is clear: the strength of the spiritual kinship of the monks (possibly reinforced by the natural kinship of the brothers) abolishes all distance and any amount of time. The spiritual family of the monks escapes any constraints of geography, just as the cyclical time of the monks—"calendaric" time completely ordered toward the celebration of the "anniversary" (of the deaths) of the brothers— is never ending.

Thus, there was something contemporary about tales of apparitions, even when they involved dead monks and abbots or warned the living to be assiduous in praying lest, in the future, dead brothers return in outrage at being neglected (1998, 68). It is this experience of an extended present that encompasses the past and the future within the present that I mean by a sense of time as "coeval."

In the centuries immediately after the start of the new millennium the monastic orders were particularly aware that they were living in an extraordinary present unlike that of the past and not necessarily tied to the end of time. Schmitt (1998, 61) cites several sources who call attention to the distinctive character of their own age, which was the outpouring of apparitions:

Thus an awareness of the value of the contemporary began to be formed in the minds of the monks and clerics who were able, perhaps for the first time, to pull themselves out from under the weight of traditions (so fundamental in the Christian culture) and out from under a reading of history directed exclusively toward waiting for the end of the world.

Rather than feel that the only encounters with the dead worth talking about were the ones that were authorized by tradition, they had their own stories to tell.

There is in this process a radical increase in the range of social and emotional possibility. Under the cloak of monastic obedience there was a rebellion against the prevailing distribution of authority and of satisfaction. Had there been a Herbert Marcuse of this period he might have written of a change in the "performance principle," just as a Sigmund Freud would have understood this to mean that there were tidal shifts in what passed at the time for the "reality principle." Freud himself would have been particularly sensitive to the tendency to let passions for the dead interfere with the full enjoyment of the present, and he would have seen the refusal of fraternal orders to constrain their emotional obligations to the dead as a radical rebellion against reality itself.

The attempt by monastic orders to rid themselves of the weight of traditional authority is part of the larger story of how the West was won by more or less democratic forces in their struggles against patricians and noble families—the knightly class—for the ownership and control of mercantile activity and the government of cities. It is a tragic story, or at least ironic, since attempts at liberation so often had the effect of giving traditional authority a new opportunity to reassert itself in and under the forms of urban guilds and councils. It is a story that underlies Freud's own preoccupation with the tendency of individuals to repeat unpleasant experiences and to remain unconsciously obedient to parental authorities even in the act of rebelling. It is also a story that helps to account for the continuing preoccupation with the hidden operation of external forces even in societies that have relatively clear boundaries with the outside world. Thus, it is a story that will help us understand the operation of the Sacred in disguise.

When the monastic orders sought to declare their own spiritual freedom in relation to the dead and thus to expand the borders of their encounters with the Sacred, they were part of a larger rebellion against traditional authority. That rebellion was endemic to patrimonial societies, in which the power of the patriarchal family was expanded to include control over not only inheritance but investment in and the use of property, the flow of capital, offices of administration, retinues of servants, and their own militias. For instance, the first-century rebellion and civil war in Jerusalem was directed against patrician landholders and absentee landlords, as well as against the administration of the Temple and the Roman garrison; it was one of many debt revolts and was typical in seeking to destroy the records of indebtedness in the city treasury. In that revolt, which was critical to the origins of early Christianity, we see an example of the continuing warfare between peasants, artisans, and merchants, on the one hand, and the knightly classes, noble families, with their centralized powers of administration, on the other.

The story of the West is, as Max Weber (1958, 156) reminded us, largely a saga in which "the old charismnatic noble clans lost their legally privileged positions and were forced to share or completely yield power to the *demos* of Greece, to the *plebs* of Rome, to the *popolo* of Italy, to the *liveries* of England, and the *guilds* of Germany." In this process it is fraternities, brotherhoods, tied together by solemn oaths of mutual allegiance, that challenge the authority of patriarchs and patrician families.

The story as Weber tells it, however, is continually one of the subversion of the fraternity by outside, and typically patrimonial, interests. The urban brotherhoods, whether of burghers or merchants and artisans often sought to exclude from their members any individual with a noble pedigree or who had taken on the life of a knight and was thus potentially eligible for noble status. As Weber pointed out, the nobility had charisma: a form of the sacred that was beyond the reach and the control of the rising urban classes. That form of the sacred was thus potentially subversive and indeed dominated some of the earlier attempts to free the city from traditional control. Weber (1958, 111) speaks of the "revolutionary usurpation" of city councils by the old families who controlled the right to vote and hold office. Indeed, it was during the eleventh century, at the beginning of the new millennium, that the cities sought at first unsuccessfully to initiate a new age in which the fraternity of urban dwellers would be free from traditional controls: the same time at which Jean-Claude Schmitt finds the monastic brotherhoods staking their own claims to the sacred and expanding the degrees of their own spiritual freedom.

It was not easy for the new city councils to get rid of what Weber called "the internal remnants of feudalism," however, any more than it was easy for the monastic brotherhoods to rid themselves of their obligations to the past. Among the brotherhoods, as we have seen, the ghosts came to remind the living of their obligations, which usually were to discharge the debts of the departed. As Weber (1958, 154) puts it,

Inevitably and with characteristic irony as the guilds became the sole avenue to civic power forces formerly outside the guilds penetrated them and transformed them from within. Theoretically membership in the guild was acquired only through apprenticeship and initiation. Actually, membership was increasingly obtained through inheritance and purchase.

There is a reason for this; it is the past intruding again, not only in the form of the influence of old families but of the importance of inheritance itself. Later in this chapter I will go into more detail about the institution of *consortium*; it is the basis for fraternal obligation in ancient Rome and required of the living that they share mutually and without limit in the responsibilities as well as the rights of common ownership of inherited property and wealth. The city, so to speak, was a confraternity: an extension of the brotherhood to be found in families and clans. That fraternity was extended through voluntary choice, through oaths, and it became not only a metaphor but a model for new forms of association among philosophers and those with common economic interests.

In other words, the city in the West remained, even in the beginning of the second millennium, very much as it had begun in Rome: a federation of brotherhoods based on the responsibilities and liabilities of inheritance. These liabilities were immense, in some cases, since individuals could be held responsible for inherited debt, to the limit of their liability to pay. To put it another way, there was a purgatorial ethic at work in the ancient city that found its way into the mainstream of Western culture through monastic orders but also survived even in the cities that were, like some monastic brotherhoods, bent on declaring their freedom from the weight of traditional authority.

Thus, sociologically speaking, it is not surprising that the bounds of legitimate association and of social possibility were being pushed outward from within, although the impetus, in the form of apparitions, appears to have come from without. Perhaps an analogy would be the experience of the present, at the turn of the millennium. The sensitivity of the current generation to apparitions cannot be doubted; consider only the range of interest in angels, alien visitors, and in extraterrestrial life. Similarly, the range of association and of social possibility has been extended by women and gays. These changes, of course, are not restricted to the end of one millennium or the beginning of another, but when they occur during such periods they are conducive to the people's belief, described by Jean-Claude Schmitt with regard to the monastic orders of the eleventh and twelfth centuries, that they are living in a remarkable and perhaps unprecedented time.

Historicist illusions to the contrary, the monks who were beginning to relate to the dead on their own terms were still living under the weight of the past. Even while the monks were seeking to lift the weight of traditional restrictions from their shoulders in order to expand the range of communication and of free association among themselves and with the dead, they were also, perhaps unwittingly, fulfilling the possibilities inherent in the Roman institution of *fraternitas*. Certainly the liability of living monks for the debts of the departed, like the common ownership of the entire wealth of the fraternal order, had its roots in the Roman past.

In her fine study of "fraternal ideology" in Republican and Imperial Rome, Cynthia Bannon (1997, 14) notes that

> Ideas about brothers and *consortium* engage with the laws on inheritance and with economic and personal aims to circumscribe the practice of family life and of being a brother at Rome. Such ideas do not present us with a photographic image of the Roman family, but rather they represent possibilities, choices, and values . . . that Roman brothers invoked in what they said and in what they did."

Fraternity was thus sacred, and it pointed to a realm of social possibilities that may have begun in the family but did not end there. It extended to the entire range of legitimate association and suggested possibilities for resolving conflict and shaping loyalties that informed the social imagination as well as the letter of the law.

In the above passage, Bannon links Roman ideas about fraternity to something called *consortium*. Coming out of Roman laws governing inheritance the fact of *consortium* endowed each member of the family included in that inheritance with access to—and responsibility for—the whole estate: "Instead of providing equal shares for all heirs, as in later Roman inheritance law and practice, *consortium* granted a kind of totalizing equality in that each heir owned the whole estate" (Bannon 1997, 73). Think, then, of the monastic principle that permits a dead monk to ask the living to bear and relieve his burdens. There is no limit to the liability of the living for the debts of the departed, and their inheritance casts on each of them the responsibilities as well as the rights of joint ownership. *Consortium*, as Bannon (1997, 14) put it, "offered a paradigm for fraternal *pietas* and its expression in brothers' roles in the family."

Because it had a metaphorical, as well as a more literal, legal usage, the idea of *consortium* extended to those who shared one's fate and not only one's inheritance. As a metaphor, then, it suggested the presence of mutual interests, common character, and shared liability. It was thus the dominant form of the sacred because it pointed to the range of social and emotional possibility that could only be partially institutionalized in any single time and place: "This flexibility in connotations of *consortium* reveals its symbolic or ideological force as a paradigm for social relations that is rooted in the relationship between brothers" (Bannon 1997, 21–22). It was a paradigm, I have suggested, that retained its force throughout the Middle Ages and legitimated the rise of urban brotherhoods and fraternities among artisans, burghers, and merchants in their struggle against the feudal order that continued to dominate urban government.

There is in this tradition of *fraternitas* a heavy bias against any sort of division or individuation. The rights and responsibilities of brothers eventually became a model of a social order in which sharing a common lot, a given tradition, even the land itself, was the basis for partnership. There is here not a shred of the voluntary or consensual basis of solidarity that is later to inform fraternal relations in Western cities; more on that shortly. Here it is simply the fact of a common fate that is crucial: a common lot, whether it was a family inheritance, a particular philosophy like the Pythagorean, an economic venture, or common values. Even animals, according to Pliny, simply by virtue of sharing the earth with humans had the same rights of common ownership as did people themselves (Bannon 1997, 23–24).

Despite the lack of voluntarism, however, there is a heavy burden of social responsibility that weighs on the individual. It is the individual, after all, that underwrites the common enterprise. Bannon (1997, 24) quotes a Roman jurist, Ulpian, to the effect that people who are partners in a common enterprise "still ought to be held liable for what they can pay or for what they fraudulently avoid paying." Like the individuals who underwrite the risks insured by Lloyds' of London, the common ownership of partners makes them in the end wholly vulnerable to the liabilities and costs of the enterprise itself. Their lives, one might say, are not their own.

The somewhat Christian overtones in the last sentence are intentional. It would be impossible to read Bannon's account of brotherhood as a metaphor and inspiration for social life in ancient Rome without thinking of the Christian version. In the Pauline churches, of course, there were divisions, but these were supposed to be overcome in the spirit of fraternity. Each person was a coinheritor of Christ, and Christ himself was not divisible into equal shares. On the contrary, being a common inheritor of Christ meant that each person was responsible for the welfare of the whole. Their lives, too, were not their own, but had been mortgaged, so to speak, by the fact of their inheritance.

Indeed, inheritance for Paul was the overriding model for understanding the relationships of Christians to one another and to those who did not receive the inheritance, the Jews. As in Roman law, in Pauline theology it was recognized that not everyone would receive exactly the same share as everyone else; each would receive, however, what he or she needed to take part in the common enterprise and thus to be joint heirs, with Christ, in the new household of God. Precisely because there were so many rivals to Paul for apostolic authority, it is wholly understandable that he would have fallen back on the Roman notion of *consortium*; as Bannon (1997, 18) points out, it is "an alternative to selecting a single heir."

Not only were the Roman notions of *consortium* and *fraternitas* crucial for understanding the relation of Jews and Christians to one another, then, but they were essential for resolving the conflict set up for the succession to the authority of the founder of the new spiritual enterprise. What began in Roman law as a way of resolving conflicts over succession and inheritance ultimately became a model for a society based on common commitment and responsibility or on more "abstract notions of unity and similarity" (Bannon 1997, 18). Not only Christians but Pythagoreans modeled themselves in this manner after the brotherhood who shared a certain lot in life (Bannon 1997, 20–21).

Note the contradictions in this development of the Christian community as an extended brotherhood. Claims to the rights of brotherhood to common ownership in the inheritance end up by saddling the brothers with the burden of responsibility for the entire legacy. The early Christian emphasis on each person being the coinheritor of the Gospel results in the believer no longer having a life of his or her own. The medieval monastic's claim to be the recipient of visitations from the dead led to new obligations to relieve the burdens of the departed. Medieval monastic notions of being part of a new age obscured the obligation of the present to the past. Claims to widening the range of social possibility are, in both cases, easily substantiated; brotherhood became the norm for new relationships and obligations that extended beyond the immediate fraternity of the early Christian community or the monastic brotherhood. On the other hand, these new possibilities created or perpetuated forms of exclusion that are only now being remedied in some quarters toward the end of the second millenium. These are, notably, the exclusion of women and of those who do not share the inheritance of faith. For Pliny, animals may have shared the earth with humans as part of a common *consortium*. For Christians it is still not clear whether they will share the same lot in life as those who worship at different altars, and among Christians themselves women are still in the process of overcoming centuries of exclusion or, at best, marginal status in the household of God.

As I suggested earlier in this chapter, in discussing Max Weber's view of the city, not only did the revolutionary federations in medieval cities seek to usurp the feudal classes' authority and eventually, over time, entirely to eliminate them from the cities; these feudal authorities, like ghosts, kept coming back to haunt the urban confederates. In the north of Europe, Weber (1958, 23) notes, the old families and, in some cases, bishops retained their influence in the cities, and even in Italy the nobility and knightly classes were not completely excluded from the cities. Similarly, northern fraternities not only functioned as protective associations and guaranteed the welfare and economic survival of their members; they also engaged in prayers for the salvation of their members' souls and had conflicts over ritualized demonstrations of social status (1958, 112–113). Weber's point was that here, too, the urban association breaks open the old social boundaries imposed by clans and creates a new range of social possibility.

We have seen how what Weber called an ethic of responsibility allowed urban dwellers in the West to come together in ways that were not available wherever the power of the clans kept people locked in sacred communities. That is, it was the power of the Sacred to break down old barriers and create new forms of association that allowed the Western city to emerge from under the weight of notables and knights. Elsewhere, particularly in China the powers of caste and clan prevented the more inclusive and flexible forms of urban association from developing (Weber 1958, 119).

In the West, one sign of the outpouring of the Sacred was in the increasing number of visitations by ghosts; the genie of the dead, so to speak, was out of the monastic or ecclesiastical bottle. New spiritual and social possibilities were being opened up to the laity and the clergy alike, to the secular as well as to the monastic. As I have already suggested, however, the ghosts were a sign with a double-meaning. The apparent advent of a wider range of social possibility came with fresh reminders of the obligations of the living to the dead. The ethic of responsibility that once created a moral community based on fraternity in Rome, and that had been carried through monastic orders, had broken loose from its sacred confines, but it made for a perennial sense of unfulfilled obligation.

It would be hard to miss the echoes of *consortium* and *fraternitas* in this passage from Weber (1958, 118): "In the beginning, active membership in the burgher association was bound up with possession of urban land which was inheritable, saleable, exempt from compulsory services and either rent-free or charged only with a fixed amount." That is *consortium* indeed: a partnership forged out of the fact of common ownership and inheritance. From that fact came the moral responsibilities of individuals to uphold a social system and pay one another's bills to the limits of their ability. In this urban development we are still a long way from the limited liability corporation of Western capitalism, but we are closer to the Roman model of the city as a community that laid heavy moral obligations on its members.

The reason for the rise of the Western city, then, was Rome. If it was necessary for the development of the occidental city that it should have been based on the Roman model, it was not sufficient. Without the embodiment of the spirit of fraternity in the monastic system, the notion of *consortium* might have died with Rome itself. Again, however, unless the Sacred had been allowed to break through in order to create new forms of social solidarity and experimentation, fraternity may have remained locked up within clans and the monastic system rather than breaking open to legitimate new forms of confederation in the Western city. In that process it was the new dialogue between the living and the dead, in which the living undertook to save the dead from the ongoing flames of purgatory, that created an acute sense of social obligation and schooled new classes to pay their bills and live up to their word.

The Sacred, as a distant horizon of possibilities both for social life and for the integration of the psyche, may be approached in ways that do indeed create new forms of solidarity and a new depth to humans' experience of themselves. On the other hand, the sacred may be embodied in ways that call for the sacrifice of certain loves and friendships and for the imposition of new forms of psychological repression. It is not surprising, of course, to see the Sacred turned into idolatry. As the range of unfulfilled human potential, the Sacred may open up vistas of spiritual development or the experience of the individual psyche; on the other hand, the sacred may become embodied in ways that limit growth and development to forms of experience that do not threaten the authority, for instance, of men or of elders.

With the discovery of a wider range of social possibility comes an acute sense of the present. No doubt the discovery of an enduring present that is not only hospitable to the past but also open to the future, a present without limits, was indeed crucial for the emergence of the Western city. Both the early Christians, at the beginning of the first millenium, and the monastic orders, at the beginning of the second millenium, felt themselves to be in a unique present that was open to unprecedented spiritual visitation. Indeed, the generations were coeval; they belonged, as I have suggested, to the same time zone. However, that temporal community among the generations made the present generation liable for the debts of the old while endowing the present with the entire inheritance of the past.

To be sure, there is a cybernetic space that opens up in which communication between the living and the dead constantly expands the range of possible opportunities and associations. In this process, furthermore, new relationships are grafted on the old, as the dead bear messages to the living and the living carry these messages to one another. In such a community there is in principle no limit to the possibilities for free association or mutual obligation. A monk can return to his brothers with a request that they lift his purgatorial burdens by their own devotions. Thus, there is also no statute of limitations on past debts, and the next generation, while fully owning the spiritual legacy of the past, also inherits the guilt of those who have gone before.

It is not as if one could look back at the past and see it as a mere preparation for the present; on the contrary, those living in the present must be prepared to entertain visits from those who have passed away. Only later does it become possible for progressive ideologies to distinguish the past from the present in a way that relegates the past to an inferior level of development. There is among brotherhoods a commonwealth of time, so to speak, that allows no generation a priority in relation to the eternal. All are equidistant from the center of time.

Of course, this spiritual democracy was not perfect, and in some monasteries something like patriarchal authority did reemerge to inhibit the spiritual inventiveness of the monastic community. Schmitt (1998, 64) notes two monasteries that were particularly indebted to St. Benedict for inspiration and authority; each claimed to be the possessor of his body. Unfortunately for them, this authoritative antecedent took precedence over the individual monk's own experience of the dead and monopolized messages from the afterworld. In other monasteries, however, where no such quasi-patriarchal authority was present, the spirits ran more freely and the brothers were able to receive a wider range of visitors from the dead.

This is not surprising. Translated into language about the range of social possibility, the difference between these monasteries simply means that spiritual brotherhoods were more able to explore and mine the Sacred, to investigate it and transform its mysteries into information, when they were not barred from doing so by a concentration of the sacred in a particular figure, like St. Benedict, and by his body. The body of the great saint, I would argue, had thus become an idol, in the sense of the word that I have been using in this book. It stood for—and sought to embody—the Sacred, but in effect barred access to it. Thus, in the monasteries endowed with this potent relic, the monks were unable to investigate the full range of social and psychological possibilities that inhere in the Sacred or to make good use of its mysteries. In particular, they were deprived of access to messengers from the dead other than St. Benedict himself, who had a monopoly on authoritative intelligence from the beyond.

It could well be argued that brotherhoods could themselves take on the function of idols, in the sense that they embodied one set of possibilities at the expense of others. For instance, Schmitt (1998, 62) notes in passing that female ghosts were scarce in monasteries. Thus, the brotherhoods themselves were deprived of access to that huge range of social and psychological possibility represented by women. Instead, the monasteries poured their adoration into the cult of the Virgin; some monasteries, Schmitt (1998, 63) notes, created gold statues of the Virgin and child, reliquaries, that were "quite close to pagan idols." It is interesting that Schmitt himself does not make the connection between the paucity of female ghosts and the penchant for gold statues of the Virgin. However, his primary interest in telling the story of the near-idol of the Virgin was to call attention to how, in a dream, a dead abbot lent his blessing to the innovation.

Although blood brothers were often united in these spiritual fraternities, the brotherhood itself is based purely on contract. It is a fundamentally secular organization: voluntary, intentional, contingent on fidelity and obedience, and thus part of the temporal order. It is not surprising, then, to find Schmitt pointing out that the brotherhoods had an affinity for other ties that were also contractual. They sought to strengthen, through tales of returning ghosts, the more fragile solidarities based on the contract between husbands and wives, or the covenant between godparents and godchildren (Schmitt 1998, 66–67).

Because they are a temporal order, then, brotherhoods were in competition with other forms of solidarity that claimed more enduring sources of affinity or authority. The priesthood was of course a natural enemy: ordination through an apostolic order giving the priest a form of authority that mimicked the succession of the generations in providing an organic tie with the past. As for the family, it was the contractual solidarities rather than the organic ones that monks reinforced through their own prayers for the dead.

So contractual was the brotherhood that even guilt itself could be transferred from one monk to another in exchange for a promise of prayers and offerings to lighten penances in this life and the next. That sort of solidarity, in which the living bore the guilty burdens of the dead, underlay the entire penitential "system of equivalency, of compensation and of exchange with the living" (Schmitt 1998, 67). Those who see the modern system of contract and of voluntary exchange and commitment as being rooted in the Enlightenment thus miss the contribution of spiritual fraternities and the penitential order that placed the living and the dead in the same temporal framework. They were both "doing time," in the modern sense of working off a debt to society.

We are now in a better position to understand why it is difficult to rebel against a complex, modern society. One of the answers, as we have seen in the first chapter, is suggested by Marcuse; it is that the control of the younger generation by the older is no longer personified in the father. To be sure, the father is the center of control over infantile rebellion, but he now operates as a representative of the society as a whole. It is the whole society's division of labor that is getting reproduced in the family: a whole system that seems more rational than repressive, because on it depends the continuity of life from one generation to the next. The survival of the whole society depends on its ability to recruit members into a wide range of roles. It therefore seems rational for individuals to subordinate their longings for love and comfort in the service of the larger society because their own future depends on it:

> "The guilt of rebellion is thereby intensified. The revolt against the primal father eliminated an individual person who could be (and was) replaced by other persons; but when the dominion of the father has expanded into the dominion of society, no such replacement seems possible, and the guilt becomes fatal. Rationalization of guilt feeling has been completed. The father, restrained in the family and in his individual biological authority is resurrected, far more powerful, in the administration which preserves the life of society, and in the laws which preserve the administration." (Marcuse 1955, 83)

Whether or not this system of domination is really rational, of course, is another story. Clearly, in some societies it is not rational, since there is so much less pleasure than the society could actually afford. To make this point Marcuse brings up the subject of surplus repression, and by that he means the amount of renunciation of pleasure that is no longer necessary but is sustained by an aggravated sense of guilt. The amount of surplus repression is much like Freud's notion of unnecessary suffering, but it is even more like Marx's idea of the surplus value created by workers in complex industrial societies. What they produce has a value far beyond the effort that it took to produce it, and yet that value is not given back to the worker but is siphoned off by those who control the way goods are produced and exchanged. It is the system at work that makes repression of any kind a surplus, beyond what was actually necessary on the part of the workers and citizens.

To put it another way, simply being part of a system that is a "given," that is far beyond the person's knowledge and control, puts unnecessary constraints on the way a person thinks and imagines. The real possibilities for making enough to live on, for getting by, for making love, for having time to oneself, are obscured by the way a social order preempts the imagination, the ability to think of any way of life other than the one that seems so apparently universal and inescapable.

That is precisely what Catherine Bell had in mind when she was explaining the power of ritual. On the one hand, ask anyone who is taking part in a ritual what they are doing and why they are doing it, and many will be able to tell you that they are breaking bread or singing hymns or baptizing babies because that is the way people praise God or raise the young or show that their hearts are in the right place. On top of this open-minded and clear-sighted goodwill, however, the ritual imposes another structure: a set of fetters on the mind and the imagination, which is all the more powerful because it is implicit and unobserved. To paraphrase Bell on this point, two processes are going on in a ritual: what the participants are doing, and what the ritual is doing to them.

What the society is doing to those who voluntarily participate in it escapes notice and yet accounts for the unnecessary suffering, the surplus repression, that makes people unnecessarily dutiful and therefore unhappy. The accumulated feeling that one has unnecessarily forfeited one's life increases with civilization, and yet there is no clear place where one can put the blame for this unnecessary sacrifice. As in a ritual, complex societies seem to impose their pressures on people without any overt sign of coercion or domination; it is as if people willingly take up a burden that is unnecessarily heavy without realizing that they could refuse or lighten the load.

Marcuse speaks movingly of a sense of betrayal that afflicts the civilized, but it is a betrayal of their own innermost selves, their potential. The soul dies slowly, by inches, in the course of doing the right and the reasonable thing, over a long period of time during which one learns to be serviceable to community and the larger society.

There is another sense in which a complex society is far less rational than it seems. It seems strange that modern societies, with their capacity to produce goods and services far exceeding the needs of their own citizens, should have homeless persons in the streets, despair in the inner cities, a huge incarcerated population, a daily diet of violence, and high rates of infant morality and suicide. It also seems strange the the question "Who cares?" should be difficult to answer. In making work and renunciation seem inevitable and reasonable, however, modern societies have required less affection and loyalty. Unlike a father who needs to be loved by those who fear him, modern societies have not succeeded in mobilizing affection to the same extent. One is not likely, then, to have a sense of affection for those parts of the society that are struggling to stay alive, and one suppresses them through administrative and legal channels without anger or bias. "In cold blood" becomes the mantra for the signing of brutal legislation in welfare and immigration even by a president who claims to feel the pain of the people.

Where are we to look, then, for the origins of a social order in which so much privation is voluntarily undertaken and where authority is all the more ruthless for not being patriarchal? The answer is clearly in the brotherhood. On this point Marcuse is not quite so clear as he is on the question of surplus repression. Nonetheless, he does trace the evolution of modern societies' rational and impersonal forms of domination to the role of brotherhoods: "From the primal father via the brother clan to the system of institutional authority characteristic of mature civilization, domination becomes increasingly impersonal, objective, universal, and also increasingly rational, effective, productive" (Marcuse 1955, 81).

In the brotherhood, there is no father to blame, but as we saw in the preceding chapter, only the brother who appears to preempt the role of the father. As power becomes more widely shared among the brothers, it is more difficult to fight against any particular set of rules or to imagine a social order where certain privations are less necessary. The brotherhood at Qumran, for instance, is a prime example of a brotherhood that was in total opposition to the power of the patriarchal rule under Herod the Great, and yet it exercised near total domination over its members.

The hero is the one among the brothers who most effectively leads the others. There is strong ambivalence toward the hero, however, because the hero can then claim most effectively to represent the father. The story of Joseph in Egypt is the prototype of all later hero stories. The despised younger brother, who dreams of lording it over his older brothers as the favorite of his father, then becomes a hero who saves the family and the brotherhood from starvation. He alone is the one who is able to engage in exchanges with external powers without becoming polluted by his contact with them. In this brother's humiliation and exile are the seeds of a later triumph that allows him not only to be vindicated against his brothers but to become the father of his people. As Marcuse (1955, 57) points out,

> Freud's hypothetical history of the primal horde treats the rebellion of the brothers as a rebellion against the father's taboo on the women of the horde; no "social" protest against the unequal division of pleasure is involved. Consequently, in a strict sense, civilization begins only in the brother clan, when the taboos, now self-imposed by the ruling brothers, implement repression in the *common interest* of preserving the group as a whole. And the decisive psychological

event which separates the brother clan from the primal horde is the development of *guilt feeling*. Progress beyond the primal horde—i.e., civilization—presupposes guilt feeling: it introjects into the individuals, and thus sustains, the principal prohibitions, constraints, and delays in gratification on which civilization depends."

Thus, voluntary waiting becomes the mark of the brotherhood. Once imposed by a father figure who could keep people waiting for whatever bits of property or gratification they should eventually be allowed, now it is the brotherhood itself that imposes its own time constraints on satisfaction. Think, for instance, of the long periods of hazing and apprenticeship that are required of recruits to the army, to guilds and fraternities, or to the ranks of an occupation, whether in medicine and the law or in the academic world. The period of probation is undertaken voluntarily, by those who wish to seek entrance into a community of those who regard themselves as peers.

More important, the entrance into this peer world requires that one undertake a burden of guilt for crimes that one has not committed. It is as if the civilization based initially on brotherhoods has created a legacy of guilt that requires all future generations to do a certain amount of time. The burden of proof is on those who would seek admission to the community of peers who control, as once did the father, the scarce resources of privilege and recognition, achievement and satisfaction.

Thus, the father succeeds in dominating the sons even when he has been removed from power. In fact, he is even more authoritative and repressive now that his power has been taken over by the sons. They rule by guilt, and here Marcuse makes an interesting move. Not only are the sons forever guilty of a crime that later generations have only imagined but never committed—the elimination of the father; they are guilty for quite another reason. In accepting the rule of the brotherhood and the self-imposed restrictions on pleasure they have sinned against the possibility of genuine freedom and liberation. In the end there is a second crime, committed against the self: the crime of keeping oneself waiting for gratification (Marcuse 1955, 62).

To be sure, there have always been brothers and junior brotherhoods that responded to the impulse toward freedom. In the hills of southern France one can still see the remains of the fortifications where the Cathars made their last stand against the older brothers from Rome who could not bear their presumptions and pleasures. In every heretic and upstart brotherhood there surfaces a younger brother who represents what originally inspired the brothers to proclaim themselves free from the oppression of patriarchy: the desire to let love have its way. Jesus is simply the first of many younger brothers who incorporated women into the fellowship of the free and were therefore abhorrent to their older brothers. Still, the struggle against liberation continues:

The image of liberation, which has become increasingly realistic, is persecuted the world over. Concentration and labor camps, the trials and tribulations of non-conformists release a hatred and fury which indicates the total mobilization against the return of the repressed. (Marcuse 1955, 65)

So long as the sacred is well established, the struggle between the brothers is controlled by a common obedience and by a shared sense of guilt. That, indeed, was Freud's point about the origins of the sacred in the first brotherhood. Having eliminated the father, the brotherhood had to keep its own rivalries under control in order to permit life to go on (Marcuse 1955, 58).

Once the sacred begins to weaken, however, rivalries and separate interests again come to the surface, and some of the brothers dream dreams of suppressed desires for satisfaction. Women once again appear to be available as sources of gratification, and their presence increases the costs of obedience and asceticism. The conflict between patriarchal and fraternal authority thus increases as certain brotherhoods move in the direction of women and freedom. Jesus's "Woes unto the Pharisees" are a case in point, just as was the Pharisees' attack on Jesus and his followers for being undisciplined, gluttonous, and sacrilegious.

At any given time and in any particular society, of course, the sacred may take on a wide range of forms. To locate them would be the first step in understanding the contradictions that are at play in that society. In Thailand, for instance, the sacred has often been centralized in the monarchy, the court, in certain texts, and in the brotherhoods of monks that are alone given access to these texts (Reynolds 1977, 277). On the other hand, the sacred is also at times to be found among dissident brotherhoods of monks who develop their own followings and may pose a threat to the king. More than one Thai king in the last two centuries has found it necessary to control charismatic monks who had escaped royal discipline. Not only was the sacred centralized in the monarchy and the court with its attendant monks, however. It was also concentrated—sometimes in the person of the king himself, but increasingly in certain rituals and in the revised texts of certain cosmologies and teachings. Following a coup and the beginnings of parliamentary democracy, however, the sacred became more widely dispersed. The national leadership made common cause with a populist Buddhist sect and trained monks "to counteract Communist influence, to help in the integration of hill-peoples into Thai society . . . and to assist the government in the attainment of its objectives in the areas of community and national development" (Reynolds 1977, 279).

If this were the only description we had of Thai society, we might think that the sacred was primarily centralized in the government and monarchy but occasionally dispersed according to the needs of the government to mobilize the population. Frank Reynolds (1977, 280) goes on to mention, however, that even in the 1970s, when his article about Thailand was written, the sacred had become more decentralized and, I would add, more diffuse. Not only were leftist monks associating themselves with various trade unions and occupational groups; at least a few apparently had Communist sympathies and may have formed what in the West would have been called an underground. The term suggests the presence of unseen forces at work with the capacity to shift the basis of the social order. Popular Buddhism was no stranger to the sacred in its more diffuse forms, both at the center and in dispersion.

The possibility of a secular society thus depends on the capacity of radical confraternities to break their ties with the past and to free themselves from the diffuse obligations of the individual to the larger society. The more that radical confraternities can break the bonds of *consortium*, the more they may relieve themselves from obligations to the past. To shrink social obligation to the size of what can actually be controlled is a step toward the further secularization of societies. The alternative is a social system that lays on its citizens a heavy debt of responsibility for what they cannot control.

5

TOWARD A THEORY OF A SOCIETY WITHOUT IDOLS

From Civil Religion to Public Religiosity

W e have begun to make more progress toward answering the question, "Under what conditions is a secular society possible?" One such condition is that the Sacred not be institutionalized. Indeed, a secular society may never again be able to put the genie of charisma into any bottle. The Spirit, to use the metaphor of the New Testament, blows wherever it listeth. The divine Kingdom is in the midst of the people, but it is neither here nor there. Least of all is the Sacred institutionalized in a cultic center, where access to it is controlled by priests for various forms of tribute.

If the Sacred is not institutionalized, however, it may have lost whatever protections and boundaries it once enjoyed. The emperor is notable for his lack of clothes; the vestments of the priests are sold for revenue. The demands of the state are no longer easily buttressed by claims to a special mission or a holy covenant, let alone a divine right. The sacred emanates from various quarters, but never wholly reliably or for long at a time.

Under these conditions it is difficult to know whether religion, as it describes and defends the nation as a whole, is a freestanding and well-integrated body of belief and practice or merely a rhetorical dimension of the polity. It is hard to know whether one is dealing with the religious aspects of the political system or the political aspects of the religious system. Whether the sacred comes from the people or from some more highly orchestrated source of public rhetoric is also difficult to determine, as is the difference between popular and official religiosity.

When the sacred loses its institutional center and protection, the center may scramble to recover at least the vestiges of its old monopoly on public religiosity. In the Middle Ages, for instance, Rome may have appointed a priest who appears to have the ascetic discipline and simple ways that commend the religious to the people. Conversely, wayward and seditious monks may have started dispensing the sacraments and absolutions once monopolized by the center. In our own era, the president of the United

States has been seen in the company of ministers who are favorites of the people in an attempt to salvage his popularity when his credibility and authority are weakened. That is another way of saying that it is difficult to know whether a particular issue, for example, the failings of President Clinton, is an offense to the most sacred traditions of American society. Some would regard his lies and indiscretions not as an injury to what is held sacred in American society but merely as the failings of an artful dodger with an extraordinary capacity to trip on his own shoelaces. (I will return to the subject of his impeachment later in this discussion.) Just as it begins to appear that pundits are right to doubt whether any morals are sacred in the United States, the people show support for evangelists who run for public office and even for the presidency itself. Populist tendencies may become fascist patriotism may become chauvinist, and ethnic pride may turn into ethnic cleansing.

Certainly these ambiguities make it difficult to render any clear and consistent judgment about the role of religion in complex and secularizing societies. Of course, sociologists are informed participants in their own societies, and some are keen observers of other societies. As informed participants, however, they may not be able to transcend the ambiguities of their own contexts. That is because their own societies lend themselves to multiple interpretations and are sufficiently ambiguous to create controversy even among the sociologically like-minded. Take Robert Bellah, for example. In speaking on one occasion of what he called the American civil religion, Bellah (1976b, 57) sought to settle some of the controversy on that subject by making a useful distinction:

> Therefore I think it might be useful to distinguish two different types of civil religion, both operative in America and distinguishable perhaps more in the minds of the analyst than in the consciousness of the people. These two types I would like to call special civil religion . . . and general civil religion . . . It is the essence of general civil religion that it is religion in general, the lowest common denominator of church religions.

In this passage Bellah distinguishes a "special" from a "general" form of the civil religion, which he calls "religion in general, the lowest common denominator of church religions." He goes on to relate it to what in the past has been considered "natural religion" and to find in it the basis of social order, civility, and government itself. Without this general form of civil religion a people may lack the essential predisposition to allow themselves to be governed. In describing this general form of civil religion Bellah cites Rousseau's notion of a public piety that required belief in the existence of God, a life after death, a final accounting, and so on. What Bellah (1976, 156) calls the "fundamental function of general civil religion" is "the basis of public morality and so the indispensable underpinning of a republican political order."

As a participant in American society Bellah understands that people may not see much of a difference between the "general civil religion" and the "special" type that seems quite clear to an informed observer like Bellah himself. Going to church, preparing for an afterlife, being willing to face a final judgment, and believing in a God who controls history and the fate of nations may seem to be part and parcel of a more "special" covenant between God and the United States of America that requires the faith and obedience of an Israel. To an observer like Bellah, however, the covenantal side of this civil religion seems to be part of a more ancient tradition with roots in Biblical faith. One is more traditional, the other more utilitarian:

> "The biblical interpretation stands, above all, under the archetype of the covenant, but it is also consonant with the classical theory of natural law as derived from ancient philosophy and handed down by the church fathers. The utilitarian interpretation stands, above all, under the archetype of the social contract and is consonant with the modern theory of natural rights as derived from John Locke. (Bellah 1976b, 65–6).

Unfortunately, even Bellah as a highly trained and perceptive sociological observer leaves room for plenty of confusion in his observations. On the one hand, he sees the distinction between the two types of civil religion as merely analytical: clearer to the observer than to the participants. On the other hand, however, he sees the two civil religions as independently "operative" in American society. The distinction is not only real; it is functional. This tendency to have it both ways, of course, is not unique to Bellah, but it is characteristic also of his earlier (1966) article on the civil religion that renewed sociological interest in the topic. There he also asserted both that civil religion is merely a dimension of American society and also that it is quite separate from other forms of religious culture.

No doubt Bellah has been vague about whether the civil religion is alive and well in American society or is a part of a" broken covenant" that remains shattered and empty on the historical landscape. The American religious landscape is littered with relics of the sacred, some of which seem to have retained a certain vitality of their own. Referring to his 1966 article Bellah (1976b, 72) later opined that "Looking back now it seems that the article and the widespread response it evoked reflected some kind of break in the line of American identity. Civil religion came to consciousness just when it was ceasing to exist, or when its existence had become questionable." On another occasion, however, he thought that the civil religion may have come into existence when he published his 1966 article.[1] I will return to these alternating appraisals later in this chapter.

In tracking these variations and inconsistencies in Bellah's work we are finding more evidence, if any were needed, that in modern societies it is hard to tell whether religion is ephemeral or substantial, marginal or of central importance to the polity. We are finding out that the sacred in complex, modern societies is elusive and episodic; it does come and go. Difficult to institutionalize, it loses the air of permanence, even when in its frequent returns it seems perennially significant. As an informed observer of the sacred in American society, Bellah is reflecting not only his own quandaries but those of anyone who understands that the Sacred is an environment that may or may not penetrate all aspects of the society. Rather than being an environment external to the system, therefore, the sacred is an aspect of the society that must always be taken into account.

In Bellah's inconsistencies, then, we find the inevitable turnings of the mind of someone trying to come to grips with the Sacred when it is no longer safely institutionalized, no longer confined to certain texts or monuments, and is therefore likely to put in unpredictable appearances on such obvious occasions as the American bicentennial. Disappointed with the tawdry glitz of these latter festivities, Bellah was not alone in feeling that what used to have been sacred about the American experiment had now been lost.

The more secular the society, the more will the sacred be evanescent rather than substantial. Indeed, the sacred will increasingly behave in the way charisma is supposed to behave. That, presumably is what Martin Marty (1974, qtd. in Regan 1976, 141) had in mind when he commented on the episodic quality of the civil religion: "Civil religion is a kind of cluster of episodes that come and go, recede back to invisibility after making their appearance; only gradually are they institutionalized and articulated in organizational form."

In Bellah's view, the special form of civil religion exists in certain texts that reify the sacred, fix and locate it in ways that render the sacred immune to public awareness or response. These texts, whether constitutional or presidential, are themselves not only the signs of the sacred but its very embodiments. There is in Bellah's high regard for these sacred texts what Robert Scribner (1993, 484) has called "a distinctive Protestant form of sacramentalism." After destroying the sacred in the form of icons and images or of particular practices that seemed magical, the Protestant Reformation nonetheless found the sacred in various texts, whether the Bible or the texts used in liturgies and instruction.

To Bellah's critics, this position has seemed unnecessarily concrete, rigid, and divisive. Modern Protestants tend to pour the sacred into the mold of a fixed text. There is an idolatry of the word that turns even the Bible into something of an amulet. Like medieval amulets, the Bible, or the taped words of a preacher, can be circulated to ward off evil influences and to disperse charisma from an evangelical source to the periphery.[2] It is therefore not surprising that Bellah, too, unnecessarily fixes the meaning of civil religion in textual concrete. Indeed, one astute observer, Amanda Porterfield (Hammond et al. 1994, 10), addresses the reification of the sacred in Bellah's thinking by suggesting that these texts should better be seen as suggestive of a wide range of sentiment rather than as the repositories of fixed meaning: "[I]t seems more accurate to speak of a concurrence of various religious feelings around an important speech than of a civil religion distinct from these." Finally, the divisiveness of Bellah's view of the sacred has been noticed by James Moseley (Hammond et al. 1994, 15):

> To the extent that a strong sense of the otherness of God is downplayed in the language of civil religion, a corresponding sense of the humanity of people who are not defined as citizens of the republic may also be lost, along with their rights, their property, and their lives.

The more diffuse is the sacred, the more difficult it is to fix its meanings, to restrict the range of their reference and application, and to limit those who have access to the sacred.

To understand Bellah's reification of the sacred we have to appreciate the fact that there is for Bellah something revelatory about these texts. They are the core not of the "general" type of civil religion mentioned above but of what he considers to be a peculiarly American and therefore "special" edition of civil religion. In the passage in the Gettsyburg Address in which Lincoln calls for "a new birth of freedom—and asserts that government of the people, by the people, for the people shall not perish from this earth—"Bellah finds "the heart and soul of the civil religion." Granted that this is one form of the civil religion and that it "has never been shared by all Americans," still Bellah (1976a, 153) was able in these few words to point to the very essence of the thing itself.

This reverence for the text is very close to a reification of the sacred, if not to an idolatry of the word. If that seems too strong a view, consider that Bellah (1976a, 154) went on to define the civil religion as "faith in certain abstract propositions which derive ultimately from God. If the 'larger society' does not conform to them, so much the worse for it." Thus, in Bellah's view the civil religion hypothesis is exempt from empirical testing, since its existence is guaranteed by the text of the Gettsyburg Address, along with other presidential speeches that he cited in his 1966 article. "If I am right about where the objective existence of the civil religion lies then no number of public opinion questionnaires can prove its existence" (Bellah 1976a, 153).

In order to make it clear that Bellah himself sees certain key texts as the very embodiment of the sacred, I have underlined his use of the term "objective existence of the civil religion." An idol by any other name, one might say, is still an idol. Indeed, it is to exempt the sacred from empirical testing that an idol exists, to which offerings may be given in the search for favors. To take the mystery from the sacred, however, is to open it up to inquiry and testing, and in the process to expand the degrees of human freedom and responsibility.

Here, then, are the key elements of the case brought against Bellah's notion of the civil religion: that it was itself a theological statement rather than a sociological analysis; that it was based on a reification and reduction of certain texts viewed as sacred; and that this reduction of meaning was more costly to some groups than to others. To be sure, Bellah would reject the notion that his own approach was idolatrous; it was he, after all, who was seeking to prevent an idolatrous conception of the state from taking over American politics; indeed, Bellah was against the conservative reaction that has in the 1980s and 1990s introduced its own form of biblical literalism into American politics. However, as Porterfield (Hammond et al. 1994, 8–9) put it, even in his attack on idolatry, "Bellah introduced theological principles that he presumed overarched the state and the religions it protected." That is, he fought one form of political idolatry by introducing another from, based on certain extrapolations from particular texts.

More is at stake here, of course, than one sociologist's preferences for a particular conception of sacred words. Behind every such attempt to reduce the scope of the Sacred and to fix its meaning and location, lies a special interest. Here is Porterfield (Hammond et al. 1994, 9) again:

> "In its appeal to an overarching set of theological principles, Bellah's concept of civil religion can be seen as a vestige of the de facto religious establishment supported by U.S. courts throughout the nineteenth century . . . [which] supported a set of religious beliefs on which a particular notion of American society rested."

Porterfield was not alone in her suggestion that the restrictive notion of civil religion advanced by Bellah as "special" placed certain groups, for example, women, Native Americans, and Mormons, at a political and moral disadvantage. John Wilson also has argued that Bellah was seeking to revive a Protestant culture that once had enjoyed a near monopoly in political influence and authority. In his view, as well as Porterfield's, Bellah's civil religion hypothesis was a rear guard attempt to restore a cultural hegemony that had been lost:

> On the one hand, civil religion as a subject concerns the possibility that specific social and cultural beliefs, behaviors, and institutions constitute a positive religion concerned with civil order in society. On the other hand, political theology is a specifically theological program concerned to place questions of the political order in more universal perspectives . . . It seems to me an error to confuse civil religion with political theology, for the one concerns religious expression of particular social orders, while the other seeks to relate transcendent and universal perspectives to claims made about particular civil orders." (Wilson 1986, 111)

The "mistake" to which Wilson refers is, of course, the one that I have been attributing to Robert Bellah. There is no doubt that Bellah himself would agree that he was seeking to provide "more universal perspectives" for Americans who had forgotten or never known the religious dimensions of their political inheritance. Once, indeed, Bellah (1978, 22) referred to the bicentennial and the presidential campaigns of 1976 as a "vague and list-less allusion to a largely misunderstood and forgotten past."

If consensus on something like the civil religion is very hard to come by in the United States, where religion and politics have long been inter-twined, such a consensus might be more easily achieved in France, where the political center has been liberated from the control and tutelage of the church, Such, however, is not the case. One commentator, Jean Willaime, argues that France has always had trouble deciding whether it is the daughter of the Church or of the Revolution. Not surprisingly, the public sphere remains the place where this uncertainty is discussed and where national identity is formulated and contested (Willaime 1993, 571–80). He argues that there is a perennial need not only for public religiosity but for a civil religion, since France, as a nation-state, must alleviate the fear that it will come to an end in another revolution or, as we have seen, in another war with its historical enemies to the east. To be legitimate as well as effec-tive, the nation must be seen as able to score a victory over the passage of time and to transcend all the chances and changes of a life that is forever mortal:

> Il s'agit en effet de conjurer la crainte latente de désintégration du corps social et donc de renforcer sans cesse l'unité au niveau sym-bolique. Le culte des origines joue ici un grand rôle (notamment l'évocation des luttes passées et du sang verse), ainsi que la référence a l'universel. (Willaime 1993, 571)

Note the implicit reference here to perennial fascist tendencies. It is neces-sary, Willaime writes, for the larger society to stir up anxiety over whether it can survive and stay together. It is these very fears of disintegration and pollution by outside influences that create a demand for a return to the original inspiration and authority of the republic. However, and paradoxi-cally, it is in returning to its origins that the public sphere finds itself facing again the fundamental flaw in the body politic: the fissure that divides the memories of the revolution from the authority of the church. One might as well ask the United States whether it is the child of its revolution or of the great religious awakenings of the eighteenth and nineteenth century.

For some, like Bellah and Willaime, it is virtually impossible to imagine a democracy or a parliamentary monarchy without public religiosity. The polity is a framework within which souls are prepared through pedagogy and citizenship for the life to come. Even for Rousseau, the core of the so-cial contract is respect for the laws, reinforced by beliefs in the punishment of vice and reward of virtue by an all-wise and provident God (Demerath and Williams 1992; see Hammond 1980). Others are not so sanguine about the blessings of a civil religion. Therefore, Richard Neuhaus would agree that civil religion is not a fiction. Indeed, he finds it in authoritarian and totalitarian quarters and fears it in the United States: "Rousseau spelled it out in theory and, in our time, we have seen its practice in, for example, both Nazism and Marxist-Leninism. Civil religion is not a fiction, but *American* civil religion is not the past or the present or, I pray, the future" (Neuhaus 1986, 101). For Bellah and the Durkheimians, then, a secular society would be a contradiction in terms, whereas for Neuhaus a society with claims to a civil religion is a clear and present danger to civil liberties and the Christian faith.

Whether or not one agrees with Neuhaus on American civil religion, he has clearly understood the problem: the need for a secular society as opposed to one that can harbor McCarthyism, Nazism, or any of the authoritarian versions of the civil religion to which the twentieth century has been subjected.

Certainly the fascist tendency exists at one end of a spectrum of civil religion: close to the far left, as it were. Reading from left to right along this spectrum one will find a range of civil religious systems. At the far left end, as I have suggested, is one would find theocratic states and societies where religious institutions maintain the rule of God. Just to the right along this imaginary spectrum one would find the ideologies cited by Neuhaus that have provided coercive and brutal forms of legitimation and cohesion to certain nation-states. I will return to this spectrum shortly. It is not only a way out of the ideological controversy between Bellah and Neuhaus but also a way of ordering a wide range of studies on societies as different from one another as the United States and Sri Lanka, or as Norway and Japan.

It is toward the middle of this spectrum, as in the United States and in France, that there is no consensus on the proper role and limitations of religion in the political sphere, let alone on whether the nation itself is bound together by a sacred covenant or by a common declaration of the freedom to pursue life, liberty, and happiness. Here is the place for Bellah's notion of a decline from the values of the Declaration of Independence to the interests enshrined in the Constitution: a fall at the very foundation of the republic itself. In the United States as in France, the cult of the republic (civil religion) comes from a secularized Christian eschatology. Public religiosity is an even more secular faith, in that it restores to humans the task of their own redemption and self-regeneration, not through the offices of the state as the only means of a rational and instrumental collective agency, but through a laicist movement to capture the collective imagination. It is just such a movement, I have argued, that appeared in McCarthyism and continues to hold a fascist potential.

In the United States, as in France, there is a fundamental division between the memories of a secular or utilitarian republican tradition and a more biblical tradition of a nation covenanted together under the providence of God. In France, moreover, as in the United States, the existence of religious, ethnic, and cultural differences, alongside individuals who have been trained to think and decide for themselves, has shaken the civil religion, both in its civic-Republican and its common-religious-Christian sides. The claim of individuals to freedom from collective judgment and constraints has reduced the state to being merely a manager of a pluralistic society. And regional, ethnic, and class differences contest with each other in a public sphere where there is no single arbiter or common vision of national identity and destiny.

Not only is France faced with greater internal conflicts but its environment has become increasingly complex and risky. Thus, added to France's internal cultural and social conflicts are the greater uncertainties and opportunities of a nation-state in an increasingly European and global context. When a nation faces an environment, both internally and externally, that is increasingly filled with possibilities, uncertainties, risks, threats, and opportunities, the stakes of public policy become greater: the outcome becomes more uncertain and the costs of failure more devastating. Under these conditions it is not surprising that some seek to restore an original authority and purity to the nation. Such efforts are made more necessary and are destined to be more futile by the very fact that, as Willaime points out, the sacred is being diffused and its identity is contested.

If there is a civil religion in France, it is—like that in the United States—not clearly separated from the religious and political aspects of the French nation. The sacred is likely to be dispersed to a wide range of times and places rather than to be enshrined only in the cathedrals or in pious, collective memory. The sacred is all the more likely not only to have escaped institutional and professional controls but to be diffuse and evanescent: difficult to fix and locate in any single time or place, practice or observance. That is, the sacred becomes more charismatic, opposed to routine, antithetical to organization, and ambiguous enough to be continuously open to contest and reinterpretation. That is why it is as difficult for Willaime to offer a single and consistent version of the sacred in French society as it was for Bellah in his inconsistent attempts to locate the sacred in American society. Like Bellah, Willaime not only has to distinguish between what an observer might consider sacred and what inspires popular devotion. Like Bellah, Willaime makes analytical distinctions between the traditional religious identity of the nation and the more diffuse and popular religion of the people: in the case of France, their "christianitude." As did Bellah, Willaime multiplies the use of terms in order to distinguish the popular ethos of the country from its public institutions or ethos. Finally, like Bellah on occasion, Willaime does not seem to be clear as to whether there is indeed a civil religion in France or whether there is a vacancy in public religiosity needing to be filled.

Unlike Bellah, Willaime does not appear to be worried that there are contests over the civil religion or that minorities and subgroups would find any particular version of the civil religion repugnant or contestable. That is one of the functions of the civil religion: "La religion civile peut entretenir des rapports trés variables avec les religions constituées et constituer un important enjeu de luttes entre les forces agissantes d'une société, que celles-ci soient politiques, sociales ou religieuses" (1993, 573). Neither is he worried that the concept of the civil religion gives too much authority and power to a state that is itself less representative of some peoples and interests than of others. On the contrary, he argues that in France the job of the state is in effect to create the nation, through capturing the imagination of the people and through creating a society out of individuals who are otherwise atomized. The state is the generator and educator of the people out of their atomic condition as individuals or out of their many cultural diversities.

It would be a mistake to underestimate these diversities and the difficulty of forging them into a collective system of allegiance and devotion. For instance, the management of the calendar, of days of remembrance and times for observing heroes in the calendar, reveals the coexistence and also the tension between the secular civic religion of the republic and the public religiosity, the "christianitude," of the people. Thus the National Front prefers 8 mai (Joan of Arc's liberation of Orléans) to 14 juillet (Bastille Day) (Willaime 1993, 577). Because time is marked by Sunday, Easter, Christmas, Ascension, and Pentecost, along with the secular calendar, Willaime (1993, 577) is able to claim that a sort of "syncrétisme s'est opéré entre la religion civique et la *common religion*."(italics in original). Others, we have noted, detect distinct Gallic and Celtic strains in French identity, both of which compete with each other and with the Roman or European identities of the larger society. Thus, these temporal and ethnic honors signify conflict and disunity, as well as a problematic and ambiguous mixture of memorials. No wonder Willaime calls on the state to take the initiative in helping the nation to imagine itself under the auspices of a new civic religion.

No wonder, also, that there seems to be something missing in the discourse of the French political and cultural center. Ethics has replaced the political dimension as the register in which differences are discussed. That is hardly an endorsement for a civil religion in which contending parties can find their commonalities while asserting their differences. Public discourse is further strained by the tendency of the state to come into conflict with the demands of individuals for control over their own affairs. What is needed, Willaime (1993, 577–98) believes, is a new value to be placed on the state as the one agency that can help to reformulate the collective imagination: "un nouveau civism" based on human rights. Indeed, it is human rights that will provide the integrating value-system for the new Europe. If the syncretism were satisfying and complete, Willaime would not have described ethics as the public discourse of a French broker-state.

We are on familiar territory with this analysis. If we treat Willaime as we did Bellah, that is, as a trained informant and participant, we can understand why his description of the civil religion in France raises many more questions than it answers. Is civil religion the way in which France as a whole expresses itself in relation to its historical meaning and destiny; or is France reduced, as it were, to a form of public religiosity that is inevitably less consistent, more occasional and episodic, and more highly contested than civil religion? If public religiosity is more diffuse and less separate as an entity in itself, is it even still possible to identify a civil religion in France? How is the civil—or civic—religion at the level of the state related to the religious and philosophical beliefs of the people themselves? What relationships survive between traditional religion and public religiosity in France?

That is, on what basis can one speak even in France of a devotion to the unity of the social body? If the answer for France is as tendentious as the attempt by Bellah to reify the sacred in certain texts and occasions of national importance, it may also therefore be wishful thinking for Willaime (1993, 573) to assert that "La sacralisation de l'unité sociale mobilise des ressorts les plus profonds du sentiment collectif et sollicite des imaginaires chargés d'histoire et résonnant encore des conflicts passés." It may be wishful thinking partly because in mobilizing the sentiments and loyalty of the people, the contradictions in France between the civic religion of the state and public religiosity may yet come into play. Even more difficult is the task of mobilizing religiosity that is caught up in local places and particular times rather than in the great collective moments of national celebration or in the centers of public devotion that, like the cathedrals, are now largely empty and lack immediate significance to the people themselves.

Under these conditions it is difficult to see how any putative civil religion itself is capable of orchestrating local pieties and national conflicts into a common theme, with movements of varying complexity and pathos, that culminates in a celebration of national confidence. Even in Israel, Willaime notes, there is a civil religion with a political orientation fostered by a political elite, and another one with a purely social orientation that is more local and communal, but with a religious dimension. The latter, I would argue, is public religiosity: a more diffuse form of the sacred not likely to be contained by the political center. Thus, there is conflict in Israel, as in France, between these two ways of imagining the society: public religiosity and the civic religion; between the more diffuse form of the sacred and the more institutionalized; and between the more popular piety and the times and occasions of a more centralized and official public devotion. Once again, we are on familiar analytical territory, even if it is still poorly mapped. Certainly, one question is the degree to which the sacred is diffuse, difficult to institutionalize, popular, and evanescent.

Another question concerns the degree to which the sacred is so contested that the larger society is unable to establish clear symbols of its own transcendence over the passage of time. Whether France gives central honors to Joan of Arc or Bastille Day determines its symbolic claim to a victory over time and answers the question whether the nation is the daughter of the church or of the Revolution. Until that debate is settled, the place of the nation in history, its claims to continuity and identity over time, and finally its sense of its historical mission and destiny will remain perennially contested. So long as these claims are not resolved, the nation cannot resolve the anxiety to which Willaime pointed, that is, the fear that the social body itself will not stand the test of time but will decay or disintegrate. Signs that the social body will disintegrate can bring out the more militant and even vicious forms of idolatry: witness Yugoslavia, Bosnia, and Kosovo.

It is just that fear of national disintegration that lies behind the current revival of Celtic idolatry that I mentioned in the preceding chapter. There, you will remember, we found Vercingetorix, that old Gallic antagonist of Caesar's, now doing double duty as a heroic symbol of a new Europe. On the one hand, Europe is claiming to be unified by its Celtic heritage: never mind that much of Northern Europe is not and never has been Celtic. On the other hand, French leaders like Le Pen are also claiming Vercingetorix as the guiding spirit of their own resistance to the encroachment of Paris and to its rapprochement with Europe. Vercingetorix was indeed a favorite of Marshall Petain's until the marshall decided to subsume France in Germany; before him Napoleon III decided that he himself was not only an avatar of Vercingetorix but an emperor in the line of Roman rule. Thus, the celebration of Celtic heritage in general and of Vercingetorix in particular is like a symptom: at once a sign of resistance and submission to the powers of disintegration.

Like Willaime, Bellah cites fears of national decay to justify the renewal of a civil religion. Remember that Bellah (1976b, 70) makes the conventional argument that the utilitarian interpretation of the social contract on American shores owes much to Locke and informs the Constitution, whereas the covenantal interpretation owes much to the Bible and appears in the Declaration of Independence: "Indeed, if we can say that virtue is the spirit of the Declaration of Independence, then interest is the principle of the Constitution. Between the two documents there is a great lowering of the moral sights." I disagree. In fact, the Constitution, and with it Lockean notions of a contract, are (pace Bellah) not merely subject to the play of interests but are forms that the sacred takes in modern societies (see Hammond 1980). Indeed, Locke provided an argument for turning the polity into a school for the soul. In Locke's view, the purpose of education and pedagogy is to prepare children for citizenship in ways that cause them as little psychological harm as possible. That means that there would be fewer moral and emotional sacrifices required, and as adults citizens would not be plagued by memories of a painful or lost youth, nor would they be haunted by fearful memories and by the terror of the infantile imagination. While the executive branch of government would take the role of the servants in administering physical punishment and executing the laws, it would be up to the legislature to represent and advocate the best interests of the people and stand in for them as parents. The legislature would be the object of the citizens' affection, just as the executive branch would inspire the citizens with necessary respect. In any event, this rationality in public institutions and discourse was intended to fit the soul for the life to come. Social discipline would require, at least among Christian citizens, that they live under a new dispensation: their former sins forgiven, but their future mortgaged until the citizen had given sufficient signs of bona fides. That is, citizens would be expected to live up to the moral requirements of a Christian community in which one lives and acts in a way that displays the fruits of repentance. The core of social life, for Locke, was just this dispensation from sin combined with a penitential discipline. Without it, what Bellah and others take to be a utilitarian social contract would not only make no sense; it would be impossible. Thus, in Locke's view, the central government and its religious dimensions are united with popular religiosity through the sort of pedagogy that makes individuals follow public opinion under the illusion that they are walking to the beat of their own, internal drummer.

Some sociologists, of course, find it hard to imagine a wholly secular society. Especially those sociologists who, like Bellah, stipulate their adherence to Durkheimian assumptions, find it very difficult indeed to conceive of a viable, enduring society that lacks a set of sacred symbols, principles, or texts that constitute a civil religion. Others, still Durkheimian in their assumptions, would deny the existence of something as discrete and systematic as a civil religion pertaining to the nation-state but would allow for a pervasive public religiosity that could at times be mobilized for the purposes of the nation-state. Either alternative is, for someone like Neuhaus, a form of idolatry itself.

Let us return to our hypothetical spectrum: that is, a range along which we may describe societies with regard to how they institutionalize the sacred. At the far left end of the spectrum, I have suggested, would be societies that do indeed merge their political with their religious institutions and who subscribe to a theistic notion of the universe, Islam and Eastern Orthodoxy being obvious cases in point. Belgian sociologist Karel Dobbelaere (1986) does take note of civil religions that are closely tied to the state, from Islam and Eastern Orthodoxy to Soviet Marxism or Nazism. However, I would place the latter two ideologies, Marxism and Nazism, slightly further to the right along the spectrum among societies where religion remains central to their political systems but has been somewhat transformed into less traditional forms of display and ceremony. Here also belong civil religious beliefs and practices in the Netherlands, Japan, and Sri Lanka under this rubric. Still further to the right along the spectrum are societies that merely have the vestiges of a civil religion that once was

"established," in the sense of being closely tied to dominant political institutions. At this point civil religion decomposes into a species of public religiosity: Norway, for instance, may belong about here in our analysis.

Toward the far right end of this imaginary spectrum we may expect to
find a wide range of societies that are in agreement only on basic procedures rather than principles. For instance, Dobbelaere goes on to discuss a
more hypothetical possibility: a secular civil religion, if that remains the
right word, that lacks any explicit dependence on belief, traditional or modern, theistic or humanistic, or on practices that invoke the supernatural or
divine. Dobbelaere (1986, 136) is quite clear that the function of such a secularized civil religion would be simply to legitimate the *procedures* by which
the various parts of the society relate to one another; "integration is based
on cognitive rather than normative mechanisms." The rules governing the
system focus on routines and procedures rather than on ultimate ends or
general values, and the civil religion itself, Dobbelaere (1986, 136, 137)
notes, is therefore "operative" rather than "conventional."

One advantage of this spectrum is that it avoids the impulse to create
another typology. Along the spectrum civil religions lose their unique basis
in the nation-state, decompose into public religiosity or political ideologies,
and finally produce a consensus on procedures that are held sacred but are
nonetheless open to revision and negotiation. Centralized forms of public
religiosity become dispersed. Institutionalized forms of religiosity become
deinstitutionalized. Highly focused forms of civic piety become diffuse.
Elitist forms of public religiosity become more democratic. Official forms of
national piety become more laicized, and so on.

Another advantage of the proposed spectrum is that one can see how a
single society moves along it over time. Take, for example, A. I. Wierdsma's
1987 study of civil religion in the Netherlands. The inauguration of Queen
Beatrix to the throne of the Netherlands in 1980 followed a ritual that had
not changed since William I ascended the throne in 1815. By 1980, however, the sacred, once centralized in the church and the monarchy, had
been decentralized to include a wide range of actors, some of whom might
have been surprised to have a sociologist call their flag in the inaugural parade a proud emblem of the sacred. Appeals were made to the sacred, but
less to the signs of concentrated charisma such as the crown and the
scepter than to a spirit of working together and of a national solidarity
based on shared and unspecified values. In the eyes of one commentator
even the music was not religious but might as well have been supplied by
the Beatles. (Wierdsma 1987, 42).

In the Netherlands, then, the sacred has become more widely dispersed
and, rather than being concentrated in specific personages and emblems,
increasingly is to be found in the highly diffuse world of abstract values or
in the spirit of the people. It has not always been so, of course. Like other
nations with a strong Calvinist spirit, the Netherlands, at the time when
William I became king in 1815, had ideologues who would refer to it as a

new Israel, "the Israel of the West," in the course of summoning a people to arms in a battle, with God wholly on their side. The sacred was concentrated in the person of the new king, who ruled by divine calling and presided over a nation that itself would be called to national days of prayer for the remainder of the century (Wierdsma 1987, 31). At his inauguration in 1815, the sacred was also concentrated in such visible symbols as a copy of the new constitution along with the crown, a scepter, and an orb. One is reminded of the Buddhist kingdom of Thailand under Rama VI discussed in the previous chapter.

As in Thailand, so in the Netherlands: over time the emblems of the sacred became less the monopoly of the nation-state and more the property of a rather diffuse public religiosity. When Queen Juliana was inaugurated in 1948, the press did not find in the event the symbols of a Christian monarchy but merely a celebration of the values both of the House of Orange and of the country as a whole, although there was some consensus that the Netherlands was still a Christian nation and the people deeply religious. (Wierdsma 1987, 41–42). That in itself represented a radical dispersion of the charisma that had been so thoroughly concentrated in the monarchy and in the church during the days of William I early in the nineteenth century. Later, in 1980, Queen Beatrix referred to an even more diffuse and abstract constellation of the sacred: a "working-together-in-oneness of spirit" and a certain "restricting-ourselves in freedom" for the sake of the "human dimension of solidarity," hardly the sacred tokens of a new Israel or of a nation-state specially favored by a Calvinist God (Wierdsma 1987, 31).

To mobilize for war, however, and to create a democratic constituency it is necessary for the sacred to be dispersed at least to the representatives of the people. In the Netherlands the separation of the church from the state was necessary because of a continuing Roman Catholic presence before and after the secession of Catholics to Belgium. By the time of the inauguration of Queen Wilhelmina in 1898, there was no doubt that the sacred had been dispersed from the center enough to include Catholic and Protestant workers' unions; by 1980 even the Socialists displayed their flag during the Queen Beatrix's inaugural parade.

That same separation (of the church from the state) made it necessary for the monarchy to find a more informal relation to the churches and to adopt a more diffuse symbolism for the sacred. As Wierdsma (1987, 37) put it, "The less explicit the figures of speech became, the more the Catholics were eventually also able to stand behind them." When the sacred becomes more diffuse, however, there are always voices that call into question what, if anything, is the substance under the appearance of national consensus. No wonder that some found the inaugural of Beatrix to be far less sacred than secular, less awe-inspiring than entertaining.

Thus, the changes in the Netherlands over the last few monarchies illustrate some of the transitions along our hypothetical spectrum. The nation-state loses its monopoly on the sacred. Public theology introduces a less concentrated, more dispersed set of symbols and observances. The symbols themselves become more abstract and thus more suitable for a political ideology. The sacred becomes not only more dispersed but more diffuse and therefore more difficult to identify in specific events, times, places, and personages. The sacred becomes at once less centralized, less elitist and official, but more laicized, democratic, and dispersed among a wide range of organizations and constituencies. In the end there is an implicit agreement on procedure, but even these may become increasingly negotiable and dependent on circumstances.

At the far end of the spectrum, then, we find that civil religions have been reduced to agreements, to quote Queen Beatrix once again, to "working-together-in-oneness of spirit" for the sake of the "human dimension of solidarity." What is striking about this end of the spectrum, however, is that those who wish to be able to draw a line between the religious and the secular, the sacred and the profane, will have a difficult time of it. It is not only the relative absence of theistic or supernatural forms of religion but the blending of the sacred with other aspects of social life that signals the process of secularization at a fairly advanced stage. Who is to say that those who stand together in "oneness of spirit" are not standing on holy ground? But who is to say that they will indeed stand together on another occasion when calls for sacrifice may be made to an indifferent or even hostile audience?

Precisely this same question is raised by another description of civil religion: this one about Rumanian Jews in modern Israel. Rina Neeman and Nissan Rubin (1996, 197) investigated an ethnic association of Rumanian Jews that legitimates the identity of the Rumanians and relates them to the larger Israeli society by mobilizing them for various tasks. It is a cultural rather than political organization composed of Jews who are irreligious and largely nonobservant.

There is very little of a critical or prophetic tone to their ideology. The past as reconstructed is largely fictional and ignores the conflicts and differences that fragmented Rumanian Jewry. The emphasis is on providing a picture of solidarity and of continuity with the past. Religion is far more an intellectual pursuit than a source of piety or object of commitment. These Israelis are fundamentally nonideological: "[T]he meaning of the Jewish tradition is existential rather than religious, and as such, acceptable and even desirable even among non-practicing people" (Neeman and Rubin 1996, 202).

Even Hanukkah is celebrated as a moment of solidarity among Jews rather than in memory of the prophetic revolt of the Maccabees against the assimilation of the Temple to Syrian culture. The prophetic element is missing. For them, even in connection with Holocaust Day, the election of the Jewish people by God for a special role as a suffering nation is divorced from any religious connotations, such as observance. It is more "cosmic" or "existential." Not only does this form of Israeli civil religion lack any substantive "religious" frame of reference or set of practices. It is a form of public religiosity that makes it unclear as to what is sacred and what is secular. Contrast this secularized form of civic observance with what we may expect to find toward the left end of our hypothetical spectrum.

At various points along our hypothetical spectrum individuals are more or less defined or even subsumed by the symbols of national identity. This identification is partly due to national efforts to mobilize individuals' loyalty and energies, but it is also due in part to the tendency of individuals to find an anchor for their selfhood in the public formation of the sacred. Wherever civil religion is part and parcel of the nation-state, of course, the self finds itself not only anchored but enmeshed in a social order that claims prerogatives over life and death and seeks to transcend the passage of time. The times of the individual are clearly orchestrated with the seasons in the life of the nation. The lifetime of the individual is only a blink, so to speak, of the national eye.

This is another way of saying that for individuals to find their lives defined by the events and memories, the rhythms and prospects of the nation itself, it is necessary for a civil religion to subsume the days and moments of a person's life into the major times of the nation-state itself. Take, for example, the organization of Shinto, which is clearly about the social orchestration of time (Dobbelaere 1986). As Dobbelaere makes clear, the years of youth are brought into increasing contact and harmony with the celebrations of the larger community and of the nation, as children at the ages of three, five, and seven are introduced to Shinto ceremonies. The beginning of new chapters in the life of a family or institution are also observed by Shinto rituals. At the same time as these rituals celebrate significant moments in the life of the individual, they also dignify and celebrate those who have helped to ensure the survival and continuity of the group or organization. The celebration of the start of life is thus harmonized with the commemoration of individuals who were instrumental in the founding or growth of the nation, the community, or the institution. These latter heroes are secular saints, as it were, and they are called upon for blessings to ensure that the living "will endure" (Dobbelaere 1986, 138). Those who have stood the test of time, then, are called upon to enable the living to persevere. Those who have died for the nation are especially honored, and in honoring them the devotees of Shintoism act out their belief that those who enable the nation and social group to endure will themselves be guaranteed their own transcendence over the passage of time. Even the criminal code, going back to the nineteenth century, made it a crime to make "'false' defamatory statements on the dead" (Youm 1990, 1105).

The individual, however, is always a poor totem for the larger society. Few can claim to incarnate the collective order in themselves; of even fewer is it said that on their life and death hinged the fate of the society. The individual as bearer of civil religion always also carries smaller identities, identifies with particular groupings, and pursues quite personal interests. However, as Peter Takayama (1988, 331) goes on to point out, societies still seek to bridge the distance between these lesser, more circumscribed identities and the ones provided by the larger society:

> Whereas state Shinto centered on veneration of the emperor, early and communal Shinto centered around the animistic worship of natural phenomena . . . Totemistic ancestors were included among the *kami*, or deities worshipped, and no line was drawn between humanity and nature."

In Shinto, therefore, the local and communal *kami*, the totemistic ancestors who transcended time because they were partly human and partly divine, became part of the pantheon of the nation-state and were subsumed in devotion to the emperor (Takayama 1988, 331). In Japan, the role of the kami has been to incorporate local loyalties to place and clan into the civil religion. Thus, Shinto provides a pantheon of heroes that transcends both place and time.

Even in Japan, however, there has been a movement from the civil religion of the nation-state to a more diffuse public religiosity. State Shinto relied on the earlier tradition of turning emperors into "visible gods." Emperors were made to transcend time, and this form of transcendence sustained the attempt to defend Japan from westernization. Even after the Second World War, when Japan was open to the secularizing influences of the West, Shinto provided the spirit that mobilized the nation around democratic reforms:

> Japan was able to rebound from the ashes of defeat to become committed to building the "new democratic" nation-state because it kept its traditional cosmology and religious values and sentiments. Certainly, national symbols for postwar Japan have been universalistic and secular, and the ideal of secularization and democratization has been vigorously pursued. Yet the traditional values and institutions have facilitated the actual nation-building. In this perspective, one understands that the Japanese state (or government) was able to obtain enormous commitments from the citizens in the 1960's, although the national goals were obviously secular (e.g. the slogan "greater gross national product"). (Takayama 1988, 330)

Thus, the nation had moved from civil religion and (later) from public religiosity to a secular political ideology of democracy and progress given the appearance of legitimacy by the older public religion. Japan is moving to the right along our imaginary spectrum.

Takayama thus finds two somewhat decomposed forms of civil religion in Japan. One is modern, democratic, egalitarian, peaceful, and "very successful." However, there is a "vacuum of moral values" and a lowered "concept of the state in the consciousness of Japanese individuals." Therefore, it is not surprising that there have been attempts in Japan to revitalize public religiosity. These have drawn on surviving elements of Shintoism: for example, "communal rites and festivities," and an optimistic cosmology. (Takayama 1988, 330).

Thus, the opposite ends of the spectrum can be illustrated by two periods in the history of Shinto. During the Meiji restoration of the late nineteenth century, "Mass media were employed to spread among commoners the archaic imperial mythology which in the past had been the serious make-believe of aristocratic and military alone" (Davis 1977; qtd. in Takayama 1988, 331). Thus, the Japanese nation-state was effective in rooting civil religion in local observances and public piety. In recent years, however, the social basis of Shinto has shifted from the village and the clan to the corporation and the nation. Shinto, Dobbelaere now argues, has been developed in corporations to instill social discipline and a sense of solidarity among workers. There it is increasingly seen to be less effective and compelling: more rhetorical than substantial (Dobbelaere 1986). As the social functions of a religious culture become more explicit, and the interests behind those functions become more transparent, religious culture itself becomes more clearly a way of ensuring the smooth functioning of the social system.

Not only is it now easier to see through the masks of the sacred; the forms of Shinto are no longer clearly either sacred or profane, public or private, national or local, but a problematic mix of the two. The domains of the individual and the larger society, and their relative claims to loyalty and commitment, are thus more problematic and contestable. That is about what one would expect of public religiosity toward the far right end of the spectrum. Toward the secular (right) end of our hypothetical spectrum we find that the sacred has been split off from the political and cultural center and exists, if at all, on the periphery. There it may come into play in national politics from time to time; its appearance would be episodic at best, however, although the aspirations for the sacred to have a dominant role at the center might occasionally be the source of reactionary or reformist movements.

I have been suggesting that secularization alters the form and function of a wide range of phenomena that are more or less traditional. The more secularized a society becomes, the more difficult it is to discriminate the new from the old, the modern from the traditional elements in the culture. Under these conditions, civil religions lose some of their traditional authority and become largely reduced to ethnic and cultural festivities, that is, to public religiosity. Civil religion therefore is often visibly contrived and correspondingly less compelling. Take, for example, Daniel Regan's (1976, 98) analysis of civil religion in Malaysia:

When Islam is harnessed to governmental five-year plans and development projects, what seems to occur is a politicization of religion, but not necessarily a convincing sacralization of worldly activity and national life . . . In terms of elaborating civil religious elements, therefore, the Malaysian case seems quite different from that of Buddhist Ceylon, for example, where for 1500 years civil religion has fostered the unity of nation and religion.

This degeneration into public religiosity is captured by Regan's (1976, 98) sharp comment that "official support for religion amidst a pastiche of particularistic holidays remains far from the image, projected by Bellah, of the binding rituals of civil religion." I would simply add that the loss of sacred mystery and authority opens the door to motivations, impulses, memories of old grievances, and possibilities for human satisfaction and achievement that had been foreclosed under tighter and more authoritative religious controls. That would lead us to expect periods of high dynamism and volatility in Malaysia as well as progress toward a more termitelike state with happy and diligent workers entirely mindful of their social duties.

Similar comments about the degeneration of civil religion into public religiosity could also be made about Indonesia. There, as Susan Purdy (1982/83) has pointed out, is an ideology, Pancasila, with many of the trappings of a civil religion, but it remains to be seen whether it can succeed in integrating so complex and pluralistic a society and legitimating the authority of the state. Where there is much ambiguity about whether certain aspects of a society are sacred or profane, civil authority may have difficulty in functioning during crises or at critical moments in the life cycle.

Another case in point is a recent celebration of Indian culture in the United States. Here I rely on the report of Sandhya Shukla (1997), who uses the concept of "imagined community" to describe the production of Indian nationality and ethnicity in a cultural festival organized by a Gujarati religious organization. The festival combined colonial and postcolonial, traditional and New Age symbols, overcame local-global distinctions, and tried to produce an image of Indianness as being open, tolerant, and without boundaries. A closer examination of the cultural event reveals, however, elements of traditional intolerance, for example, hostility toward Sikhs, the usual sexism, and notions of Hindu cultural superiority.

That is, in this festival it is clear that the sacred and the secular elements are mixed up in a melange of cultural celebration. On the other hand, it is not clear that Indian culture, as conceived in this festival, has moved to the far—secular—end of the spectrum. Veneration is still in order, and the traditional elements are juxtaposed with rather than reduced to the contemporary. I will return to this degradation of tradition to cultural festivity shortly.

First, however, I want to point out that the festival of Indian nationality on American soil apparently mixed the local and the global. That is precisely what we would expect as traditional and relatively insular societies become caught up in a global marketplace of ideas and symbols, people, and food, not to mention microbes and currency. Dobbelaere (1998) puts it more strongly. He argues that the new global culture will become the context in which particular cultures will become expressed and be defined. In that context, however, it will be difficult to distinguish the local from the national or global, the particular from the universal, and claims to uniqueness from claims to superiority.

The global culture will not be a religion so much as a sacred ethos that will identify or proclaim certain values as universal; it is in the light of these values that various regional or national cultures will be defined. Not even the new emphasis on human rights will be legitimately universal, since in the eyes of some nations, as Dobbelaere argues, it is the product of a European, particularly French, tradition and ethos. Dobbelaere (1998, 85–87) goes on to point out that even the Soka Gakkai in Great Britain cannot distinguish what is truly Nichiren (universal) and what is properly Japanese, any more than the Roman Catholics have been able to distinguish the indigenous from the Roman according to clear criteria and have remained paternalistic and particularistic in their assertion of universality.

It is difficult to place an entire nation at one point along our spectrum, since the center is often out of step with the periphery. On this point, there are aspects of a recent report on Norway that are particularly germane. Inger Furseth (1994, 48) finds very little evidence of a civil religion in Norway during stable times. Even during the turbulence of Norway's declaration of its independence from Sweden in 1905, there was very little popular or official reference to the divine, to God, to Christianity. In fact, there was opposition to "a civil religious understanding of the monarchy, at least among the politicians." Not only did the politicians reverse the Constitutional amendment permitting coronation under the auspices of the church; they eliminated any reference to the king's selection by the grace of God. To be sure, at the inauguration of the new, popularly elected king, "Bishop Wexelsen said in his sermon that the King was chosen by the people and given by God" (Furseth 1994, 48). Nonetheless, here was an entirely secular king elected only by the representatives of the people and by popular consent.

Not even crisis brought a possibly latent civil religion to the surface. No doubt 1905 was a critical year in the history of Norway. The people severed their connection with Sweden by an overwhelming majority. Nonetheless, Furseth points out, there was not the slightest hint of piety or prayer in the Storting (Parliament) during that upheaval, whereas in the years immediately before and following there had been the usual requests for God's blessing on the acts of the people's representatives during the closing of the session. As Furseth (1994, 48) put it, the working class and the liberal sectors of the country were beginning to outweigh the already weakening "alliance between the church and parts of the civil servants and bourgoisie."

Here, then, we have evidence of a split between a center that was increasingly secular and a periphery that remained nostalgic, if not always hopeful, for a return of Christianity to a central place in the nation's life. Only among the conservative sections of the country, the southwest in particular, were there expressions of lay piety regarding the move to independence. Support for the notion of Norway as a Christian country still came from the so-called Bible Belt in the Norwegian southwest. There the hope is expressed that, as a teacher named Svanholm put it, "we still have the possibility to become a Christian people" (Furseth 1994, 46). However, the churches and the lay movement in the southwest have had relatively little impact on the center; they remain peripheral or compartmentalized. Even if the monarchy itself should hanker for access to Christian sources of legitimation, political rhetoric and the press seemed largely devoted to the secular discourse of liberals and the working class. Legitimacy came from the legal system, and its values were largely secular (Furseth 1994, 50–51). In this regard it resembles Canada, where religion is less central to the polity than in the United States but is comparatively more significant and enduring at the popular level. Thus, Reimer finds that in Canada there is a stronger correlation between religious belief and religious practice than in the United States. Religion in Canada is less conventional and taken for granted, and so among Canadians there is more salience to religion in everyday life than in the United States.[3]

For some sociologists it is very hard to imagine any society as being without a civil religion. In part that is because they agree with Rousseau that most societies require some sort of social contract. Without a belief in God, in the afterlife, in the punishment of vice and the reward of virtue, the foundations are presumed to be missing for social duty. These reminders of a law-abiding universe are alleged to be necessary to reinforce the demands of the society on the individual. Without them one might have people thinking entirely for themselves, withholding payments of various kinds of tribute, and even refusing to bear arms or sacrifice their lives for the good of the larger society. At the very least one might have a society riddled with individualism. I would hope that the discussion in this chapter would at least give sociologists of this persuasion reason to be more optimistic about the possibility of a secular society.

For sociologists who adhere to the notion that societies inevitably produce the required civil religion, something more than functional arguments is sometimes required. Societies are precarious enough without having their worldviews made to seem trumped up and artificial: a contrivance in order to keep people compliant. Beyond the functional argument one therefore sometimes finds sociologists making an ontological claim that reduces individuals to a chip off the social block. On this latter asumption, it is societies that are real, and without them individuals would scarcely grow up to be human. Without social life the human is like a feral child, an animal, and is unable to speak, think, reason, and be what we all too easily take for granted as "human." These arguments, based on the development of the infant to the adult, are sometimes cited as the warrant for arguing that societies have ontological priority over individuals.

If Durkheim had been entirely clear and consistent at all times, it would be easy to say that this view of the society as reigning ontologically over the individual is Durkheimian. It is, but Durkheim also referred to societies as based entirely on cultural fictions. At one point he even suggested that societies exist only in the minds of the individual. They are fundamentally psychological, and without some sort of collective imagination the social order itself would appear to be as precarious and flimsy as it really is. As we have seen in this chapter, there are societies whose cultural heroes, calls for sacrifice, and claims to transcendence over the passage of time are increasingly seen to be contrived and precarious.

The awareness of societies as being self-made, revisable, and open to negotiation inspires some sociologists to come up with ontological reinforcements. Bellah supplied them in an article on what he called "symbolic realism." In that article he claimed that it did not matter whether anyone can find empirical evidence for the civil religion in, say, the responses of individuals to interviews or questionnaires. The civil religion exists in the realm of symbols, and these symbols live, move, and have their own being, as it were, quite apart from popular or individual recognition. The civil religion will persist whether or not people know about it or care.[4]

Notwithstanding, some commentators have been discouraged by what one has termed Bellah's "broad and diffuse use of the term" civil religion and by the "theoretical instability" of his model (Crouter 1990, 161). On this view Bellah becomes a mere "preacher" given to admonishment and exhortation. As John Wilson noted, Bellah was writing in the middle of the 1960s, when American society seemed torn by irreconcilable social movements, and he sought to revive a sense of American national identity and purpose. In the next chapter I will explore further the inhibitions on sociologists' imaginations that have made a secular society inconceivable. Here it is simply worth reflecting that a secular society is perhaps frightening because it fails to reduce the Sacred to manageable proportions.

Why then cling to the notion of a civil religion, even when it seems to be ephemeral, however central it may still be to several cultures and polities? That is the question I take up in the next chapter.

6

STIFLING THE
SOCIOLOGICAL IMAGINATION

The reasons for any attachment to the argument for a civil religion have to be found in basic assumptions about social life and about human nature. One such assumption is simply that individuals are incurably hungry for meaning and that they will not be satisfied until they can relate their short time on earth to something more lasting. This hunger for transcendence cannot be satisfied unless societies can claim the ability not only to survive but to embody enduring values and ideals. A wide range of sociologists might well agree that social life is serious precisely because it bears the existential burdens of human beings.

It is a short step from such assumptions to arguing that a secular society is inconceivable except as a contradiction in terms. Not only do individuals seek existential confirmation from societies that mediate transcendence; societies themselves inevitably find ways to symbolize their identity and enshrine their ideals in monuments and myths, in texts and narratives of heroism and sacrifice. For instance, Christi and Dawson (1996, 320; quoting Bellah 1989, 147) note that, although Bellah has tried to distance himself from the term "civil religion," he still asserts that "the religio-political problem [addressed by the concept] will not go away whether we use the term "civil religion" in thinking about it or not" Indeed, Christi and Dawson (1989, 320) go a bit further and state that "In fact the notion of civil religion remains a most useful device for the elucidation of the fusion of the political and religious horizons (under certain conditions and at certain times) in the development of modern nation states . . . " From these arguments about how societies function some sociologists might make ontological statements about religion being fundamentally social or about societies being fundamentally religious.

That is precisely the problem. So long as Bellah can hyphenate religion and politics, or others like Christi and Dawson can speak of the "fusion" of the two, the notion of a civil religion appears to be rooted in some fundamental reality. On this view, some belief, some historical narrative, some collective memory will inevitably be found to be the civil religion of an apparently secular society. In a very comprehensive and keen analysis of some of Bellah's positions, Daniel Regan (1976, 96) finds that, for Bellah, "every modern nation is presumed to have one [a civil religion]." (Indeed, just that argument has been made about history in Australian society [Regan 1976, 161]). That may be because, for Bellah, societies have a tendency to interpret their experience in transcendental terms; it may be because societies that have a political center require a civil religion. Indeed, for Bellah Islam would quite logically be a civil religion. On these terms, then, it would be problematical if a society with any history at all, let alone one with political dimensions, were to lack a "civil religion." The notion of a civil religion is thus almost a tautology, religion being inherent in the way a society transcends itself and comes to symbolic terms with itself. It would be in such moments of Durkheimian confidence that Bellah opined, "If you think the civil religion is dead, just wait until 1976" (1973, 14) and "I do not think the American civil religion is dead or dying" (1973, 19), as opposed to the more despairing note, "Today the American civil religion is an empty and broken shell" (1975, 142).

However, it is not always true that the religious and political landscapes offer a fusion of horizons; the political perspective may indeed be very different from the religious viewpoint. That is why, in the next chapter, I cite at length speeches in the United States Senate about the alleged failings of the highly flawed American president, William Clinton. There we find that for some the political horizon indeed overlaps very nicely with the religious, but for others the political horizon hardly offers any vistas toward the Sacred at all. The point is simply that not only for some sociologists but also for some political actors, the notion of a society as being thoroughly secular seems to fit the nation's political life better than some notion of civil religion.

In this chapter, then, we take a further step toward challenging the axiom of Durkheimian social thought that all societies, given time, will find a way to express and identify themselves in sacred symbols. No matter how difficult it may be for some sociologists even to imagine a social order incapable of generating a sacred worldview by which to commend its institutions, legitimate its authority, attract loyalty, and justify calls for sacrifice, some historians, however, are able to do so. John Wilson (1986, 120–21), for one, states quite flatly that "It is simply no longer assumed that there is, or will be, a common religion of the society but rather that there will be contention between a variety of religious positions for influence, if not hegemony within the society and its culture."

Is America a Babel, marked by confusion and conflict rather than consensus, solidarity, and the signs of covenantal obligation? A number of scholars besides Wilson appear to think so. Jonathan Sarna (Hammond et al. 1980, 21) argues that we need "an alternative hypothesis rooted in the pervasive sense of cultural conflict that characterizes much of America's past. Sarna (Hammond et al. 1980, 21) goes on to cite Wuthnow's analogy to Babel's "confusion of tongues" and to argue that the past is a record of conflict over the nature of America as each group seeks to fashion it in its own image: "Civil religion, like all religion, turns out, on close inspection, to promote both *communitas* and its opposite" (Hammond et al, 1980, 22).

Even these allowances for cultural differences and conflict, however, do not come really close to the exercise of sociological imagination that I am advocating in this book. To have different groups promoting their own notions of the sacred is to have a war of the idols. That war may indeed be taking place, as those who tout the sacredness of oaths, or life, or the family pit themselves against those who tout the sacredness of human rights. Certainly, Wilson (1986, 119)would agree:

> What has happened since mid-century is not a decrease of religious behavior and belief in some absolute sense, but a turn away from what we might term the presumption that religions in their different expressions are in fact one. It is the distinctive aspects of different religions that have been increasingly pronounced since roughly 1955, when Herberg wrote his book.

The more open and secular the center of American public life becomes, the more do various groups seek to place their own idols, so to speak, on the public stage. Each group wishes to define itself as over and against what it takes to be the emptiness at the center of American life. If the center is now the presumed territory of "secular humanists," one can define oneself only in opposition to that moral vacuum as the bearers of the sacred. In this process even Bellah's own attempt to promote his conception of a civil religion appears to be sectarian. Wilson (1986, 122) argues that any claim that there is a civil religion is easily ummasked as a

> scarcely veiled revitalization movement, perhaps intensely reactionary in its program, dedicated to returning a culture to the value complex believed to have dominated a previous time . . . highly selective, prejudicial, indeed, one among other religious movements contending for control of the society in question.

Bellah knows, although many Americans may well have forgotten, that these foundations were laid on top of the remains of ancient Athens and Jerusalem as well as of Rome. To fill what he perceives as a vacuum in public discourse he argues that social science should function as "public philosophy and even as public theology (1986, 90). In his view, sociologists as public philosophers would be all the more necessary because even the best nation can do terrible things and because individuals need to be reminded that they find their true dignity only in community. Besides, for Bellah technical questions are never best discussed in a moral or social vacuum but only in the light of notions of what makes for a good society and for economic democracy. Finally, Bellah would have our notions of a good society replenished from traditions of natural law and moral philosophy.

It is not surprising that Bellah should have drawn on moral philosophy in his constant attacks on "individualism." In reminding the society of the needed balance between the public and the private, the personal and the collective, he is engaging, as I have suggested, in public philosophy, under the guise of sociological analysis, and his ideals have therefore driven his descriptions of a loss of social responsibility.

Bellah himself thus stands in a long rhetorical tradition, not only of the jeremiad but of Greek philosophy, as he warns of the effects of anomia on the republic. In his article on Thucydides as an exponent of an Athenian civil religion, Donald Neilsen argues that the Greeks did indeed celebrate their ability to hold public interests in harmonic tension with the private sphere, and so with work and play, peace and war. One was never pursued at the expense of the other (Nielsen 1996). It was only when the plague decimated Athens that we find citizens devoting themselves exclusively to their private interest; Thucydides, like Durkheim over two millennia later, used the term *anomia* to describe that total breakdown of social order and solidarity: "Thucydides needs to follow Pericles's idealized picture of Athenian virtues with his plague narrative in order to achieve the desired moral and pedagogical effect. . . . In sociological terms, 'civil religion' and 'anomie' need to be joined, yet opposed to one another" (Nielsen 1996, 399).

Thucydides describes the total breakdown of social order during the plague. Only individualistic, egoistic self-interest then ruled. People burned their dead on others' pyres and left without staying for any honors or pieties. They looked out only for themselves, with regard to their most material interests. This was the apotheosis of tendencies that had set in during the expansion of the Athenian economic and political empire.

What is lost here is the harmony of opposites, celebrated by Pericles in his funeral oration. There he had praised the Athenians' ability to engage in their private pursuits while taking full regard of the public interest, whether in work and leisure or in times of war. The plague created "a loss of the balance and harmony among the constituent elements of the Greek value system. The extremes of conduct became accentuated, and all sense of measure was lost. It is not surprising that the term *anomia* should be used to describe this situation" (Nielson 1996, 401).

Bellah's rhetorical efforts assume the existence of a people hungry for moral instruction from sociologists and philosophers. In a secular society, however, individuals, and indeed groups and communities, may interact with others around their own values and interests in the act of creating a moral community that is constantly open to revision and that can defend itself only on the grounds that decisions have been made fairly according to procedures that continue to be revised in the light of new participation and information, new contexts and contingencies. Its laws, like the laws of nature, will evolve with the social system itself.

In a secular society, where there used to be a symbolic world in which each part of the republic could find its proper place, there is merely a congeries of interests competing for a place in the symbolic or political sun. Religion, rather than articulating a broad range of social values, is already more likely to be engaged in single-issue politics. Instead of a steady pull on the direction of social change, religion increasingly exerts a temporary, however intense, influence during spurts of social mobilization. Less a national conscience than a set of partial ideologies, civil religion itself is better conceived as "a confusion of tongues" speaking from different traditions and offering different visions of what America can and should be" (Wuthnow 1988, 244; qtd. in Billings and Scott 1994, 178).

Under these conditions those who wish to engage in public philosophy sometimes justify their role by stipulating that there is a gap in public discourse. Individuals are thus alleged to have lost the ability or the language to put their own interests in a larger context. However, I would argue that this vacancy in the symbolic center of American society opens the possibility of the United States becoming a genuinely secular society and requires sociologists to try to imagine what such a society would be like.

I have been arguing that the place of the sacred in many contemporary societies is very ambiguous indeed. The sacred takes a variety of forms, none of them very stable, and comes from a variety of quarters, none of them entirely predictable. The sacred is therefore evanescent, diffuse, and disturbing rather than institutionalized and thus maintained within relatively safe boundaries. Thus the Sacred continues to contain a great deal of information that may be essential for any society: information about unsatisfied desires and longings, about unsettled grievances and unrealistic demands for satisfaction or revenge; information about human potential that is not well used or directed; and information about attachments and loyalties that go far beyond the confines of the society in question.

If what is required in the way of sacrifice is ever to be lessened, or if what is offered in the way of hope for satisfaction and fulfillment is ever to be enhanced, it will be necessary to demystify the Sacred. To see in the Sacred the residues and markers of wasted lives, the signs of unnecessary suffering, is also to find the potential for a society that is more flexible and dynamic, more resourceful and rewarding than the present social order.

The Sacred indeed has a place in secular societies, but it is diffuse and suggestive rather than focused in the political center or fixed in certain texts and monuments. This more widely available form of the Sacred releases previously repressed aspirations for personal and social satisfaction, articulates longings to restore past forms of solidarity, and expresses impulses long suppressed but now available for play, creativity, or the development of new forms of technology or social life. The search for alternative ways of living, for authority from alien traditions, for the expansion of conscious experience may no longer be politicized, as it was in the 1960s. However, in a more secular society this search may also be allowed to flourish in an area that is neutral to economic or political interests in certain forms of order. In this way capacities may be developed that might have seemed seditious in an earlier period but now may be allowed. In these capacities, furthermore, there may also be found resources for basic science, new technologies, the creative solution of social conflict, alternative forms of family life and political organization, or cosmopolitan literature and arts.

Interestingly enough, just such a renaissance appealed to Bellah and others with an interest in some version of an American civil religion. Bellah, as we have seen, thought that he was reviving lost elements of the sacred: not quite a "crusade for the lost ark" but nonetheless an attempt to recover the covenantal dimension of the American political system. Not only would the civil religion revive the sacred dimension of the American polity; it would provide the foundation for a global political system. One reviewer pointed out that one of Bellah's coauthors, Phillip Hammond, saw American civil religion as the basis for a world civil religion: "[T]he American civil religion has its own manifest destiny" and "this volume is its manifesto" (Weddle 1983, 198–99). Indeed, speaking of his 1967 article, Bellah (1989, 147) wrote: "The argument of the article seemed obvious to me. It is the sort of thing any Durkheimian would have said. I still think that is the case. I have never recanted my position on civil religion." Sociologists do not "recant" social theories, but like everyone else they might be tempted to recant a "genuine apprehension of universal and transcendent religious reality . . . as revealed through the experience of the American people" or a statement of faith in "American civil religion b coming simply one part of a new civil religion of the world" (Bellah 1967, 12, 18).

Not every historian or sociologist during this period lost the opportunity to take an expanded view of the Sacred or to see the possibility of the United States becoming a genuinely secular society. John Wilson (1986, 118) with characteristic caution, gave a minimal assessment of this possibility:

> I think it is difficult to maintain that there is now a recognizable spiritual ethos in the culture that is the common religion of this society in anything like the way Protestantism, Catholicism, and Judaism in their presumed commonality were in the immediate postwar era. From this point of view the last decades may be viewed as representing a decisive departure from the century-and-a-half-long tradition of American society centered on a common religion defined in terms of an increasingly broad interpretation of Christianity finally becoming the presumed Judeo-Christian tradition."

To fuse religion with politics, to demand a state founded on traditionally religious principles, and even to apotheosize the king are tendencies that were neither foreign to the world in which the early Christians lived nor, therefore, to Christianity itself. Both Judaism and Christianity have been at times civil religions: the symbolic and rhetorical expression of the collective life of a people under a central political authority. If Boniface, working for the Carolingian monarchy, could bring the Saxons to their knees, where they begged for peace and the sacraments, it is not surprising that Christianity would henceforth be intolerant of any government that claims religious authority for itself under a more eclectic religious framework. Indeed, it is partly the very tolerance of civil religion in America that antagonizes those, like Bellah, who speak with veiled contempt of a civil religion that is the "lowest common denominator."

Thus, it is the claim by the political community to have its own sources of legitimacy apart from those owned and controlled by the established religious traditions of Judaism and Christianity that presents the greatest threat. No wonder, then, as Will Herberg (1960; qtd. in Fairbanks 1981, 221) put it, that "Jewish-Christian faith has always regarded such religion as uncurably idolatrous." No wonder that Bellah sought to define a civil religion that was conceived on more narrowly defined biblical foundations.

It is not surprising, then, that as the faith of the early Christian community became the core of a Roman civil religion or of later kingdoms and nation-states, it acquired a more problematical and contested claim to effective universality. As Richard Fletcher has argued, however, those claims were not entered in the first few centuries of the Common Era; indeed, barbarians remained beyond the pale of salvation, and the faith was extended, often by force, primarily to all those within the sphere of what was left of Roman civilization.

To adore a king either could be an act of political protest or a form of civil devotion. When Julius Caesar was declared to be a god, for instance, stories were told of the ascent of Romulus to heaven as "a way of understanding, justifying or attacking the recent (and contested) elevation of the dead dictator" (Beard et al. 1998, 4–5). It would not be surprising to find that the early Christian community also developed stories of the ascension of Jesus as an antidote to the Imperial cult, just as they may have portrayed Jesus as messiah and king to combat the influence of other messianic movements, for example, those heralding the restoration of a united kingdom under Agrippa I in the years shortly after Jesus's death. I cannot begin to pursue such a speculative argument here.

The point, however, is that the biblical tendency to honor the king could and did lend itself to public protest and to rival political movements, as well as to allegiance to the political center. That divided tendency has made discussions of civil religion all the more torturous, with some scholars focusing on the chauvinistic and others on the prophetic aspects of American religious culture. Both tendencies are consistent with the Christian tradition under various conditions, as David Martin has so thoroughly and lucidly argued in various works, especially *Does Christianity Cause War?* (1998).

The Sacred, whenever it is reduced to the sacred, thus introduces distinctions that can only be chauvinist and invidious. In the case of a civil religion, the society as a whole is given a dignity and mission that sets it apart from other nations. For example, in the previous chapter I discussed Japanese Shinto. As Japan found itself in competition with Western nations in the latter half of the century, it needed to mobilize the nation around a new set of loyalties to the Meiji emperors. Not only did state Shinto give to the Japanese nation the right and duty to govern the other nations of the world; Japan itself was seen as an exemplary nation with a mission to enlighten them (Coleman 1970, 71). This century's war in the Pacific with Japan, then, was a conflict between two nations, each with a sacred mission to global expansion for the sake of the less favored nations of the world. Even though the nation—like Israel—is given responsibility for setting an example to these other nations and for creating a universal fellowship based on justice and peace, the nation itself is given a charisma that places it first among other nations.

Even more invidious is the internal distinction between those responsible for conserving and propagating this civil religion and those who refuse—or are denied—the vision. Indeed, a civil religion creates a world of second-class citizens among those who were not regarded as recipients or carriers of the national vision. Take, for another example, the Moroccan oath of allegiance of people to a leader:

> "Alawists posit the existence of a direct relationship, sanctioned by divine decree, between the sovereign and his subjects . . . Those who hold such views assert that this primordial relationship is expressed in the solemn oath of allegiance (*bay'a*) presented by the community—as represented by the ulema, or doctors of Islamic law—to the candidate of its choice at the outset of each new reign. This oath of allegiance, renewed every year on the great Muslim feast days, constitutes an unbreakable bond between the people and the king. It also places the king above any cleavages which may divide the community . . . As a descendant of the Prophet, the monarch incarnates in the eyes of the people the miracle of his ancestor, namely the emergence of a community which restores the primordial Word and builds a new order." (Hammoudi 1997, 12–13)

Granted that not all Moroccans subscribe to this view of monarchical authority. Authority there derives from other sources as well: trade unions, separate communities, rival brotherhoods, and chiefs who earn the favor of their people. That is precisely the point: that a civil religion is inevitably a source of division. As surely as patriarchal authority is offset by the authority of brotherhoods, or as surely as the center breeds its own sources of resistance on the periphery, so claims to represent the whole inevitably create partisanship.

Similarly, the Israelite priests returning from exile in Babylon carried a mandate from Cyrus the Persian to administer the Temple and to collect tribute and taxes from a colonized population. Those who did not acknowledge the authority of the Temple cult and the satellite regime run by the priests were soon stigmatized as the people of the land: far from the seat of grace and outside the boundaries of the true Israel.

A secular society will have to endure the high levels of conflict and uncertainty associated with the Sacred. Especially contested will be the role of religion in public life. As the boundary separating the public from the private changes, so will the sense of what lies beyond the legitimate scope of public knowledge and control.

If nothing is inherently Sacred in a secular society, the public sphere will at least be entertaining and occasionally even shocking. In the midst of the impeachment hearings and the trial of President Clinton, one of the overriding issues concerned whether the public sphere, not only through the media but the public prosecutor, had invaded what was properly private. Not only intimate conversations but confidences extended to the clergy or to lawyers were being broadcast and published to an extent that caused concern among pundits and among those celebrities whose private lives long have been the object of public fascination. The voyeuristic interests of the public were titillated and among some more than satisfied. Not incidentally, the president's ratings in public opinion polls kept pace with the rate of new revelation. In a secular society the Sacred stimulates wonder, if not admiration, and is often reduced to a demand for public access and collective ecstasy.

No less controversial than the limits of the sacred in a secular society is the role of religion in the public sphere. Madison, and perhaps Jefferson, had confidence that the public could sort out true religious opinion from the false. Partly because of their own faith in the rule and ultimate triumph of reason, and partly because of a republican confidence in the will of a properly informed and deliberative majority, they wished to see religion allowed full play in public debate with neither help nor hindrance from the state itself. Occasionally Americans continue to be lectured by religionists that Jefferson in particular wished the government to place no limitation on religious opinion, whether it were voiced individually, through religious institutions, or even by a majority. As for the excesses of a majority, these, too, can be checked by minorities fully apprised of their own rights under the Constitution. What is at stake, we are told, is "not the access of religion to the public square" but "the full and unencumbered participation, of men and women, of citizens, who bring their opinions, sentiments, convictions, prejudices, visions, and communal traditions of moral discernment to heart on our public deliberation" (Neuhaus, 1992, 15).

Those who justify the role of religion in the public sphere by appealing to the sovereign rights of public opinion may be appealing to a disappointing or unfriendly court. Public religiosity lacks the stability and authority of tradition. Furthermore, while public opinion is the court of last resort in a democratic society, it may not always satisfy those who define religion in traditional or particularistic terms. The traditionalists, like Neuhaus himself, may find that God's ways are not their own ways. Public opinion also may not be very kind to those who define religion exclusively in their own terms. During the impeachment hearings and the trial in the Senate, these public deliberations were constrained by public opinion that offered little support for the proceedings. I will turn to those proceedings in the next chapter. Here the point is that those who have beaten the drums for religion in the public sphere must occasionally accept a popular verdict that rules religious convictions out of order on the floor of Congress.

How will societies cope with the high levels of controversy and divisiveness that attend all public discourse in areas that have been considered sacred? To begin with, we can expect that pressure will increasingly be put on the meaning and authority of public speech and personal testimony. Even more fundamental than religion as a social institution is language itself. When religious beliefs and practices are put before the bar of public opinion, and when public testimony crosses the boundaries of the sacred into areas previously considered private or even sacrosanct, the institution of language itself has to bear the burden of the contest for authority.

Without idols, the door to the Sacred remains open, and no confidence may be respected, no privacy or secret remain inviolate. The secrecy of Swiss bank accounts has been violated in order to provide information, and a modicum of justice, to the survivors of German concentration camps and their descendants. As the files of the KGB and the East German secret police are opened, or the hitherto secret records of the Nixon administration, there is little room left for illusions about the decency or fairness of public officials or the guardians of public safety.

As the level of conflict and uncertainty increases, so does the risk of making any decision. There are serious dangers entailed in missing or taking an opportunity, in disclosing or concealing information, in realizing or ignoring a threat, and in trusting any source of information. Those dangers are enhanced when no one is sure what may be safely left to the realm of mystery and what must instead be disclosed. No one is sure who has the right to keep what secrets or to make certain revelations. Neither is there certainty as to the validity or veracity of speech that claims to be based on religious authority or conviction but may instead be mere opinion or a statement of special interest.

7

AMBIGUITY, CONTROVERSY, AND THE LIMITS OF LANGUAGE AS THE BEARER OF THE SACRED

As David Martin has argued in a variety of contexts, the soul is naturally tied to the world of the intimate, face-to-face community of family, friends, and neighbors. Thus, to link the soul to the fate of a larger, more distant and abstract social body like a people or a nation requires that symbols be stretched, meanings be made more ambiguous, and language be filled with double entendres. As symbols are expanded to cover a wider horizon and a longer span of time, their semantic range also is stretched to cover meanings that may become antithetical. Hence, it is possible for the civil religious aspects of Christianity to be both prophetic and priestly. With a wider range of meaning, of course, advocates and interpreters can claim to find in them more universal significance and application. They can also claim that religious meanings and rhetoric have been stretched beyond recognition or belief. Civil religion is a case in point.

Not only is civil religion divisive, then, but it places a severe strain on language itself. As loyalties become stretched or even torn, between the family, say, and more complex or distant sources of authority, language bears the freight of multiple and inconsistent meanings. In this context loyalties are often called into question and emphasis is therefore placed on promises and oaths that are tests of allegiance. Speech itself becomes problematical when there are truths too dangerous to be uttered and loyalties too compelling to be denied even under the force of political circumstance. I have argued this case more fully with regard to the context of Palestinian Christianity in the first century. In this chapter, furthermore, I will examine the tensions surrounding language as sacred as an oath of office in contemporary American politics.

While the United States does not turn the president into a deified king, it is nonetheless true that the president's office until recently has carried with it the duties of a religious and moral leader. Indeed, a strong case has been made that even presidents with far less to recommend them than

Lincoln have discharged these duties at least rhetorically. Some have called attention to the mission of the country and its obligation to fulfill a high set of moral standards; others have relied on a rhetoric that merely evokes the continued blessings of a favorable providence. It is routine, however, in times of crisis and during presidential inaugurals for some reference to be made, however banal or prophetic, to the religious obligations and providential prospects of the nation.

During the near-impeachment of President Clinton, in fact, it was this moral and religious dimension of the office that was being weighed in the balance of public opinion and political interest. I will explore this subject further in this chapter, but first I wish to point out that the nation may have reached a clear decision, if not a consensus, on the relative weight of these symbolic aspects of the presidential office. It may not be the president that has been found wanting in this debate so much as the traditional expectation that the president should exemplify as well as evoke the religious and moral dimensions of the nation-state. If, as some have argued, it is the civil religion that gains substance from the presidency and not the reverse, the Clinton years may have brought religious rhetoric connected with that office into irreversible disrepute (Fairbanks 1981, 218).

In the references by presidents to religious beliefs and themes, there have been two contrary tendencies. One has been to see the nation as living only by the grace of God and with a mission to be exemplary because it has been chosen and favored; thus, the nation stands under the claim of God, whose favor exacts obedience. Other presidents, however, have exalted the nation itself, sometimes by name—America—and sometimes under the aspect of the sacred Union, as being the fount of blessing and even of religious liberty and of faith itself; thus, it is to the nation that one's highest and most sacred obligation is owed (Fairbanks 1981, 226).

In the American context, the desire to elevate the king to divine status is only slightly disguised by democratic institutions and rhetoric. Consider this description of an American high feast day:

> The single greatest celebration of the American civil religion was the 1970 July Fourth celebration in Washington where Billy Graham, Bob Hope, and other political leaders and entertainers led millions in an Honor America Day. Some saw it as the beginning of a new political movement in which the chief spokesman for American Protestantism had joined forces with the high priest of the religion, Richard Nixon. Graham, the main speaker, used the biblical injunction to "Honor the King" as the reason why Christians should join in honoring the state. Graham went on to review the various virtues which made the American Republic particularly deserving of honor, ending with the claim that there has been "woven into the warp and woof of our nation faith in God." (Herberg 1960; qtd. in Fairbanks 1981, 218)

Not only have recent incumbents in the office of the president debased civil religious discourse in American society. By endorsing the public use of religious symbols, the Supreme Court has managed to secularize religion even further. In various decisions it has adopted the view that symbols like the creche have long since lost their sacred potency by association with other symbols:

> Where a practice or symbol is perceived as integral to American culture, or where the context of a display which includes religious articles creates an impression of mere holiday celebration or religious pluralism, the symbols will be recharacterized as secular . . .
>
> "Symbols and practices which were at one time religious can lose their religious significance (for purposes of constitutional analysis) when surrounded by nonreligious items or when consistently included in national celebrations over the course of history. According to this theory, history, time, and culture somehow diminish or erase the religious import of practices and symbols which continue to be used and invoked by religion. (Furth 1998, 591–93)

Such "constitutional analysis," argues Alexandra Furth (1998, 59–93), can offend people who like clarity and consistency in judicial opinions, or who like to keep their religious symbols pure of secular pollution, or who like to keep their holidays safe from the encroachments of the sacred, or who fear governmental endorsement of religion because it is a prelude to regulation:

> [E]ven a seemingly innocuous acknowledgement of Jewish or Christian culture constitutes government identification of these religions with American national culture; the result is a diminution of the tradition itself, a preferment of religion over no religion, of Christianity over the others, and a marginalization of those who wish to keep their belief separate from their politics, who do not want their beliefs diluted in public discourse, whether they are religious or atheist beliefs.

Let us agree with Furth (1998, 596, 601) that the Court is not equipped to be "an arbiter of cultural semiotics" and that "if the state may aid or co-opt religion, it may also regulate it." Nonetheless, in muddling its way through to decisions that dilute religion even while accommodating it, the Court may be expressing precisely the confusion of the sacred with the secular that is a hallmark of societies undergoing the process of secularization. To put the creche next to a reindeer may be taking the mystery out of the creche. It may also be adding a bit of much-needed sanctity to an otherwise tacky reindeer. Those who like purity in their religion and in the law are going to be sadly disappointed with a Court that cannot easily distinguish what the larger society itself has confused.

What, then, is devisive in these proceedings? It is not the Court that is to blame. If it is ambiguous and patronizing of religion, it is because the larger society is equally so. Rather, what is divisive is the very existence of a civil religion that enjoys official patronage. Because public religiosity is civil, those who seek to keep their faith unalloyed with ordinary convention will be unhappy to have their beliefs and practices reduced to secular custom by the Court. Furthermore, those who seek to keep the sacred free from the hint of coercion will find it objectionable to have a Court giving positive sanction to their beliefs. Because it belongs to the center, those whose notions of the sacred differ will find themselves further marginalized. As Furth (1998, 604) herself notes, secularization is a process by which religious conviction does become conventional, and religion becomes a "social fact rather than a spiritual choice."

What is needed, however, is a further secularization of the civil religion. The ambiguity as to what is sacred and what is secular will not go away, but the offense given by officialdom and centrality can be minimized by placing these matters outside the scope of judicial review. That would leave communities on their own to work out their own forms of the sacred: a process that would further take the mystery out of the sacred and turn veneration into discourse.

Rather than wait for the Supreme Court to secularize the political center of the United States or to dignify the religious beliefs of people on the margins of American society, some groups have taken the matter into their own hands. Some, like the Seventh-Day Adventists, have done what peripheral groups often do: tried to replace the center by imitating it. In becoming a mirror image of the center, however, peripheral groups often reverse the meaning of symbols: the cross is transformed from a sign of political authority to a symbol of the meekness of the poor who plan to inherit the earth (see Martin 1998). Thus, the Seventh-Day Adventists changed the Sabbath from the first day of the week to the last and replaced a view of steady progress toward a final millenium with a view of a Christ whose coming in judgment would initiate the tribulations of the damned and the reign of the righteous:

> The early Adventists . . . fashioned their ideology into the mirror-image of contemporary civil religion. Having defined themselves in opposition to the state, Adventists sought to replicate its institutions, thereby creating a network of health, educational, and commercial enterprises which cater to every stage of the life-cycle. (Bull 1989, 178)

The Adventists thus secularized America and Protestantism; time was running out on them; and the ways of marking time, notably the Sabbath, therefore had to be reversed. The first [day] would be the last.

Nearly two thousand years ago two other societies, one centered in

Rome, the other in Jerusalem, also paired off in mutual symmetry and opposition to one another. The Palestinian periphery claimed to have a divine kingdom that would outlast the Roman empire, while Rome itself claimed to be exercising a providential rule with an emperor who was the savior of the world. Each consigned the other to the world that was passing away while claiming for themselves a purchase on the future at the beginning of a new era. The result was the disastrous civil war of 66–73 C.E. that left Jerusalem in ashes but did not burn out the drive toward messianic kingship. The dynamic between Seventh-Day Adventists, who assign the Sunday Sabbath the mark of the beast in Revelations, and the larger society with its claims to a providential role in history has been a pale reflection of that earlier dynamic struggle between Rome and Jerusalem.

More is at stake, however, than a contest between a center and periphery over the signs of the sacred. Even at the political or cultural center there is a division between those who close the circle of meaning and significance around their own interpretation of constitutional and sacred texts. They sacralize the language of these texts in reaction to the elusiveness, openness, ambiguity, and transience of the Sacred itself. The divisiveness of the attempt to sacralize particular texts and practices continues, as zealots seize the center of the national stage in an attempt to purify language of all ambiguities and the nation of all impurities. Opposing them not only on the periphery but in the political and cultural center are those for whom the sacred is more episodic and elusive, diffuse and dispersed, evanescent and uncertain, ambiguous and multiple in its possible meanings. For these latter protagonists it is difficult to institutionalize the sacred even in the oath of office. They have become used to a society in which no form of the sacred can claim priority for very long at a time. That is, they are at home in a society where some groups are identified as carriers of the spirit of the nation, while others are allowed to sit at the edge of the pantheon and venerate those within. Each group has its own set of heroes and definitive moments, and each tends to minimize or ignore the similar attempts of other groups to sacralize persons and events that have stood the test of time. The Sacred is everywhere, but nowhere in particular: pervasive but evanescent. Some aspects of the past are exalted and sacralized, others rendered part of a shameful history of servitude.

If the United States bears any mark, it is not that of the beast but of a former colony unsure of its future and ambivalent about its past. As the mark of a former colony, such chronic uncertainty about national identity can also be found in Australia. Speaking of Australian attempts to create an ideology for the nation out of versions of its history, Mark Hutchinson (1990, 193, 195, 197) finds in the historiography of the Australian colony

overt support for a particular structure in political relationships; a vision of the future shaping the interpretation of the past; mythologization of particular individuals and events and the denigration or exclusion of others; a division of history into the sacred and the profane consequent on this mythologization; a practical imperialism, or evangelization of the public through the press; and a devotion of the work to particular publics and audiences, at whom the message is aimed . . . The inevitability implicit in this view of colonial history is teleological in effect, depending for its justification on a state of affairs that is not verifiable or historically provable, because it has not yet happened . . . As belief, it partakes in the essential nature of religion . . . [N]ot only were the faith-based descriptions of the future essentially religious, but the past was seen as morally charged, divided according to the rationalist version of the "sacred and profane."

A very similar attempt to mythologize the future and the past and to sacralize certain utterances such as oaths and promises can be found in the heroic rhetoric of the debate in the U.S. Senate over the articles of impeachment directed at President Clinton. Sacred persons and events were clearly enshrined as idols of civil religion. Both parties to the debate interpreted the past, but those who interpreted it most narrowly defined the range of meaning and significance the sacred past might have for the present and sought to inhibit any attempt to turn sacred texts into discourse. Those who sought to defend the president tended to find the sacred as more complex, ambiguous, evanescent, and diffuse, and they were less likely than the advocates of impeachment to enshrine particular meanings or acts of speech.

Language has long been the institution on which the sacred and religion relied for various forms of conviction. Consider the following abbreviated list of forms of speech that have been relied on to penetrate and disclose mysteries and to resolve uncertainty: oracles, promises, blessings, curses, oaths, covenants, confessions, eyewitness testimony, petitions, absolutions, verdicts, sentencing, commissions, commitments, declarations, and pronouncements of marriage or death. It is no wonder that when the foundations of a society are laid bare the highest of premiums is placed on the right to speak, the authority of the speaker, the credibility of testimony, the authenticity of confessions and promises, and the meanings of words themselves.

The more secular a society becomes, then, the more strain is placed on language to bear the weight of—and to produce—conviction, but speech itself is very slippery ground on which to stand. Oracles may be ambiguous or false; promises may be insincere and misunderstood, or the speaker may be incompetent to fulfill them; blessings may be rejected or come back empty; and curses may be neutralized by sorcery or even backfire on those who gave them. An oath may be profane, and the giver may not be faithful to it; covenants can be broken, confessions partial, and testimony either false or controverted by other witness. Petitions may be inappropriate or may fall on deaf ears, while absolutions and verdicts may be given by those who lack the authority to have the last word. The notion that "In the beginning was the Word" can be offset by a voice that asks, "Did God say . . . ?"

Secularization, then, like the serpent in the Eden myth, underscores the importance of language while undermining the authority and force of any particular speech. That is the fundamental contradiction of a secular society, and it is the direct result of increasing ambiguity concerning the always contested boundary between the sacred and profane.

Lacking speech that can stand the test of time, moreover, a society legitimately wonders about its own ability to reproduce itself from one generation to the next. An entire generation of young people may not know the books of the New Testament, let alone what is in them. There may be widespread ignorance about the Declaration of Independence and the Constitution itself. Promises may be made to be broken, and false testimony under oath may become the routine practice of law enforcement officials. Research reports may be falsified and exonerating evidence withheld. There may be no agreement about the rules for interpreting texts as important to the foundations and continuity of the society as the Bible and the Constitution. No one may know what is meant by "high crimes and misdemeanors" or what to do about a president who lies under oath.

In the impeachment hearings many senators as well as the "managers" from the House of Representatives voiced concern about the continuity and the survival of the United States. They based this concern on their conviction that the president had violated, as Sen. Strom Thurmond (1999) put it, "his sacred oath to faithfully execute the laws of the United States." Thurmond's (1999) testimony evoked the question of what is sacred: that is, of what is beyond the legitimate realm of public inquiry, and he resolved that ambiguity by resorting to the sanctity of speech itself as the foundation of social order:

> Regardless of the bounds of private conduct and of the importance of allowing people to keep their private lives private, those bounds are broken when someone violates an oath to tell the truth in a court of law. Those bounds are also broken when someone interferes with a court of law in its efforts to find the facts and find the truth."

Once the bounds of the sacred have been broken, it is a short step to the last line of defense of the sacred against being reduced to the uncertainties of discourse, and that last line of defense is speech itself. Thus, an oath is sacred and must not be broken, any more than should testimony under oath violate the integrity of the courts, whose existence depends on their ability to recognize and validate credible speech and to make authoritative statements.

Earlier we noted that traditional language constrains the responses of all those who take part in certain rituals by evoking traditional authority. It is a means of social control. The taking of oaths is precisely such a case, where the oath taker is reduced to saying "I do, so help me God" or to some similar formula. Those who have taken oaths of office may then engage in the use of traditional language to exert their own authority over others. However, they do so at a price. As Bloch (1989, 29) has noted, this is done at the cost to the superior of losing his own freedom of manipulation. He can enter into a mode of speaking which compels the hearers, but since the mode predicts his speech at the same time, he also severely restricts himself in what he can say." That is why President Clinton's slippery use of language, under oath in courtroom testimony but also to the American people in press conferences, was noted with such care. At stake in these proceedings was the ability of the courts and of the state to circumscribe the use of language through the adoption of traditional forms of ritualized communication and rhetoric. Along with the link of the nation to its own past, at stake in these proceedings were the authority of the nation's leaders and the range of options that any leaders, political or religious, would have open to them.

Once the threat to the institution of language has been recognized, it is another short rhetorical step to utterances questioning the continuity and survival of the social order itself. Here I quote Sen. Jesse Helms's (1999) statement before the Senate in closed-door testimony as a case in point:

> So many decisions are made in the Senate—be it on the fate of treaties, or legislation, or even presidents—decisions having implications, not merely for today, but for generations to come, reminding [us—rkf] that if we don't stand for something, the very foundations of the Republic will crumble.

> Perjury and obstruction of justice are serious charges, and nobody knows better than you, Mr. Chief Justice, charges that have been proved in the course of this trial. Therefore, the outcome of this trial may determine whether America is becoming a fundamentally unprincipled nation, bereft of the mandates by the Creator who blessed America 210 years ago with more abundance, more freedom than any other nation in history has ever known . . . We have the facts before us and we should heed those facts because truth must become the legend.

> We must not permit a lie to become the truth."

Secularization does indeed make principles subject to inquiry and to revision. A "fundamentally unprincipled" nation is one that can no longer rely on authoritative texts, or agree on their interpretation, or authorize incontrovertible speech. In such a society there are no boundaries to define what is suitable for public discourse and what must remain private and thus safely beyond public knowledge. The boundaries that define the realm of legitimate obscurity, once opened, leave little if anything sacred and make it possible to probe the mysteries of intimate relationships, secret understandings, subversive attitudes, and private devotion. The same openness also makes it legitimate to reinterpret the Bible or to acquire knowledge of genetic codes and to use that knowledge to affect the evolution of species. Secularization places immense strains on language and makes all forms of mystery problematical.

I interpret the debate in the Senate on the articles of impeachment, brought against President Clinton, as a decision about the scope of the sacred in public life and thus about the nature of the system itself. In doing so I am adopting not only a sociologist's viewpoint; such was the view of many of those who did the voting. I have already quoted from two senators who saw the sacred at stake in these events. The sacred was found not only in the realm of the private but in the seriousness of confessional speech that discloses the private sphere to public scrutiny. The sacred was found in speech that promises under oath to defend the law and to speak the truth. Finally, the sacred was found in speech that constituted an inheritance from previous generations and that would constitute the legacy of this generation for years to come. All these forms of sacred language proved to be not only ambiguous and divisive but highly contested as well.

It is the capacity of language to stand the test of time that renders it sacred. One senator, Wayne Allard of Colorado, in closed-door hearings prior to the final vote on the articles of impeachment, based his entire speech on the sanctity of the oath. Referring first of all to his own oath of Congressional office, he referred to a federal district judge who had been impeached in 1989 for violating his own oath of office to tell the truth. The senator's point was that to lie under oath is not only perjury but an obstruction of justice, and he went on to remind his fellow senators of their oaths of office. These oaths, he pointed out, are living testimonies required by the Constitution, and the meaning and efficacy of the Constitution in turn depends on the sanctity of the oaths taken by those who hold public office. Drawing on Washington's Second Inaugural Address given on March 4, 1793, he reminded his colleagues that Washington himself took the presidential oath with utmost seriousness:

> Previous to the execution of any official act of the President the Constitution requires an oath of office. This oath I am now about to take, and in your presence: That if it shall be found during my administration of the government I have in any instance violated willingly or knowingly the injunctions thereof, I may (besides incurring constitutional punishment) be subject to the upbraidings of all who are now witnesses of the present solemn ceremony. (Allard 1999)

Senator Allard went on not only to quote from Supreme Court decisions that confirmed the seriousness of perjury but also to cite the importance of oaths among the Boy Scouts, police and military officers, and a wide range of civic offices.

Speech, whether given before a court of law or inscribed in texts that define the foundations of the social order itself, is sacred to the extent that it provides a word that will stand the test of time. Only such enduring language can become the core institution of a social order that itself claims the ability to transcend the passage of time. The following excerpt from a speech by Senator Abrahams (1999) tells the story:

> We are a great nation because, in America, no man—no woman—is above the law . . . Our tradition of chartered rights—rights laid down in laws, which no king, Parliament or other official could breach—culminated in our Constitution. That Constitution, which is itself only a higher law, protects us from tyranny. Once the law becomes an object of convenience rather than awe, that Constitution becomes a dead letter, and with it our freedoms and our way of life.
>
> Mr. Chief Justice, my grandparents did not come to this country seeking merely a more convenient, profitable life. They came here seeking the freedoms that were given birth on Bunker Hill and in the Convention at Philadelphia.
>
> I know some people mock as self-righteous or feckless the piety many Americans have toward their heritage and toward the Constitution that guards their freedom. But I will never forget that it is not the powerful or those favored by the powerful that need the law's protection.
>
> If we set a precedent that allows the President—the chief magistrate and the most powerful man in the world—to render the judicial process subordinate to his own interests, we tell ordinary citizens, like my grandparents, that Americans are no longer really equal in the eyes of the law. We tell them that they may be denied justice. And we thereby forfeit our own heritage of constitutional freedoms."

It might seem too harsh to suggest that what we have in these speeches is an idolatry of the word. Certainly, societies do indeed rely heavily on language as the institution that guarantees all the others, including religion itself. Take away the sanctity of the word, and there is very little left. Language is the final screen against uncertainty and the terror of living in a society that is unknowable and unpredictable.

Nonetheless, the sanctification of oaths of office, and particularly of the president's word given at inauguration ceremonies, effectively reifies the sacred and reduces the scope of the uncertain and the unknown. What may occur in the future remains beyond human ken and perhaps beyond human control, but the invocation of divine help, the laying of the presidential hand on the Bible, the presence of the clergy, and the appeal to the faith of the people all seek to guarantee that the future will be a continuation and renewal of previous blessings. Despite all its transformations and changes the future will therefore be recognizable as an extension of the providential past.

This is the direct opposite of a world in which all communication is anticipatory, interactive, provisional, and in the dark. This is the world of "double-contingency," to use Niklas Luhmann's awkward but apt term, in which "black boxes" communicate with each other in anticipation of certain cues that have not yet been given. Such communication is open-ended, continually revised, and consists only of a tentative exchange of symbols and messages. This is the world of the cybernetic universe, in which strangers communicate according to the improvised rules of the mass media or of chat rooms on the internet. It is the world in which a president can announce that his previous statements on a certain subject are "inoperative," as did Nixon himself—"inoperative" being a code word for "unbelievable."

Even more to the point is the problematical nature of the oaths taken by government officials to uphold the Constitution of the United States. In an acute comment on this subject, David Smolin has pointed out that the ceremonies in which these oaths are taken bear almost all the trappings of a coronation: the absence of an archbishop or the pope is offset by the presence of a leading American evangelist. In certain key respects, when Washington took the oath of office, his action was very much like the coronation of King George III (Smolin 1997, 15). Smolin's point, however, is that those who administer and witness the oath are the same justices who then rule that religious utterances and endorsements, even certain religious symbols, should be kept out of the schools, the municipal buildings, and indeed out of any governmental property or occasion at the local level. What is suitable for the center is a prohibited degree of state involvement with religion when it occurs on the periphery.

It is not merely the inconsistency here and the possibility of sham that are troubling. It is that the oath of office itself, even while being administered and taken, is itself compromised by a knowing complicity in double meanings and exceptions that allows for the princes what is prohibited to the people:

> There are several possible reasons why elected officials do not insist on strictly secular inaugurations and public events. One cynical possibility is that public officials who participate in these ceremonies, including Presidents-elect and Supreme Court Justices, believe such ceremonies to be inconsistent with the Constitution, but continue these traditions for fear of alienating the unwashed American public. The possibility makes the unhappy suggestion that government officials are willing to violate the Constitution in the very act of swearing allegiance to it. (Smolin 14)

Any oath is an idol, in the sense that it functions to reduce the complexity and mystery of the unknown to manageable proportions. In short, idols do indeed provide a Maginot Line that separates mystery, possibility, potentiality, threat, and promise from profane gaze and secular knowledge. To take someone at his or her word is thus to close the door on the mysteries of motive and intention; it is also to suspend inquiry into threats and surprises that have been precluded from foreknowledge and further discussion precisely because the word has been given, the promise made, the threat believed, or the covenant made. However, oaths taken under ambiguous conditions and with uncertain motives are easily seen to have the proverbial clay feet of the idol.

Now, it was the purpose of the hearings and the trial to explore the possibilities of subversion and danger to the republic that presumably had been foreclosed by the presence of serious speech, such as oaths. The Senate intended to inquire whether Clinton had intended to lie or simply refuse unnecessary assistance to lawyers asking him about his relationship to Monica Lewinsky. The hearings also needed to discover whether Clinton, in rehearsing cover stories with his aides and with Lewinsky herself, was trying to influence testimony or merely to refresh their memories. Some senators sought to remove ambiguity from the discussion of perjury by referring to the relevant statutes; others referred to Blackstone's *Commentaries on the Laws of England* (Hutchinson 1999). The realm of relevant ambiguity, however, did not stop there.

To explore beyond the text of transcripts and depositions, of oaths and affidavits, requires entering into the spirit rather than the letter of communication, and this entrance is usually granted only to those who are able to meet face-to-face. That was one reason that some senators insisted on a trial in which they would have a chance to observe the tone of voice and demeanor of key witnesses. Other senators evoked not the spirit behind certain testimonies but the spirit of the times. Some pleaded the spirit of a people who appeared to be weary of the proceedings and who allegedly thought of the offense as trivial and of the inquiry itself as demeaning not only to the president and the Congress but to the American people themselves. Others, however, pleaded the spirit of the age and argued that history would find Congress guilty either of Puritan morals and prurient interest or, conversely, guilty of undermining the attempt of parents to pass on standards of candor and truthfulness to succeeding generations. Of possible implications and looming threats there seemed to be no end.

That sort of open-ended discourse, with its endless elaboration and its appeals to generations of precedent and possible consequence is precisely what one would expect when the boundaries between the sacred and the profane have been effaced. One is then in a territory in which the line separating the relevant from the irrelevant, the knowable from the unknowable, and the unspeakable from the all too speakable is nowhere durably drawn to anyone's satisfaction.

Such unbounded discourse, furthermore, is entirely suitable to a social system in which every part has to take into account the interests of every other part. In a society such as the contemporary United States there is therefore no end of relevant attributions. Thus, speakers in the Senate were able to derive their concerns and base their positions on the president's case not only by reference to past and future generations; the senators and the "managers" from the House could involve the attitudes and interests of all plaintiffs and defendants past and present, all officeholders and civic officials, all parents and youth, the entire military, as well as those with an interest, one way or another, in public policy on gender harassment.

The senatorial scope of reference also extended backward in time and outward in space. As for time, the proper reference is to Adam and Eve, who, according to at least one senator, Dale Bumpers, set the precedent for the president's lack of perfection. In terms of space, the senator went on to discuss the president's achievements in foreign policy and the high regard in which he is held throughout the world. Among those quoted or cited as having praised Clinton's efforts for peace were Carlos Menem, the president of Argentina, Vaclav Havel, and King Hussein.

The point is that with so high a level of accountability and interdependence, and under the weight of this much complexity and uncertainty, no single statement, let alone any particular interpretation, could withstand much scrutiny. There were too many alternative viewpoints and allusions to be taken into account. As a case in point, let me cite Senator Bumpers's discussion of the Vancouver Bear.

The bear in question was a small stone sculpture apparently bought in Vancouver by the president as a gift for Lewinsky. When testifying before the grand jury Lewinsky described the bear as an "Indian symbol for strength, you know, to be strong like a bear" (U.S. Senate 1999, 156) Asked whether she interpreted the gift as a reminder to be strong in concealing her relationship to the president, she said flatly, "No." In the eyes of those conducting the inquiry in the House Judiciary Committee and representing the case for impeachment to the Senate, however, Lewinsky's denial was unconvincing. The incriminating bear (like other gifts) was "a tacit reminder to Ms. Lewinsky that they would deny the relationship even in the face of a federal subpoena" (U.S. Senate 1999, 157). This, said the presenters of the case, was "the only logical inference." Senator Bumpers suggested that there were indeed other logical inferences, one of which was that she meant what she said when she replied "No" to the suggestion that the gift was a reminder to be quiet.

Here we are entering a hermeneutical jungle where no viewpoint is privileged and no interpretation authoritative. What did the president mean by this gift? How did Lewinsky receive it? How did it refer to prior understandings that were intimate and secret? After all, as Lewinsky herself pointed out in that context, she and the president "never questioned that we would ever do anything but keep this private and that meant to take whatever appropriate steps needed to be taken to keep it quiet." To a simple-minded analyst, that statement might well mean that she planned to say "no" to any question asking whether she had entered with the president into a conspiracy to obstruct justice. Such a simple-minded analyst might be excused for thinking that the Vancouver Bear was an idol to a sacred promise to keep a presidential secret. However, on this point Senator Bumpers took Lewinsky at her word when she said "No" to such a suggestion. In fact, he went on to assess the motives of those who saw "the only logical inference" as incriminating; they, he alleged, simply wanted "to win too badly."

This is not to say that Senator Bumpers was indifferent to historical precedent, to the original intention of the writers of the Constitution, to common law traditions, or to any other outpost of the sacred. Indeed, he said that the Constitution was "the most sacred document to me next to the holy Bible" (U.S. Senate 1999, 151). With regard to those who wrote the impeachment provisions into the Constitution, he recalled that one of them, George Mason, drew on English law for the phrase referring to "high crimes and misdemeanors," which referred to "offenses distinctly political against the state" (U.S. Senate 1999, 161).

Senator Bumpers's recourse to the past, however, was an attempt to put a narrow construction on the notion of an impeachable offense, just as he had sought to put a narrow construction on the meaning of Lewinsky's flat denial of being party to a cover-up. A political offense against the state appears to be Mason's requirement for impeachable offenses.

Despite this political interest in a narrow construction of constitutional language and of testimony under oath, even Senator Bumpers's own usage shows a remarkable tendency to slip into the sea of broader inference and wider meaning. Note how Senator Bumpers revises the meaning of George Mason's restriction of impeachable offenses to those against the state. Bumpers soon decodes this reference to include offenses of a broader range: offenses that are not necessarily political and therefore may be against society as a whole. Consider the following question raised by Bumpers (U.S. Senate 1999, 161) immediately after his discussion of George Mason's contribution to the definition of impeachable offenses as "high crimes and misdemeanors . . . political offenses against the state: "If, as Hamilton said, it had to be *a crime against society or a breach of the public trust*, what are we doing here?" (emphasis added) I mention this simply to indicate that even when it was in their interest to use a narrow construction of traditional language on the subject of the Constitution, the president's defenders were likely to adopt the broader, more diffuse, and open-ended habits of speech that befit a secular society.

This open-door policy to the use of language made the presidential defense unnecessarily vulnerable. For instance, one answer to Senator Bumpers's question about what they were doing was simply that the president had indeed breached the public trust (never mind offenses against the state).

We are in a linguistic arena here in which words, their meanings, their relevance and their weight, and the inferences that one draws from them are floating freely in a sea of possibilities. The lack of boundaries that would define what is to be known and discussed, what is relevant and weighty, does more than reflect a society in which all internal boundaries that separate religion from politics, entertainment from the law, politics from business, the public from the private, and the sacred from the profane have broken down, become ambiguous, divisive, and contested. It also reflects a society that has no clear boundaries separating the past and the future from the present.

Under these conditions it is entirely suitable for commentators to make extended references to a past that reached even beyond George Washington's mythic propensity for the truth first to Blackstone and King George III, and finally to Christendom and its long engagement of the church with the state. The future also hung in the balance of extended commentary on the prospect of future generations having no models by which to restrain their tendencies toward lying and promiscuity.

As if in reaction to the dangers of open-ended discourse, multiple reference, eclectic selection from the past, and a logic of inference that presented no principle for excluding alternative interpretations, some sought to recover a limited and particular frame of reference. For them the sacred could be found in a plot of ground or a cross above a grave, in a soldier's oath, in the sacrifices of prior generations, in the military's code of sacred honor, and in the president's oath and sacred promise to uphold the law and the Constitution. In these concrete particulars are embedded a universe of meaning and obligation. They stand as markers of the faith and hope that consecrated the lives of those who have gone before and who even now stand ready to give their lives in the service of the nation. If, from my point of view, they are idols that indicate the entrance to sacred territory, to certain speakers they are reminders of a covenant that remains binding even on those who ignore and forget it.

One reference to discipline and codes of behavior in the military came from Representative Steve Buyer (U.S. Senate 1999, 146) in answer to a question from several Republican senators including Thurmond and Helms:

> We must confront the fact that the president is the commander-in-chief, and I believe it is perfectly acceptable of [sic] the American people to demand of the military, the highest standard, which also means that those of whom (sic) find themselves in positions of responsibility in the Pentagon, of whom (sic) are in civilian leadership, must also live by such exemplary conduct and standards.

The high character of military officers is a safeguard of the character of a nation. The Senate, who must ratify the officers' promotion list, has repeatedly found that anything less that [sic] exemplary conduct is therefore unworthy of a commission, or further promotion."

I am not suggesting that the case against President Clinton never reached the range of historical or global reference realized by his defenders, or that the prosecution lived in a world entirely alien to uncertainty and complexity. In his concluding argument, Rep. Henry Hyde (U.S. Senate 1999, 165) did acknowledge that "we live in an age of increasing interdependence" but concluded from that fact that "the future will require an even stronger bond of trust between the president and the nation, because with increasing interdependence, comes an increased necessity of trust." Not limited to a time span that began with the inauguration of President Washington, Representative Hyde (U.S. Senate 1999, 167) referred to "3000 years of history," to the Ten Commandments, Roman law, the Magna Carta, parliamentary tradition, and this century's "great struggles against totalitarianism in which the rule of law was defended at immense cost against the worst tyrannies in human history."

At the heart of Representative Hyde's speech, however, were references to the "sacred honor" inscribed into the Declaration of Independence and to what President Clinton himself referred to as "a covenant, a solemn pact of mutual trust and obligation with the American people." That covenant is the office of the president. That trust "is the mortar that secures the foundations of the American house of freedom." Representative Hyde went on to the presidential oath and to "truth telling" as "the heart and soul of our justice system," but in further concrete imagery referred to trust again as "mortar," to "foundation stones," to the "edifice" that is American freedom, and to the rule of law as "bedrock." In referring to place and time Representative Hyde ranged from "Bunker Hill, Lexington, Concord" all the way to "Saigon and Desert Storm." In later references Representative Hyde (U.S. Senate 1999, 164–73) referred to the soldiers buried in Arlington Cemetery and in rows of crosses (he also mentioned "crucifixes") at Normandy, as well as to the Vietnam War Memorial in Washington and to the 58,000 names inscribed on it. There is a limited symbolic range here that extends to language and to monuments that will stand the test of time.

Those who wish to expand the degrees of their semantic freedom, to allow their society to be open to more possibilities as well as to more threats, and to see the meanings enshrined in the culture open to continuous review and inspection may find it hard to honor the dead. They may have to take their inspiration from a faith that encourages the dead to honor the dead and the living to find their own way into the future. What, then, is the role of the Christian faith in a secular society? That is the question that will take us into the next and final chapter.

8

BEYOND IDOLATRY

Religionless Christianity

W hat, then, are the prospects for a secular society? We know that there are some societies that live in the present with very little regard for the past. They are notably devoid of sacred times and seasons and have few, if any, heroes and ancestors whose presence they evoke through ritual on stated occasions or during moments of crisis. These are societies that are capable of living with high levels of uncertainty; indeed, they have to cope with such uncertainty if they are going to survive. Typically the sort of societies that spend a lot of time hunting and gathering, they live in a continuous present that owes very little to the past in the way of precedent. Few roles in the society are fixed or elevated above the others, and what roles they have are loosely related rather than bound together in a way that suggests something whole, organic, continuous, superior, and constraining.

The hallmark of these societies that live in the present is a relative lack of hierarchy and a dearth of rituals that impress unequal status on members of a community. Bloch (1989, 16–17) sums it up this way, speaking of an African society called the Hadza:

> [T]hese hunters and gatherers are characterized by . . . the total absence of the past as a subject matter in their discourse. They have relatively few rituals of social relations, rites of passage, birth ceremonies, funerals, ancestor worship, except interestingly enough for one major ritual which is primarily concerned with the relationship of men and women . . . The Hazda have very little instituted hierarchy except between men and women and mothers-in-law and sons-in-law, and they have little ritual communication except in respect of these relationships. Their concepts of time are almost entirely present-oriented.

It follows that, with so little in the way of ritual to mark out sacred time and space, people and events, there is also very little in the way of the profane. Few, if any, markers separate what is to be taken seriously or revered from what must bear investigation, what can be dispensed with, and what is clearly of only momentary importance. They live in a world very much like that reported in parts of the Synoptic Gospels, where the questions posed to Jesus and his answers jumbled existing categories for what distinguishes the past from the present and the sacred from the profane. As for notions of hierarchy, his words notably upset existing categories and left his followers highly uncertain about what, if any, distinctions could or should be allowed to persist in their community or would be allowed to prevail in the world.

The very distinction between sacred and profane has therefore understandably become problematical, at least for Christians, precisely because of the Incarnation. The Incarnation makes it difficult for anyone to say of any aspect of social life that it is not potentially the site of revelation. Any time or place may be the scene of an encounter with the divine or an occasion on which ultimate meanings come into play disguised as the stuff of everyday life.

On the other hand, the Incarnation also makes it impossible for anyone to say that here or there lies the Kingdom of God. The Incarnation was the Incarnation to end all Incarnations, just as Christianity is the religion to end all religions. The successful institutionalization of Christianity, then, requires a society that has been bleached entirely clean of all forms of what a theologian would call religion and of what I in this book have been calling idolatry.

My argument is relatively simple. At the heart of the Christian Gospel, I will suggest, is a tendency toward radical secularity. Instead of sanctifying the dead and enshrining their memory in sacred institutions, the Christian is instructed to let the dead bury the dead. In the same way, instead of developing a social identity that can be given the trappings of the sacred, the individual is to exercise his or her piety in secret, and the God who hears in secret will answer. Christian identity is hidden, as Paul put it, with Christ in God. Thus, any attempt to sacralize relationships and the person is to be avoided. As for those who go around in long robes and display the trappings of the sacred on their person, the Gospel calls for a demystification of their version of the sacred; on the outside they look good, but being "whited sepulchres" their interior is corrupted, and their corruption will be exposed. The Gospel is equally stringent about any attempt to sacralize extraordinary people who claim gifts of the spirit or a divine commission.

Wherever there is a tendency to turn chiefs and kings into sacred figures, the Gospel stands opposed to the attempt. Every claim by a political order to mediate the divine to the human is offset by the Gospel's insistence that there is a divine kingdom that may be anywhere and everywhere but cannot be located "Lo here" and "Lo there." Even a system that may be the instrument of divine providence or wrath enjoys only a conditional and temporary legitimacy. No political system can lay claim to being the mediator between the divine and the human.

The Christian at times has relieved, at other times has exacerbated, the tension between the loyalties that bind people to their families and local communities, on the one hand, and the claims of the state, on the other. When the state intrudes into local communities, its banners may therefore be welcome or resented. The emblems of Caesar had to be removed from the Temple, and to this day the U.S. flag is not uniformly welcome in all the sanctuaries of the land. Often the state seeks to wrap itself in the garments of local piety and to present itself as the guardian of the family and the community. The state may even invoke blessings from the same sources that consecrate the family table and the local cemetery. Often, however, these attempts by the state to mimic the piety of the periphery seem inauthentic or corrupt, and the periphery seeks to distance itself from the very symbols that the state has co-opted.

Thus, the boundary between state and local piety remains contested, and there is no agreement, for instance, on whether prayers should be offered in the schools or whether the creche, the manger scene, should be allowed to appear at city hall during the Christmas season. While those who oppose the political display of religious symbols are often regarded as the enemies of Christianity, there is a strong Christian tradition in favor of secularizing the state. If the emperor is to have clothes, they are not to be the vestments of the Christian faith.

This reading of Christianity as fundamentally secularizing may seem idiosyncratic. Among sociologists, however, it has been long understood that Christianity has tended to remove the sacred mystery from local and civic piety, just as it has always opposed the attempt of the state to take the place of the church as the mediator of divine grace. Furthermore, critical social theorists like Herbert Marcuse (1960, 265) have reminded us that the secularizing tendencies of the Christian faith work to relieve the burdens of the beleaguered human spirit:

> Kierkegaard's work is the last great attempt to restore religion as the ultimate organon for liberating humanity from an oppressive social order . . . Kierkegaard returns to the original function of religion, its appeal to the destitute and tormented individual. He thus restores to Christianity its combative and revolutionary force. The appearance of God again assumes the terrifying aspect of a historical event suddenly breaking in upon a society in decay. *Eternity takes on a temporal aspect, while the realization of happiness becomes an immediately vital matter of daily life.*(emphasis added)

Part of that "oppressive social order," of course, is the result of the church's historic attempt to gain a monopoly on the sources of meaning and to constrict the range of individual aspiration.

Certainly, in seeking to make sense of the world the church has not always welcomed competition. Wherever people or institutions have claimed inspiration or authority from sources beyond the auspices of the church, they have met with stiff resistance from the priest or the missionary, the church bureaucrat or the inquisitor. In the same way, the church's intellectuals have sought to rationalize morals, philosophy, and the sciences into an intellectually coherent system consonant with the Christian faith. This tendency toward coherence and system has produced a drive toward rationality that continues under modern auspices and that has at times turned the church itself, its beliefs and practices, into something of an anomaly. That is why I am arguing that only a secularized version of the Christian faith can free the individual from the oppressive weight of the church's attempt to discipline the soul.

It is increasingly obvious, therefore, that only a religionless Christianity can help to free the individual from the burdens imposed not only by the state or the family but by the church itself. Such a secular form of the Christian faith may not be at all difficult to achieve. The more that Christian beliefs and practices come into play in the political center, the more they are secularized. This is most obvious in the progression of conservative Christianity to the political center in the United States. The closer even very conservative Christians get to Congress or the White House, the more they have to substitute the language of compromise and problem solving for the rhetoric of obedience and faith. In learning to keep a civil tongue in their heads, Catholics as well as Protestants have become increasingly pragmatic rather than absolutist. The same progress, if that is the right word, marked the development of democracy in Scotland out of a stalemate between absolutist Presbyterian sects (see Bruce 1990). From a theological viewpoint as well, the dilution of Christian commitment by democratic and instrumental concerns leads to a utilitarian world relatively free from absolutes and ultimate conviction. Even by their successes in the political arena, Christians turn the sacred into the conventional.

From a Christian viewpoint, secularization occurs precisely—and properly—to the extent that Christianity becomes engaged and entwined with work and politics, with the everyday and the mundane. In this engagement it becomes increasingly ambiguous as to whether politics, work, or even entertainment, for that matter, is truly religious or truly secular. That is precisely the problem with deciphering the use of religious symbols in the American polity. Is a creche a religious or a secular symbol? That ambiguity spawns many Supreme Court deliberations and decisions. This ambiguity, however, is precisely what one would expect of a society that has undergone a degree of Christianization. The demystification of the sacred brings with it a radical uncertainty as to where the boundary may be drawn between the sacred and the secular. It is only when the line between the sacred and the secular is sharply drawn that one has the very conditions that Christianity has sought to avoid or prevent or transform.

Thus, I am arguing that secularization may undermine Christianity in the form of institutionalized religion, with its beliefs and practices, clerics and laity, but it will increase the very ambiguity of the sacred and the secular that is at the heart of Christian revelation. Herbert Marcuse was driving at precisely this point when he argued,

> Feuerbach starts with the fact that Kierkegaard had failed to recognize, namely, that in the present age the human content of religion can be preserved only by abandoning the religious, other-worldly form. The doctrine of God (theology) must be changed into the doctrine of man (anthropology). Everlasting happiness will begin with the transformation of the kingdom of heaven into a republic of earth."

We are still a long way from the consummation of this process of turning the vision of heaven into a constitution for an earthly republic. However, we are close enough now to be able to ask—to be required to ask— whether there indeed can be a secular society, and if so, whether there also can be a global social system of societies with, at best, a provisional set of international laws based on a contestable set of putative human rights. Can such a global social system even develop in light of the threat posed by what appears to be primitive ethnic nationalism of the Serbian variety? If religion is essential to the formation of national societies, how can it be anything other than the focal point for rival nationalisms? These are familiar questions, which formerly were asked of socialism. Now, instead of asking whether socialism can survive in one country, despite an encirclement of capitalist states, we are required to ask whether a secular society can emerge and survive in a global system of rival and sometimes religious nationalisms.

We can reduce these broad questions into a set of smaller ones. Can a nation-state survive without a national identity that is religious at least in the sense that it appears to transcend the passage of time and can legitimate state authority? Can a nation-state survive without a consensus on values that transcend special interests and appear, therefore, to be non-negotiable? Can a nation-state survive without a sense of its uniqueness or priority among the other nation-states of the world? Can a nation-state survive that is only a legal and political framework for a set of ethnic communities that share the same territory, currency, and systems of transportation and communication? Can such a society survive in view of the fact that it is not the object of moral commitments or the focus of personal identities of individuals but merely the systemic framework for moral communities based on ethnicity, language, culture, and religion?

Finally, what form would the sacred take in such a secular society? If a society itself does not lay claim to transcendent values and is not the object of fundamental moral commitments, the sacred is free from its national shrines and embodiments and may be more dispersed and diffused. Dispersed, the sacred may be embodied in the smaller communities, based on ethnicity or language, culture, or religion. Further, diffuse rather than institutionalized in particular times and places, people and events, the sacred may observe no social boundaries and will take on a life of its own. More unpredictable and ephemeral, the sacred may be manifested in movements that rely on a divine spirit, or manifested in the transformation of the self into identities that appear to be based on private sources of authority and inspiration, or in visitations of other-worldly personages, such as angels, ghosts, aliens from other planets, and other bizarre life forms.

The association of the Sacred with what is beyond and perhaps somewhat unreal locates it in the environment of a social system. By environment, I mean the sum total of all possibilities: opportunities for satisfaction and achievement, for subversion and innovation, for repression and cruelty. Many of these opportunities exist within the formal or territorial boundaries of a society, but even more exist beyond what is normally considered to be "domestic" or is accepted as standard practice. Of course, no society can be totally open at all times to every possibility that exists; if it were, it would not be a social system of any sort.

That is why the sacred so often takes on the form of what is for many people as ephemeral or potent as a ghost or an angel. For the same reason, the sacred is often identified with celebrities and saintly persons, with inspirations and visions, and with the entire panoply of the significant but extraordinary. The sacred is also found among those who speak with unusual and eccentric authority: seers and prophets, and not only among those who claim to be able to see into and speak for what is beyond the reach of ordinary knowledge and communication.

Of course, no society can be fully open to the possibilities contained in other societies, just as it cannot represent within itself the full range of human potential. Simply by virtue of being a social system, however open and fluid, a nation can at best only include a selection of possibilities from a total universe that includes, but goes beyond, all known societies both in the present and in the past. As Luhmann (1984, 4) puts it,

> The concept of system brings the difference between within and without, between environment and system into the analysis of constitution. One can think of this difference as a complexity gradient in which the environment is always more complex than the system itself. The difference between possibility and reality is one of the ways in which the system makes this complexity gradient meaningful for itself.

A society that defines or idealizes itself in religious terms will therefore make a relatively strong distinction between what is real and what is unreal: between the possible and impossible, the thinkable and the unimaginable. What Freud called the reality principle will heighten awareness of the difference between that society and all others—other societies being seen as having a lesser role to play in history or as being less developed or exemplary among nations. Conversely, a secular society will maintain only a fluid and permeable boundary between the real, as defined by its own institutions and achievements, identity and values, and the unreal. In a secular society the "beyond" or transcendent will always and everywhere be a possibility of uncertain probability. Its reality principle will be correspondingly open to suggestion and revision, negotiation and debate.

It is not surprising that some nations are open to the possibility that alien life forms not only exist but are in communication with this world, or that computers should be designed on an entirely new principle from those currently being produced, or that genes should be borrowed from the plant and animal worlds to service the human organism. The boundaries between these nations and other societies are relatively open and allow for the relatively continuous and unfettered exchange of ideas, people, food, capital, microbes, and technology. Other societies have sharper boundaries between what they consider inside and outside, real and unreal, possible and inconceivable. A truly secular society, I have suggested, is wholly agnostic about the boundary between the possible and the impossible.

In the Riddell Memorial Lectures of 1962, Denis Munby (1963, 75–6) argued (in the gender-based language of the time) that

> [T]here is no separate sphere of "religion" where God is to be found. If there is no such separate sphere, if God is a hidden God, he is equally a God who is everywhere in the ordinary everyday world . . . The secular world has its limited aims, and God respects these; there are no other alternative aims for Christians in their everyday life. But Christians, believing in God, can see these aims as *limited*, precisely because they look for *ultimate* satisfaction to God alone . . . The more choices men have to exercise, the more responsibility is thrust upon them. A secular society enlarges the area of men's choices, and calls men to greater maturity, as Bonhoeffer has made clear to us.

Munby was certainly not the first, as he pointed out, to make the argument that Christianity is a religion to end all religions. He was also not the last to distinguish religion from Christianity on these grounds: that whereas religion provides a relief from uncertainty and provides prescriptions for living, Christianity extols the life of faith that walks, so to speak, without sight.

To discuss a global ethic based on religious grounds that are at least partly Christian is at the very least problematical. It is the very absence of an ethic, global or otherwise, that makes the Christian faith what it is: a faith, a way of living into all the uncertainties that the world and life can offer, without their premature reduction into a set of guidelines and prescriptions. The God who was revealed in Christ insists that no one has seen God. Jesus is reported to have claimed that there is no one good but the Father, not even Jesus himself; that it is one's own faith, not Jesus's power, that is the source of healing; that the Sabbath is made for humans, not the other way around; as for tradition, let the dead bury the dead. Christianity radically extends the range of the imaginable and the possible without offering any particular guidance and with the assurance only that the stakes are very, very high.

This is not to say that Christianity has not at times developed a systematic ethic. Indeed, Christianity's tendency to achieve high levels of rationality in its teachings has been one factor in its success and also in its failure. It has been part of Christianity's success because the church has been able to control or eliminate deviant opinions and worldviews both within the faith and outside it while claiming a set of rules capable of encompassing a wide range of diverse contexts and situations. It has been part of its failure because, in the process of uprooting deviant, local, and anomalous forms of piety and authority, the church has sometimes found itself without a social base. Thus the church has been a strong force for secularization, especially as it proceeded to dominate Europe.

If the Christian faith, however, were to offer an ethic, it would be one that is suited to very high levels of complexity, uncertainty, opportunity, and danger. It would also require equally high levels of both personal and collective responsibility. It would also be an ethic suitable for a system that makes up its own laws as it goes along: an evolutionary system that is self-generating and self-referential. If such a social system has any rules, they are created by discussion and accepted by consent for the time being. Its rules are therefore provisional and procedural, at best, even when they appear to rely on a body of tradition. Such a system is also self-referential because those who would change the rules can only appeal to the procedures by which the rules were made in the first place; there is no higher and external tribunal outside the system itself that can listen or respond to any appeals.

That is what I mean, in part, by a secular world, and if Christianity supplies an ethic to help it get started, that is despite the fact that Christianity wears the trappings of a world religion, not because of it. Whereas Christian faith provides a rationale for living responsibly without clear guidelines in a highly complex and uncertain social environment, religion enables a society to be very selective about what it knows and remembers.

Take, for example, societies that imagine themselves as being endowed with a superior tradition or as bearing a unique mission in history. There is a vast reduction here of the complexity not only of the present but of the past, as well as a divestment of the costs of such a system for its members and its victims. The same sense of being a holy nation destined for glory can feed not only resistance to oppression; it can also feed national vindictiveness. Thus, any nation convinced that it has long been a victim and that it is now entitled to vindication will vastly reduce the complexity of the world in which it lives. It will also drastically oversimplify its memory of the past. Instead of accepting collective responsibility for its sufferings, it will cultivate a sense of entitlement to revenge.

Any nation that bears a mission to enlighten and transform other nations will be slow to relinquish its imaginary national distinction in favor of a system that treats all nations and peoples equally before the bar of an international justice. It is all the more surprising, then, that any Christian ethicist, let alone one of the stature of Hans Kung (1999, 229), should advocate a global ethic that is to be derived precisely from these same wells of national memory and experience. It is an unfortunate suggestion to the extent that these wells are poisoned by memories of humiliation and hopes for triumph, by exclusiveness and delusions of uniqueness and superiority. If there is to be a global ethic, I would argue, it will presuppose the renunciation of these dreams of national glory. That is another reason that only a religionless Christianity can help.

The seeds of cultural domination are often planted in soil that is sacred to the memory of past generations, and they are nourished by illusions of cultural superiority. When a nation also feels itself endowed with a peculiar responsibility to enlighten other societies by its example or to redeem them by its leadership, it is not likely to subscribe to international codes of ethics on human rights, the preservation of the environment, the flow of capital, or the treatment of other countries in times of war. An "indispensable nation" thus makes a poor partner.

More is needed, of course, than a process that secularizes nationalities; it is religion itself that stands in need of being secularized if a global ethic can emerge. Of course, Kung (1999, 35) deplores the "national self-righteousness" of a nation when it hides its sense of cultural uniqueness and superiority behind a crusade for "freedom and human rights." So-called civil religions could well be deplored on the same grounds. However, for Kung it is religion that is the enemy of all individualism and that is the source of personal and national self-restraint and social responsibility. Although religion is for Kung the last bulwark of traditionalism, he finds it written large enough to encompass a global economy. I would simply point out, however, that even when a religious tradition or movement has global aspirations, it is too often still the vehicle for delusions of popular and national uniqueness and superiority.

I would argue that realism requires a global ethic to be based on the secularization not only of nationality but of religion itself. It is time for Christians, at least, to announce that they have discarded any notions of a salvation that gives priority to Christians over non-Christians. This form of Christianity would simply affirm that no one is saved until everyone is saved. In the meantime, it is obvious that religion is as much the disease as it is the hypothetical cure when Christians are killing one another as well as Muslims in exercises of ethnic cleansing. Exercises of this sort have ample precedent in the Christianization of Europe, the Crusades, and in the attempts to establish a greater Israel in the centuries leading up to the disastrous civil war and destruction of Jerusalem in 66–73 C.E. That is why I have argued in this book that only a society in which the sacred is relatively dispersed and diffuse can avoid the usual delusions and horrors of national piety.

What is clearly needed here is an account of the conditions under which religion in general, and Christianity in particular, can lead to conflict and even genocide. Unfortunately, Kung's apologetics for religion—as opposed to a secular worldview— and for societies based on religion rather than on a more provisional structure of agreements and interests, gets in the way of a solid theoretical argument of the sort that David Martin, for instance, has made in his recent acute discussion of the problem, *Does Christianity Cause War?*. There it is clear that the problem depends on a wide range of variables, such as the extent to which Christian symbols and institutions are embedded in natural communities based on blood, race, and soil or enshrined in central political institutions. Other variables are the degree to which Christianity is caught up in the tension between the center and the periphery, is coterminous with the population as a whole, or is relatively marginalized and encapsulated in particular social contexts. These variables in turn control the extent to which Christianity can challenge the attempt to limit Christian symbols to the legitimation of state authority and to the prevailing distribution of opportunities for recognition and satisfaction.

Undeterred by this sort of complexity, Kung (1999, 231) simply affirms his notion that "in a "postmodern" age we should discard that neglect of the religions so characteristic of modernity in favour of a realistic assessment." It is a strange appeal, especially from one as cognizant as Kung of ecclesiastical mischief in the Balkans. To be sure, Kung (1999, 228–30) knows that religion can be fatal to international peace, but he nonetheless sees world religions as a source for a universal ethic of respect for differences, of responsibilities and self-restraints, of peaceful resolution of conflict and regard for others, especially the poor and minorities, and of the socially responsible use of property and the environment.

A global social system is already precarious enough without the additional problems caused by a nation that deems itself obligated to enlighten and emancipate other societies by its own agency and example. A secularized global system would have little place for such ideological pretensions. It would be provisional, open to constant review and revision, continuously negotiable, and contingent on the provisional consent of its members. As such, it would require societies themselves to enter a world with few, if any, illusions about their own permanence or stability. It would be understandable if, under these conditions, some societies fall back on traditions and a sense of entitlement that protects them from the risks of continuous interaction with other societies on equal terms: understandable, but tragic for the global system itself.

In such a system the stakes are very high, the guidelines vague, the penalties for failure potentially severe, and there are no guarantees of success. That is what I mean by a secular social system. It is one in which each member of that system impinges on all the others, and their interaction is continuous. Under these conditions those who participate in that system have to be extraordinarily alert to opportunities, surprises, and threats, and relatively free from fixed ideas or illusions about the system itself. There is a high premium in such a system on continuous communication, reality testing, openness to innovation, and the ability swiftly to process information and take appropriate action.

For a global system of this sort to survive, however, it will require its members to become secular themselves. Devotion to traditions or to cherished illusions about the nation would be useless and perhaps dangerous in a global system that honors equally the integrity and needs of all its members; such priorities as there are can only be temporary and provisional. While it would be legitimate for nations to ask their members to delay the satisfaction of certain needs, sacrifice would seldom be legitimate except in societies that enjoyed a relative abundance of goods and services. In a secular society or secularized global system, no sacrifice, however, would be legitimate if it represented the transformation of the system itself into one that has aspirations to transcend the passage of time.

Clearly, there is no place in such a system for a civil religion, with its illusions of national uniqueness and superiority. Neither is there any place in such a system for religious politics. Whether one thinks of evangelical inquisitions into public morals or the adventures of the Vatican in Balkan politics, these are equally recognizable as relics of Christendom and as dangerous illusions.

Nonetheless, despite his desire to avoid the extremes of moralism and realism, Kung believes that societies are always, deep down, religious at their core. Without a common commitment to something transcendent, to a set of values and morals, to the law and to legitimate authority, no society is even possible. In his view, then, it is the hard headed realists who are in fact deluded, since they fail to grasp the sacred mysteries that underlie all social disciplines. As with Durkheim, so with Kung (1999, 56): individualism is the enemy of social life and has been used to justify "all the immorality in politics."

Instead, it is necessary, I am arguing, to imagine a society or a global system that is generated by the initiative and creativity of a wide range of individual and corporate actors. To imagine such a society or system is not hard, since there is indeed already a frightening level of uncertainty and complexity in a global social system, but Kung does not trust companies and nongovernmental institutions, social movements, individual actors, and governments themselves to generate their own working agreements. Instead, he prefers international law and order to the sometimes chaotic exchanges of goods and services or the unregulated flow of currency and credit (Kung 1999, 216–217). Indeed, he wishes the world to place a higher value on things of the spirit than on material satisfactions and accomplishments, and he attacks the usual enemy of conservative social thought, individualism, whether it is exercised by personal or corporate actors.

In *A Global Ethic* there are even a few passages in which Kung's voice is unmistakably authoritarian. Although he dislikes moralism, he engages in a diatribe against people he describes as "pragmatic libertists." The culprit here is the individual who wishes to expand his or her degrees of freedom and enjoyment and to have no more obligation to the larger society than is minimally necessary or is compatible with the individual's interests. These "involuntarily prove that the Pope and Opus Dei are right (Kung 1999, 137).

In the background, behind these present-day utilitarians, Kung sees a long line of Machiavellian pragmatists with names like Richelieu and Bismarck. These personify a ruthless rationality that knows no other ethic than self-interest and the interests of the state. Lacking any universal ethic or respect for a particular tradition, they are, as Kung sees them, modern in the degraded sense of the term: lacking in any respect for religious tradition and ethics. In a word, they are "secular." Note how Kung (1999, 15) describes Richelieu as a "secularized cleric" and not a "Christian politician." In the same vein, he characterizes Kissinger as a "secularized Jew" who is "open to a variety of traditions" but beholden to none except that of Machiavelli and the amoral exercise of state power in its own interests (Kung 1999, 8). Secularized clerics and Jews, individualists and the enemies of tradition: these are the usual suspects of Christian authoritarianism and conservative sociology.

It is ironic that it is the same tradition that is responsible for much of the secularization of the West that Kung deplores. Certainly, Christianity mounted a relentless attack on local pieties and minority religious traditions. By being rational and systematic in regard to its intellectual traditions and its administration of institutions, Christianity trained the West in eliminating anomalies and incongruities and in the careful discipline of linking means to ends. By an asceticism that was impatient with scholasticism and unnecessary elaboration of tradition, Christianity also lent its moral weight to disciplined, scientific inquiry into the origins of things. By bequeathing to the world a Mediator who was to end all mediation, Christianity stripped the world of any claims to embody the Sacred. For Christianity very little, if anything, is guaranteed to be sacred; it is and has been an iconoclastic religion. Certainly, Christianity itself can take much of the credit or blame for the process of secularization in Western societies.

For Kung, however, a secular society is not only abhorrent; it is an impossibility. That is because societies, he assumes, depend on a layer of common values and commitments that make possible the agreements and commitments that are so necessary to everyday life. Without them work and politics founder in a sea of unmitigated self-interest. That is why we find Kung at times sounding very Durkheimian in his concern for the weakened or even lost moral foundations of secular societies: "Respect for the authority of the state, obedience towards the laws and a work ethic," he argues, no longer can rely on the traditional bedrock of religious commitments.

For Kung religion is the dimension of depth without which modern societies will simply come to grief on the rocks of pragmatism, irony, short-sighted self-interest, or hedonism. Worse yet, without religion humans will be left to their own devices to come up with the principles that will guide their conduct and will undergird their commitments to adhere to their agreements. Without the givenness of tradition, individuals may be able to generate a consensus of sorts by which to govern themselves, but it will be a consensus without any foundation in the past or in the nature of things.

What Kung has in mind is very similar to what has been discussed among sociologists under the heading of "civil religion." Such a religion at least appears to transcend particular interests and is received as a "given" rather than known as a social construction. Whether or not it is reactionary and chauvinistic or relatively liberal and universalistic will depend on circumstances. Some civil religions will see the nation as the harbinger of something liberating and ennobling for other nations; others will see the nation as the sacred victim that has been sacrificed to the greed and ruthlessness of other nations. In either case, however, the nation becomes the bearer of sacred meaning and the embodiment of what lies in the future for other nations, whether for their redemption or their chastisement. The nation becomes an embodiment of the human and social potential: a vast reduction of the uncertainty and complexity, of the possibilities and opportunities that in fact exist in an international system.

To put it another way, the nation becomes an idol that preempts these possibilities and embodies the sacred; it stands in the way of further exploration and innovation of the total environment of threat and possibility. Note, for instance, the view of U.S. Supreme Court Justice Judge Anthony Kennedy, who finds in America a nonsectarian "civic religion" that expresses "the shared conviction that there is an ethic and morality which transcend human invention" toward which government must remain neutral (Davis 1998, 19). This religion may be more or less nationalistic or universalistic, chauvinist or liberal, but it remains the putative source of whatever passes for a moral consensus in American society.

Contrast a clearly secular society, in which rules are clearly human in origin, clearly provisional and contingent, clearly open to continuous inspection, review and revision. That is why, for Kung, a secular society is either inconceivable or abhorrent. It is inconceivable because Kung believes that religion is not only the dimension of depth even for modern societies; it is the sine qua non of all social life. A secular society is abhorrent because it lacks any internal principle of self-restraint: "An efficient policy of interests without an ethic tends to lead to atrocities!"[1]

Kung's contrast of a society based on religion with one based on interests breaks down in specific cases. Nonetheless, he remains wedded to an antique dichotomy between the ideal world and the material, between ideas and interests, values and practices. In his logic, at least, if not in his analysis of particular cases like the church's intervention in Bosnia, there is no relief from a supposed split between the world of religion and the world of the secular. Idealism will not do for Kung; neither will a blind pragmatism that fails to discern the moral basis of apparently utilitarian practices. Their apparent insufficiencies, however, allow Kung to call religion into play as the dimension of "depth" in social life. This religious dimension then grounds the secular world even while being safely distinguished from the mere play of secular interests. No wonder, then, that the horns of the antiquated dilemma remain the same: the pitfalls of idealism or moralism, on the one hand, versus utilitarian and amoral realism, on the other; Jewish secular foreign-policy makers like Kissinger as opposed to products of international conferences on global ethics.

The world, as viewed through the eyes of the Christian faith, is not filled with dichotomies that owe more to the legacy of German idealism than they do to life. Thus, there is is no need to summon up a dimension of depth in order to find what is missing in a world that has been split by an alleged division into ideal and material interests. Instead, the Christian faith that refuses to identify the Sacred or its absence with "Lo here, Lo there." There is no way to be sure whether one is in the presence of the transcendent or the mundane. One may at any moment be engaged, unwittingly perhaps, in entertaining angels or visiting the hidden Christ in prison, or one may simply be doing what comes naturally or going about one's business. That is why there is something at once sacralizing and iconoclastic about the Christian faith.

This Christian uncertainty abut the Sacred—and openness to it—fits very well a secular society in which the distinction between the ideal and the material, like the distinction between the sacred and the profane, is empty and bankrupt. Any interests may also be described as values; commitments to the larger society may be purely self-interested or they may, at the same time, also be forms of adherence to the sacred. In a secular society, therefore, there may be no consensus on values. Certainly, there may be no agreement as to which values transcend the passage of time and which, instead, are merely the expression of particular interests.

A society without any consensus on common ideals is hardly unthinkable. Let us return to Denis Munby's (1963, 30–31) Riddell Lectures:

A secular society is a society without official images. If there are no common aims, there cannot be a common set of images reflecting the common ideals and emotions of everyone. Nor can there be any common ideal types of behaviour for universal application. Former societies glorified certain occupations, no doubt reflecting the class structure of particular epochs. All could not aspire to become monks or knights, but in a small highly-structured society such ideals were perhaps not entirely without relevance to everyday life in the Middle Ages. But today in a society of large size and enormous variety there can be no such ideal patterns of life."

Munby goes on to describe a secular society in terms that would offend any self-respecting Durkheimian sociologist. It was Durkheim, after all, who regarded utilitarianism with fear and loathing. Munby (1963, 29) does not think it is such a bad thing to pursue the greatest happiness for the greatest number:

> The achievement of the Utilitarians was to place the emphasis on actual human beings as the constituents of society and their concrete desires as the ultimate justification of society's rules. Thus they were able to sweep away a great mass of mystification about rights and the ideal ends of society which enabled people to oppress others and to neglect their actual interests for the benefit of illusory abstractions. And so the utilitarian revolution laid the basis for a truly human secular society, in spite of the narrowness of utilitarian ideas of human nature."

Durkheim, of course, thought it a contradiction in terms to legitimate social policies on the basis of what they did for the individual. It was the individual, after all, who owed his or her very being to the social order, and thus the sense of societal obligation to the individual was itself an illusion. If, like Kung and Durkheim, one is concerned about maintaining respect for authority and obedience to the law, one is very likely to look with suspicion, if not outright fear, at the "utilitarian revolution."

Of course, Munby realizes that what individuals think they want is often skewed by what industrialists want people to purchase and by advertisers who stimulate spurious needs; no market, even that of public opinion, is free from contamination by institutions or from distorted communication. However, a secular society, Munby (1963, 31) argues, "respects our variety, and cannot therefore countenance any accepted images or ideals." Furthermore, "[t]he liberal secular society, by contrast with most previous societies, does not set itself any overall aim, other than that of assisting as fully as possible the actual aims of its members, and making these as concordant with each other as possible" (1963, 27).

A secular society lacks not only a single aim or ideal but any roles that enable an individual to personify or embody that central devotion. Because law and politics, work and economics, education and the family are separated into areas that have their own logic, their own authority, rationale, and procedures, it is difficult for any individual to claim to embody the society at its best or as a whole. To be sure, particularly in the United States, presidents, for instance, often posture as religious or moral leaders, regardless of their personal demerits, and for some the presidency is indeed a sacred office on a par with a Constitution that is itself regarded as sacred. Nonetheless, a secular society is hard on those who claim to speak with spiritual authority or for the society as a whole. As Munby (1963, 25) put it: "It deflates the pretensions of politicians, but also of judges, who vainly attempt to preserve some relics of their former role as prophet-priests of the national conscience." The same might be said of ethicists, I suppose, who claim to be able to articulate an ethic for a global social system.

A secular social system respects more than the variety of nations and peoples, of communities and groups, and of individual needs and tastes. It respects the autonomy, integrity, and judgment of the person. Here is Munby (1963, 33) again (still in the gender-based language of the period):

> The positive ideals that lie behind the idea of the secular society are firstly a deep respect for the individual man and the small groups of which society is made up. It is because we have such respect that we seek not to impose on others, and not to lord it over others . . . To sum up, it is therefore because of respect for men that a secular society limits the common aims and ends of society as a whole."

Note the echoes of the New Testament in this passage. It is up to Christians—to the secularizers—not to lord it over others, as the gentiles—the religionists—do. The irony of Munby's usage at this point is very clear. It is Christian societies that indeed do lord it over others when they impose—on their own members and on other countries—the authority of their own beliefs and values, just as a Christian ethicist insists on the need to impress upon the individual the authority of the larger society and the weight of social obligation. Relatively free from a Durkheimian authoritarianism or from a Christian culture, a secular society is a zone of common inquiry and cultural invention and is thus a fit citizen of a global social system.

What Munby (1963, 33) has in mind is just such a society: one that is open to a wide range of possibilities for its own growth and development and to a similarly wide range of social possibility for all others: "Being a growing society, it is one which tries continually to enlarge the opportunities open to all men." Contrast Kung's case for the importance of religion in a global society, which he makes on the grounds that religion is the driving force behind many, even most attempts to define a people. Religion thus becomes the source of an authoritative identity of one people over and against others in a global economy. It is an unfortunate case, if only because many of these religiously grounded, populist or national identities set up oppositions within a global system rather than the much-needed openness to symbolic or other forms of inquiry and exchange. Open inquiry and communication are crucial to a global system of nation-states. Failing them, states have to fall back on intelligence services and the use of threats.

There is no mistaking Kung's fundamental disdain for what individuals and societies can do on their own, without tutelage by ethicists and without religious foundation, to achieve a tolerably just social order. Earlier I noted his belief that societies cannot generate their own agreements and commitments, their own laws and values; what is needed, he argues, is a bedrock of tradition and law that is, in its depth, religious. However, even some of his own descriptions seem to be quite compatible with the opposite viewpoint. For instance, Kung notes with enthusiasm recent efforts to bring war criminals to justice before an international court, and he deplores the delay in prosecuting those responsible for the genocides in what used to be Yugoslavia. He is also enthusiastic about the development of a retroactive jurisprudence based on conceptions of human rights that make it possible to punish East German officials for actions that were not criminal at the time they were committed. The old justifications for shooting people who sought to cross the border into West Germany are now "inoperative," notes King, because the Federal Constitutional Court has found that basic human rights have priority over positive law. Clearly, societies engaging in a secularized international system have found it possible to arrive at new conceptions of fundamental justice, and to enforce them.

Not so, Kung would argue. The German court could not have taken such an action if it were not for something prior and deeply grounded in a universal consensus: "Thus state legislation presupposes an ethic common to all human beings, a world-wide ethic of humanity" (Kung 1999, 131). This sort of pronouncement may be given in the optative mood or it may be a thinly disguised imperative; Kung liberally uses the word "must" in such contexts. Whether there is indeed an existing "world-wide ethic of humanity" is an empirical question that deserves an empirical answer.

Kung clearly subscribes to a worldview that makes such an empirical inquiry wholly unnecessary. For instance, it has long been an axiom of sociologists working in the Durkheimian tradition that the civil religious sentiments of a nation have their grounding in a universal religion of humanity. Nowhere is this more true than in the dignity accorded to the individual human being. The sacred status of the individual is grounded, in their view, on a more universal religion that enshrines humanity as such; the individual is thus the carrier and embodiment of humanity and is sacred only in this derivative fashion. That axiom thus suits the Durkheimian notion that the social order has causal and moral priority over the individual. Whether or not there is a religion of humanity, or as Kung puts it, a "world-wide ethic of humanity," from which conceptions of human rights can be derived, is itself doubtful.

However, if societies are to coexist not only peacefully but fruitfully in what is developing into a global social system, each society will have to become increasingly secular simply to embrace the widening range of social possibility with which it is confronted. This does not mean that no society would be well advised to set restrictions on the flow of capital into a country or out from it; on the contrary, such restrictions are becoming increasingly necessary for societies whose stability has been threatened by fluctuations in exchange rates and currency manipulations. This is also not to say that each society will have to become wholly transparent and accountable in its internal economy. However, access to international lending agencies does indeed require increasing levels of such openness in order to create the kind of trust and accounting that are necessary for investment.

Transparency and accountability work in two directions, of course. Societies with a surplus of managerial skills, vaccines, technology, capital, food supplies, and capital equipment will become increasingly open to demands from other societies for transfers of these goods, even when the possibilities of reimbursement or exchange are relatively meager in the near future. The temporal horizons of social planning, capital investment, and internal social policy will have to expand to encompass higher levels of possibility, complexity, and uncertainty. Again, these societies will also have to develop protections for the more vulnerable members of their own populations whose livelihoods and educational prospects suffer commensurately with the scale of overseas investment.

Whenever one society is permeated by the influence of at least one other society, social movements arise that demand a return to ancient boundaries or a recovery of traditional purity in basic institutions and ways of life. In the case of ethnic nationalisms, for instance, their revival may be due to inevitable yearnings for self-determination and democracy. In the name of self-realization, however, a people may attach a very literal and even exclusive reading to a sense of solidarity that in the past may have been sacred. This is a further reduction of the possibilities for life and death into something that is far more exclusive, fixed, and recalcitrant to revision and transformation. What these movements evoke under these conditions is a far cry from the Sacred as ineffable, transcendent, and contingent on a wide range of possibilities.

A global ethic will indeed have to take ethnic nationalism into account. I am suggesting that the way to do that is to secularize societies insofar as possible. That is not by way of suppressing ethnic nationalism but allowing it a limited expression under the auspices of a secular state. However unique and superior a people may feel themselves to be, the state will contain their enthusiasm rather than direct it outward toward the displacement and destruction of other peoples.

It may seem as if this is too optimistic an assessment of the possibilities for international as well as national secularity, given the ethnic cleansings of Africa and the Balkans as well as in parts of the Mideast. However, there is no need, as Tom Nairn has argued, for apocalyptic readings of these events. They are not necessarily a relapse to ethnic barbarism after the collapse of the large empires that held together divergent ethnic groups (Nairn 1995). The barbarism of Rwanda and Yugoslavia is due, he argues, to survivals of the one-party regimes in the old empires, Slavic or Western colonial. Where ethnic nationalism survives and enjoys a recrudescence, it is thus as a side effect of democratic impulses. Where it becomes vicious, it is as a result of a legacy of dictatorial rule.

A people claiming the right of self-determination may not easily become peace loving if it has thrived for centuries on the belief that it is the victim of other nations. If the state they acquire is indeed a relic of old one-party rule, as Nairn suggests, that state may indeed become an outlaw among nation-states. Indeed, Robert M. Hayden has argued that it was the idea of an ethnically homogenous nation that produced the ethnic cleansing in Bosnia. Through a constitution that gave legal sanction to this idealized notion of an ethnic nation-state, the Serbian regime could legitimately regard a mixed population as an anomaly that had to be removed: "the brutal negation of social reality in order to reconstruct it" (Hayden 1996, 784).

Indeed, Hayden goes on to note that the constitution of each of the ethnic republics in the former Yugoslavia speaks of a "centuries' long struggle" in the case of Macedonia, Serbia, Serbian Krajina, and of "centuries of struggle for freedom" (Montenegro). This inherited sense of victimage is taken as the basis of statehood for each ethnic group (=nation). And the word for ethnic group or nation (narod) has as its root the word for birth (Hayden 1996, 791); hence, each solidarity is exclusive, and the right to participate in the state depends not on the accidents but on the prerogatives of birth. The exception was Bosnia-Herzegovina, which could not produce an ethnic constitution for its mixed population. The nonsecular state can thus derive its power from many sources: from cultural nationalism, the turning of culture into political ideology regardless of conflicts with reality, and the intention to make social reality conform to ideological prescription.

It is thus a tragic mistake to underestimate what Hayden (1996, 784) calls "the power of a system of reified, prescriptive culture to disrupt the patterns of social life . . . that would contradict them." The ethnic constitutions of each republic effectively denaturalized the minority citizens and made them foreigners who could apply for admission, usually or often without success.

My proposal does not require that a people surrender their belief in being a victim. However, it does deprive such a people of their right to use the apparatus of the state to exact their revenge on offending peoples. To be allowed to have a state recognized by other states, a people would thus have to be willing to enter into a social system in which delusions of national superiority have no place and, when they are carried out, are suitably penalized by the collective action of other states. It is a secular system that makes its rules up as it goes along precisely in order to preserve a system that is itself open, contingent, provisional, and subject to continuous negotiation and revision. It is precisely because it is so secular that it resists the claims of any of its members to any form of priority or transcendence.

The point is simply that as societies become increasingly secular, what once seemed to be the given, the way things are, or ancient virtue becomes contingent on renewed consent, revised policies, and continuous negotiation. Wherever a "civic nationalism" predominates, Nairn (1995) suggests, it will be one in which ethnic identities can be enjoyed precisely because they are limited and transcended by a common loyalty to a single state.

One does not have to look far for an example of such a society that contains ethnic nationalisms within a secular political system. Consider Canada, where a number of factors militate against the development of a civil religion at the level of the nation-state: regionalism and the development of sub national or antinational geographic, social, economic, political, cultural, and religious interests (Kim 1993, 257–75). As Andrew Kim points out, divisive cultural and religious interests are most pronounced in the case of Ontario and Quebec, where language, ethnicity, and religion reinforce other regional differences.

The Canadian nation-state as a whole, however, lacks any mythology that would enable it to claim to be a whole greater than the sum of its parts. No model, whether that of anglophone-monarchical, bicultural, or pluralistic Canada, can overcome the inherent contradiction of two parts each claiming equality or supremacy in representing the whole. Thus, there is no part that can claim successfully to represent the whole and to impress the whole on a wide range of institutions. Each is seen to be transparently ideological and partial. Unlike the Soviet Union, whose ethnic policy seemed exemplary to Nehru, Canada does indeed manage to treat competing ethnic nationalisms equitably within a secular nation-state and could more appropriately become a model of nationhood within a global system of comparably secular states.

It is not as if in Canada there were no folk heroes and myths. It is simply that holidays and founding events all receive differing interpretations. Thus, there is no agreement on a sacred past. For instance, the Anglican version of a Christian dominion is seen by the French as a way of legitimating English domination over the French. Some groups even have a sense of being historical victims. Kim speaks of the "loser syndrome": the French and Scots lost to the English, the English to the Americans, and all were refugees at some point. Nonetheless, the Canadian nation-state leaves all claims to vindication or revenge, all delusions of transcendence, uniqueness, or superiority, to its constituent communities and minorities. While the French and the English both have viable civil religions that link the transcendent to the mundane and sacralize speech, ways of life, episodes and events, and periods in the lifetime of the individual, the nation-state as a whole remains adequately clothed without the garments of a civil religion.

Thus, a secular society has no reason for any image or embodiment of an ideal self or community, society or nation. Such an image or ideology reduces the vast amount of potentiality and uncertainty that constitutes the Sacred into a fixed image; it reduces what is unknown to what can at least be approached and perceived, if not wholly understood or explained. The idol is thus a reification and reduction of the real thing: a substitute that claims the right to attract attention, devotion, or even sacrifice.

Secular societies have no need for an idol that reduces the uncertainty and complexity within or around itself. Such a society refuses to reduce its awareness of the stakes and the risks, of the opportunities and also of the dangers that come from existing in an open, pluralistic world of rival groups and ideals. Indeed, idolatry is the antithesis of the openness and flexibility that are required if societies are to encounter each other in a global field of influence and communication that remains open to suggestion from all quarters and open as well to the future.

NOTES

Chapter 5

1. "In a sense, and not in a trivial sense, civil religion in America existed from the moment the winter 1967 issue of *Daedalus* was printed," in Richey and Jones, editors, *American Civil Religion* (New York: Harper and Row, 1974):256, quoted in Daniel Regan, "Islam, Intellectuals and Civil Religion in Malaysia," in *Sociological Analysis* 37:2 (Summer 1976):95–110.

2. "Protestant belief did not hold that the sacred did not intrude into the secular world, simply that it did not do so at human behest and could not automatically be commanded. Thus, there was no contradiction in regarding the Word of God as the most potent manifestation of the sacred in the world and so regarding the Bible as an especially sacred and potent object. By extension, this was also held of hymnals, prayerbooks, and catechisms, for they too embodied and expressed God's sacred Word. We can certainly speak of a distinctive Protestant form of sacramentalism, albeit one far weaker than its Catholic counterpart." Robert W. Scribner, "The Reformation, Popular Magic, and the 'Disenchantment of the World,'" p. 484.

3. "I argue that high levels of religiosity exist in America partly because of cultural elements that bring the secular and religious together in such a way that they seem complementary instead of conflicting. American culture-religion prompts religiosity through social convention." Samuel H. Reimer, "A Look at Cultural Effects on Religiosity: A Comparison Between the United States and Canada," in *Journal for the Scientific Study of Religion* 34:4 (December 1995):445–57, 454.

4. If Bellah had been entirely clear and consistent on this point, of course, there would be no difficulty in tracing his argument to a sort of vulgar Durkheimianism. As we have seen, however, Bellah has said on different occasions that the civil religion has not always existed but rather can be thought of as coming into being in 1967 with the publication of his seminal article entitled "Civil Religion in America." On another occasion, however, Bellah has stated that he published the same article about the time that the civil religion was becoming a dead letter in American culture.

Chapter 8

1. 1999, 128. To be sure, Kung sees religion, in the form of the Roman Catholic Church, as sometimes being caught up in the world of secular power politics. Consider the support given by the Roman Catholic Church, along with Germany, in recognizing Slovenia and Croatia as "sovereign states." After discussing the indirect help given to Serbia by England and France in the form of UN troops that failed to protect the Bosnians from Serbian repression, Kung falls back on his diatribe against "the old European policy of interests" (124). The Church's intervention in Bosnia was the result of the Vatican's "interest in seeing two more 'catholic states' in the alliance of European powers." Despite the destructive consequences of this intervention, however, Kung is willing to call it merely "unfortunate" (123).

BIBLIOGRAPHY

Abraham, Sen. Spencer. February 12, 1999. "Sen. Abraham's Closed-Door Impeachment Statement," in *allpolitics.com>storypage*, Time/CQ,

Allard, Sen. Wayne. February 12, 1999. "Sen. Allard's Closed-Door Impeachment Statement," in *allpolitics.com>storypage*, Time/CQ.

Ashberry, John. 1999. "They Just Don't Go Away, Either." *The New Yorke*, April 5: 62–63.

Bannon, Cynthia J. 1997. *The Brothers of Romulus: Fraternal Pietas in Roman Law, Literature, and Society*. Princeton, New Jersey: Princeton University Press.

Beard, Mary, John North, and Simon Price. 1998. *Religions of Rome*. Vol. 1. *A History*. Cambridge: Cambridge University Press.

Bellah, Robert. 1968. "Civil Religion in America," in *Religion in America*, William G. McLoughlin and Robert N. Bellah, editors. Boston: Beacon Press. Pp. 3–23.

———. 1973. "American Civil Religion in the 1970s," in *Anglican Theological Review*. Supplemental Series 1:8–20.

———. 1975. *The Broken Covenant*. New York: Seabury.

———. 1976a. "Response to the Panel on Civil Religion." *Sociological Analysis* 37(2):153–59.

———. 1976b. "The Revolution and the Civil Religion," in *Religion and the American Revolution*, Jerald C. Bauer, editor. Philadelphia: Fortress Press.

———. 1978. "Religion and Legitimation in the American Republic." *Society* 15(4):16–23.

———. 1986. "Public Philosophy and Public Theology in America Today," in *Civil Religion and Political Theology*, Leroy S. Rouner, editor. Notre Dame, Indiana: University of Notre Dame Press. Pp.79–97.

———. 1989. "Comment on James A. Mathison, 'Twenty Years after Bellah: Whatever Happened to American Civil Religion?'" *Sociological Analysis* 50 (2):129–46.

———. 1995a. "Coming to Our Senses." *Afterword to Theological Institute Annual Series*, vol. 4, Boston: Boston University. Pp. 161–65

———. 1995b. "How to Understand the Church in an Individualistic Society" in *Theological Institute Annual Series*, Vol. 4: Boston: Boston University. Pp. 1–14.

Billings, Dwight B. and Shauna L. Scott. 1994. "Religion and Political Legitimation." *The Annual Review of Sociology* 20:173–201.

Bloch, Maurice. 1989. *Ritual, History, and Power: Selected Papers in Anthropology*. London: Athlone Press.

Bollas, Christopher. 1992. *Being a Character: Psychoanalysis and Self Experience*. New York: Hill and Wang.

Bonhoeffer, Dietrich. 1995. *Ethics*. New York: Simon and Schuster, Touchstone Press.

Bruce, Steve. 1990. *A House Divided: Protestantism, Schism, and Secularization*. London: Routledge.

Bull, Malcolm. 1989. "The Seventh-Day Adventists: Heretics of American Civil Religion." *Sociological Analysis* 50 (2): 177–87.

Cardinal, Roger. 1999. "The Sage of Disintegration" *Times Literary Supplement*, no. 5008 (March 29).

Chriss, J. J. 1993. "Durkheim's Cult of the Individual as Civil Religion: Its Appropriation by Erving Goffman." *Sociological Spectrum* 13:251–75.

Christi, Marcela, and Lorne L. Dawson. 1996. "Civil Religion in Comparative Perspective: Chile under Pinochet (1973–1989)." *Social Compass* 43(3): 319–38.

Coles, Robert. 1999. *The Secular Mind*. Princeton, New Jersey: Princeton University Press.

Crouter, Richard. 1990. "Beyond Bellah: American Civil Religion and the Australian Experience" *The Australian Journal of Politics and History* 36(2):154–165.

Davis, Derek H. Spring 1994. "Editorial, Religious Pluralism and the Quest for Unity in American Life." *Journal of Church and State* 36(2) 245–60.

———— Winter 1998. "Editorial: Civil Religion as Judicial Doctrine." *Journal of Church and State* 40(1):7–24.

DelBanco, Andrew. 1995. *The Death of Satan: How Americans Have Lost the Sense of Evil*. New York: Farrar, Straus, and Giroux.

Deloria, Vine, Jr. 1992. "Secularism, Civil Religion, and the Religious Freedom of American Indians," *American Indian Culture and Research Journal* 16(2):9–20.

Demerath, N. J. and Rhys H. Williams. 1985. "Civil Religion in an Uncivil Society." *Annals of the American Academy of the Political and Social Sciences* 480:154–66.

Dietler, Michael. 1994. "'Our Ancestors the Gauls': Archeology, Ethnic Nationalism, and the Manipulation of Celtic Identity in Modern Europe." *American Anthropologist* 96(3): 584–605.

Dobbelaere, Karel. 1986. "Civil Religion and the Integration of Society: A Theoretical Reflection and an Application." *Japanese Journal of Religious Studies* 13(2–3): 127–45.

————. 1998. "Relations ambigues des religions à la société globale." *Social Compass* 45(1): 81–98.

Fairbanks, James David. 1981. "The Priestly Functions of the Presidency: A Discussion of the Literature on Civil Religion and Its Implications for the Study of Presidential Leadership." *Presidential Studies Quarterly* 11:214–32.

Fenn, Richard K. 1997. *The End of Time*. London: SPCK.

Flere, Sergej. 1994. "Le Développement de la sociologie de la religion en Yougoslavie apres la deuxieme guerre modiale (Jusqu'a son demembrement)." *Social Compass* 41(3): 367–77.

Fletcher, Richard. *The Barbarian Conversion*. 1998. New York: H. Holt and Co.

Furseth, Inger. 1994. "Civil Religion in a Low Key: The Case of Norway." *Acta Sociologica* 37: 39–54.

Furth, Alexandra D. 1998. "Secular Idolatry and Sacred Traditions: A Critique of the Supreme Court's Secularization Analysis." *University of Pennsylvania Law Review* 146: 579–619.

Gamoran, Adam. 1990. "Civil Religion in American Schools." *Sociological Analysis* 51(3):235–56.

Hacking, Ian. 1995. *Rewriting the Soul: Multiple Personality and the Sciences of Memory*. Princeton, New Jersey: Princeton University Press.

Hammond, Phillip E. 1980. "The Conditions for Civil Religion: A Comparison of the United States and Mexico," *Varieties of Civil Religion*, Robert N. Bellah and Phillip E. Hammond, editors. San Francisco: Harper and Row.

Hammond, Phillip E., Amanda Porterfield, James G. Moseley, Jonathan D. Sarna. Winter 1994. "Forum: American Civil Religion Revisited." *Religion and American Culture*, 4:1.

Hammoudi, Abdellah. 1997. *Master and Disciple. The Foundations of Moroccan Authoritarianism*. Chicago: University of Chicago Press.

Harvey, Mark S. 1989. "Charles Ives: Prophet of American Civil Religion." *Soundings* 72 (2–3) 502–25.

Havel, Vaclev. March 1995. "Forgetting We Are Not God." *First Things* 51: 47–50.

Hayden, Robert M. 1996. "Imagined Communities and Real Victims: Self-Determination and Ethnic Cleansing in Yugoslavia." *American Ethnologist* 23(4): 783–801.

Helms, Sen. Jesse. February 12, 1999. "Sen. Jesse Helms's Closed-Door Impeachment Statement" in *allpolitics.com>storypage*, Time/CQ.

Herberg, Will. 1960. Protestant—Catholic—Jew. Garden City: Anchor.

Hutchison, Sen. Kay Bailey. February 12, 1999. "Sen. Kay Bailey Hutchison's Closed-Door Impeachment Statement," in *allpolitics.com>storypage*, Time/CQ.

Hutchinson, Mark. December 1990. "History as Civil Religion: Writing Australian History in the Nineteenth Century." *Journal of Religious History* 16 (2): 185–201.

Kim, Andrew E. 1993. "The Absence of Pan-Canadian Civil Religion: Plurality, Duality, and Conflict in Symbols of Canadian Culture." *Sociology of Religion* 54(3): 257–75.

Kung, Hans. 1999. *A Global Ethic for Global Politics and Economics*. New York: Oxford University Press.

Lash, Nicholas. 1996. *The Beginning and End of "Religion."* Cambridge: Cambridge University Press.

Luhmann, Niklas. 1984. *Religious Dogmatics and the Evolution of Societies*. Translated and with an introduction by Peter Beyer. *Studies in Religion and Society*, vol. 9. New York: The Edwin Mellen Press.

Marcuse, Herbert. 1955. *Eros and Civilization. A Philosophical Inquiry into Freud*. Boston: Beacon Press.

———. 1960. *Reason and Revolution. Hegel and the Rise of Social Theory*. Boston: Beacon Press.

————. 1964. *One-Dimensional Man: Studies in the Ideology of Advanced Industrial Society.* Boston: Beacon Press.

Martin, David. 1980. *The Breaking of the Image.* Oxford: Basil Blackwell.

————. 1998. *Does Christianity Cause War?* Oxford: Clarendon Press.

Marty, Martin. 1974. "Two Kinds of Civil Religion," in *American Civil Religion,* Russell E. Richey and Donald G. Jones, editors. New York: Harper and Row.

Marvin, Carolyn, and David W. Ingle. 1997. "Blood Sacrifice and the Nation: Revisiting Civil Religion." *Journal of the American Academy of Religion* LXIV/4: 767–80.

Mathison, James A. Summer 1989. "Twenty Years After Bellah: Whatever Happened to American Civil Religion?" *Sociological Analysis* 50(2): 129–46.

Minogue, Kenneth. 1999. "The Ego and the Other: Why Individualism Leads to Co-operation." *Times Literary Supplement,* no. 4997 (January 8).

Munby, Denis. 1963. *The Idea of a Secular Society.* London: Oxford University Press.

Nairn, Tom. 1995. "Breakwaters of 2000: From Ethnic to Civic Nationalism." *New Left Review* 214:91–103.

Neeman, Rina, and Nissan Rubin. 1996. "Ethnic Civil Religion: A Case Study of Immigrants from Rumania in Israel." *Sociology of Religion* 57(2): 195–212.

Neuhaus, Richard John. 1986. "From Civil Religion to Public Philosophy," *Civil Religion and Political Theology,* Leroy S. Rouner, editor. Notre Dame, Indiana: University of Notre Dame Press. Pp. 98–110.

————. February 1992. "A New Order of Religious Freedom." *First Things* 20:13–17.

Nielsen, Donald A. 1996. "Pericles and the Plague: Civil Religion, Anomie, and Injustice in Thucydides." *Sociology of Religion* 57(4):397–407.

Patterson, Orlando. 1998. *Rituals of Blood: Consequences of Slavery in Two American Centuries.* Washington, D.C.: Civitas, Counterpoint.

Prades, José A. 1993. "Religion civile et religion de l'humanité:retour sur l'anthropocentrisme durkheimien." *Social Compass* 40(3): 415–27.

Purdy, Susan S. 1982/83. "The Civil Religion Thesis as It Applies to a Pluralistic Society: Pancasila Democracy in Indonesia (1945–1965)." *Journal of International Affairs* 36 (2): 307–16.

Regan, Daniel. 1976. "Islam, Intellectuals, and Civil Religion in Malaysia." *Sociological Analysis* 37 (2): pp. 95–110.

Reimer, Samuel H. 1995. "A Look at Cultural Effects on Religiosity: A Comparison Between the United States and Canada." *Journal for the Scientific Study of Religion* 34 (4): 445–57.

Reynolds, Frank E. 1977. "Civic Religion and National Community in Thailand." *Journal of Asian Studies* 37 (2): 267–82.

Schmitt, Jean-Claude. 1998. *Ghosts in the Middle Ages: The Living and the Dead in Medieval Society.* Chicago: University of Chicago Press.

Scribner, Robert W. 1993. "The Reformation, Popular Magic, and the 'Disenchantment of the World.'" *Journal of Interdisciplinary History* 23 (3): 475–94.

Shukla, Sandhya. 1997. "Building Diaspora and Nation: The 1991 'Cultural Festival of India.'" *Cultural Studies,* 11 (2): 296–315.

Smolin, David M. 1997. "Consecrating the President." *First Things* 69:14–18.

Takayama, K. Peter. 1988. "Revitalization Movement of Modern Japanese Civil Religion." *Sociological Analysis* 48 (4).

Thurmond, Sen. Strom. February 12 1999. "Sen. Strom Thurmond's Closed-Door Impeachment Statement," in *allpolitics.com>storypage*, Time/CQ.

U.S. Senate. February 9, 1999. Impeachment Trial of President Bill Clinton. Day 17. Web posted at 1:40 P.M. EDT, p. 156.

Vendler, Helen. 1999. "Scoops from the Tide Pools," *Times Literary Supplement,* no. 4996, (January 1):11.

Weber, Max. 1958. *The City.* New York: Free Press.

Weddle, David L. 1983. Review of *Varieties of Civil Religion*, by Philip Hammond and Robert Bellah ((Harper and Row 1980). *Journal of the American Academy of Religion* 51 (3): 198–99.

Wierdsma, A.I. 1987. "The Meaning of a State Ceremony: The Inauguration (1814–1980) as Ritual of Civil Religion in the Netherlands." *The Netherlands' Journal of Sociology* 23 (1):31–44.

Willaime, Jean. 1993. "La religion civile à la française et ses metamorphoses." *Social Compass* 40 (4):571–80.

Wilson, Charles Reagan. 1984. "American Heavens: Apollo and the Civil Religion." *Journal of Church and State* 26(2):209–26.

Wilson, John F. 1986. "Common Religion in American Society," *Civil Religion and Political Theology*, Leroy S. Rouner, editor. Notre Dame, Indiana: University of Notre Dame Press.

Wuthnow, Robert. 1988. *The Restructuring of American Religion: Society and Faith Since World War II.* Princeton, New Jersey. Princeton University Press.

Ho Youm, Kyu. 1990. "Libel Law and the Press in Japan." *Journalism Quarterly* 67 (4): 1103–12.

INDEX